DON'T SHOOT THE CLOWNS

THE CLOWNS

Taking a circus to the children of Iraq

Jo Wilding

Author's acknowledgements

For Spike, whose generation will have to tidy up the mess and for the people of Iraq, especially my friends.

In memoriam:

Fuad Radi
Ghareeb
Garrett Scott
Nooh Rizyami

Thanks are due to:

Zaid and Asmaa and family; Alaa; Raed, Majid, Khalid and family; Music Raed; Salam; Hamsa, Husni and family; Waleed; Chnur; Heyman and family; Ali Shalan; all at Happy Family and other Iraqi friends too many to mention and of course Imad, Julia Guest, for many things, Simonas Torretta and Pari and Paola Gasparoli and those from the Funduq al-Aghadeer, and to Abu Hassan, Hadi and others for guarding the doors, and to Tommo;

Fadhil Abbas, Devilstick Peat Simms, Amber Christis, Luis, Fisheye Sam, Uzma Bashir, Sheila Hanney, Shane, Out of Hand, Yaoh, Anna and all who supported and participated in Boomchucka Circus;

Rana, David, Jenny, Donna, Ahrar for being the finest companions in a difficult situation and the Imam who drove us out of Falluja at risk to his own life;

Joseph Rowntree Reform Trust, Methodist Peace Fellowship, Salih Ibrahim and many, many people who contributed financially;

Chris Brazier and all at New Internationalist;

Dave Peak, Jenny Gaiawyn, Alex Ross, Raed Jarrar and Kate Evans for reading chapters and Ewa Jasiewicz, Eric Herring, Justin Alexander, John Pilger, Voices in the Wilderness, Joanne Baker and Felicity Arbuthnot for helping me understand Iraq;

All at Barton Hill Playcentre, Bristol, for looking after Spike while I hammered the blog into a book;

Mum, for everything and John, my love.

DON'T SHOOT THE CLOWNS

Taking a circus to the children of Iraq

Jo Wilding

Don't Shoot the Clowns
First published in 2006 by
New Internationalist™ Publications Ltd
55 Rectory Road
Oxford OX4 1BW, UK
www.newint.org
New Internationalist is a registered trade mark.

Front cover images
Top: Jo Wilding clowning in Samawa, southern Iraq by Yoichi Watanabe
Bottom: US marines in Baghdad, Reuters/Goran Tomasevic

All photographs inside the book are by Jo Wilding except those in
Chapter 17, which are by Yoichi Watanabe

Edited by Chris Brazier
Design by New Internationalist Publications Ltd.

 Printed on recycled paper by T J International Limited, Cornwall, UK
who hold environmental accreditation ISO 14001.

British Library Cataloguing-in-Publication Data.
A catalogue for this book is available from the British Library.

Library of Congress Cataloguing-in-Publication Data.
A catalogue for this book is available from the Library of Congress.

ISBN 10: 1-904456-48-0
ISBN 13: 978-1904456-483

'When I first heard that clowns were going to Iraq, my feeling was, "That's all they need." But reading Jo's blogs and watching the film *A Letter to the Prime Minister*, I suspended my prejudices. The therapeutic value of Circus2Iraq is beyond question; and Jo's involvement with the situation, and her ability to illuminate it for the outside world, offer us priceless access. She goes further than most in introducing us to the people our taxes are killing. But, to be more positive, she also shows us the courage, resourcefulness and cheerfulness of which human beings are capable. This book is not about missionary zeal, but about being human.'

Jeremy Hardy, comedian and campaigner

'Jo Wilding's honesty, humor, compassion and courage enliven each story she tells. Teetering on stilts, blowing bubbles, and evoking sidesplitting laughter, she reached common ground with ordinary Iraqis. But the title *Don't Shoot the Clowns* pertains to nearly every paragraph of this extraordinary memoir. Wilding is a gifted writer. I hope her book, when shared widely, will fuel growing resistance to war.'

**Kathy Kelly, anti-war activist and
co-founder of Voices in the Wilderness**

'...enormous courage, a deep sense of justice, compassion and a will to show the human face of tragedy – a much needed contribution to showing the picture of modern barbarism.'

**Hans von Sponeck, Former UN
Humanitarian Co-ordinator for Iraq**

'Jo Wilding is a cheeky angel, a voice for the voiceless, a frontline unembedded reporter, a children's entertainer, and a born writer. She represents a new generation of activists who stand by those at the wrong end of the guns, and who won't be moved.'

**Milan Rai, anti-war activist, author and
co-founder of Voices in the Wilderness**

'On the worldwide web, the best "alternative" websites are already read by an audience of millions. The courageous reporting of Jo Wilding from besieged Iraq is a striking example. She is not an accredited journalist, but one of a new breed of "citizen reporters".'

**John Pilger, from his anthology of the best
investigative journalism, *Tell Me No Lies***

CONTENTS

WHO'S WHO

I make no apology for the whirlwind of characters who appear in this book. It is populated by hundreds of characters, some fleeting, some constant. That is, to a large extent, the way I experienced Iraq, meeting dozens of people every day, each with a story to tell about life under Saddam, sanctions, war and occupation, each with an identity, a history, a family, an opinion.

Many names were changed in the original to protect their owners; some have now been changed back while others cannot be. Wherever possible I've given people their real names because my going to Iraq, and writing this book, were about making them visible, un-collateralizing them, so I have not hidden them unless their safety might depend on it.

One more point about names: a child is given a first name and then, male or female, takes the names of the father. Each person has five names of this type – her own, her father's, her grandfather's, her great- and her great-great-grandfather's and then a family, clan or tribal name such as al-Hadith or al-Tikriti. She keeps those names when she marries but her children take her husband's names.

So when a person is referred to by two names, in the Western way, those might be the first name and the clan name or the first two names, not a forename and surname as in the West. I use the word 'clans' to refer to networks, also called tribes – larger than extended families – which are important in Iraq.

Many of the names I mention only appear once – you do not need to remember them. Others recur throughout the book and, to help you identify who is who, here is a 'cast list' of the major characters to which you can refer back as necessary.

Ahmed (in the first two chapters) – a huge man who worked in the hotel-apartments that I stayed in before and during the war.
Ahmed (in later chapters) – an Iraqi friend whom I worked with on a few projects during the occupation.

Ahmed, Laith and Little Saif – three little boys who lived on the street. Saif went back to his family. Ahmed and Laith moved to the shelter and then an orphanage.
Alaa – a woman I met through a mutual acquaintance, who

translated for me sometimes but
is above all a friend.
Amber – a clown from
Philadephia, with us for all of
January, responsible for teaching
me to walk on stilts.
Asmaa – a good friend, wife of
Zaid.
Bremer, Paul – the US
Administrator of Iraq following
the invasion.
CPA – Coalition Provisional
Authority.
David Martinez – an independent
filmmaker, with me on both trips
into Falluja and in Thawra.
Donna Mulhearn – an Australian
woman who co-founded the NGO
Our Home-Iraq and was with me
on the second trip to Falluja.
Fadhil – Fadhil Abbas, an Iraqi
actor who was performing with
his group for children around
Baghdad and helped us get the
circus going.
Fatih – our neighbor across the
road in Baghdad.
Fisheye Sam – a clown from
Britain, with us from February to
March.
Hamsa – a young woman I met
before the invasion when she was
a student, one of the founder
members of Iraq Indymedia.
We worked together on various
projects and I stayed often at her
family's house.
Haveman, Jim – the US 'Senior
Advisor' to the Iraqi Ministry of
Health.
Hayder – formerly a jewelry maker,
he did a lot of driving for the circus
because no one was buying jewelry,

and became a friend, introducing
us to his family.
Husni – Hamsa's dad, a Doctor
of Environmental Science, who
worked with the circus for a
while as he was unable to find a
proper job.
Imad – a Lebanese activist who
arrived in Baghdad shortly before
I did. We worked together on
various things in my first month
in Iraq.
Jenny – Jenny Gaiawyn (Guy-a-
win), a good friend from Britain
who came out to work with me
on projects with children after
the circus ended and came with
me on the second Falluja trip.
Julia – Julia Guest, a filmmaker
who travelled with me to
Iraq before the invasion and
returned twice during the
occupation.
Khalid – a kind, gentle, funny
man, blogger and middle brother
of Raed and Majid Jarrar (not
to be confused with Khalid
from the farmhouse which was
bombed).
Layla Mohammed – one of
the directors of Organization
for Women's Freedom in Iraq,
exiled in Australia by the end of
Saddam's time.
Luis – a clown from France, with
us for the whole tour.
Majid – youngest brother
of Raed and Khalid Jarrar, a
founder member of the Baghdad
Indymedia project.
Michael – Michael Birmingham,
a human rights activist
from Ireland, in Iraq almost

constantly from October 2002
till June 2004.
Paola Gasparoli – an Italian
human rights activist.
Peat – a clown from Britain, with
us for the whole tour.
Raed (Emaar) – Raed Jarrar,
my friend and housemate in
November and December, an
architect and blogger, founder of
Emaar.
Raed (Music) – a member of Aila
Saida and a good friend.
Rana – a remarkable young
Iraqi woman who was in the
ambulance with me in Falluja.
Salam – a young Iraqi man,
one of the founders of Al-
Muajaha, the Baghdad Indymedia
project, who traveled with me to
Suleimania.

Simona Pari and Simona Toretta
– two Italian aid workers from Un
Ponte Per, who helped us organize
the circus's work in schools.
Thabat – a human rights lawyer
working on cases of detainees
and injured or bereaved people
fighting for compensation.
Uzma – a British Pakistani
woman who co-founded the
NGO Our Home-Iraq and joined
the circus in February.
Waleed – my sometime
housemate, good friend, a
founder member of the Baghdad
Indymedia project and lead singer
of the Iraqi death metal band
Acras Sicauda.
Zaid – a taxi driver before the
war, he and his wife Asmaa and
family became good friends.

INTRODUCTION: CIRCUS2IRAQ

All the faces had congealed in the hot, sticky tedium of the traffic jam. Eyes gazed listlessly at the snarling razor wire and blank concrete blast walls that protected the surrounding buildings from the explosions and shrapnel that seemed to follow us all around. Like rats in a city, you were never more than a short time and space from the next blast and those times and spaces, which had seemed short enough already, were constricting all the while, closing in.

A tank blocked the way ahead and no-one dared sneak past its twitching gun. An ambulance behind screamed in the mire, emergency having lost all meaning in the encompassing trauma.

A skinny, ragged child moved between the cars, offering newspapers, chewing gum, sweets, toilet paper, growing old as the minutes passed. Suddenly his sunken eyes swivelled back, new life amid the lethargy, to confirm what they thought they had seen. The man in the car took another ping-pong ball from his mouth. And another. The boy started to smile, to giggle, to laugh out loud. He called to other children, who abandoned their columns of cars to come and look. Another man in the car took a cloth from his pocket and made it vanish. A woman began pulling improbable faces and the children, a small crowd of them now, reciprocated.

Soon the people in the cars were looking too, and laughing. As the cars edged onwards the crowd followed, absorbing the ancient women who begged for pity and dinars, until finally the road widened, the tank peeled off towards its base and the vehicles began to disperse. The children drifted away too, but with a bounce, a chuckle, a wave. It wouldn't feed them but it would keep them going for another few hours.

That's what our circus was all about. It carried people, just for a little while, took the weight off them, shoved some of the violence and destruction from their minds and eyes for a moment. Without trivializing – as if it could – what they were going through, it oiled the daily grind with laughter, not only for the children.

We had safety guidelines taped to the wall of our living room, some serious, like telling someone where you were going and walking against the direction of the traffic (so cars couldn't pull up ahead to kidnap you) and some frivolous, like never going in the toilet after Sam. And in there somewhere was: 'Keep a low profile'. But we couldn't do it: we couldn't help doing magic tricks when stuck in traffic or persuading the children on our street to rediscover their inner clowns.

One day Amber and I needed to practise a new plot involving stilts and skipping ropes. Even after the demise of the ceiling fan there wasn't room in the apartment to swing a ten-meter rope, or even a cat, so we went outside to the forecourt. In minutes we had all the kids from the street taking turns to jump over the rope, one at a time, in pairs, then threes.

Our street was in the merging point between the Christian and the Shi'a communities. For all that people denied there were divisions, there were often quite defined areas occupied by each sect and, of course, each class, centred on the mosques or churches. Karrada was relatively affluent, always rammed with traffic, hooting at inanimate objects as if that might ease the gridlock. There was a juice shop on the corner where any fruit in season could be liquidized for you, a tea-and-falafel shop opposite, the smells of popcorn and petrol mingling every Thursday evening around the weekend shoppers.

The women didn't come out on the street to join our game but laughed and waved from the balconies. Fatih, our opposite-neighbor, and his little girl, Fadia, hung out of their window cheering everyone on. Men tried to get each other to take a turn, each with an excuse for not having a go himself – I'm too old, I'm too fat, until Coco braved it, managing six or seven jumps over the rope before getting caught in it, giggling, to huge applause.

Peat stood on the balcony doing the thing he always did with ping pong balls in his mouth, where it looked like he kept taking dozens and dozens of them out, then he and Luis did their new juggling act. We had to go and get our kit together to go and do a show, but when we left everyone was playing in the street, kicking a football between themselves, running about blowing bubbles, the men as well as the children. A bit of play transformed the street completely, transformed the faces.

Then as we walked home in the rain that night a small voice called from a doorway. 'Bacher?' he asked hopefully: tomorrow? Would there be another circus in the street tomorrow? And men popped out of other doorways to ask the same thing, still laughing, still playing. It was good.

✳   ✳   ✳

'We are farmers. We are farmers.' The woman kept repeating it through her rage and grief and incomprehension while the orderlies mopped the blood from the floor, picked up the rags of clothing, torn and then cut off the body. She was Fatima, mother of four children.

It was 24 March 2003 and Baghdad was under bombardment. I and some other foreign observers had gone to the Kindi hospital to interview some of the casualties from the day before – no one official was doing it – when the doctor was called to the emergency room and told us to come with him. A family had just arrived from a farmhouse on the outskirts.

Ajama, Fatima's father, who owned the house, had a head wound and a laceration to his arm but was relatively lucid and was able to explain that there were still family members buried in the rubble. His son Khalid had got married a week earlier. As Ajama was wheeled through, Khalid gripped him and asked where was his wife, Nahda. A shake of Ajama's head, a few words and Khalid crumpled to the floor.

'The bride missing,' Ajama explained. 'We don't know where.'

Fatima held one child after another, clothes patched with their blood. Her nine-year-old daughter Zahra was dead, taken away in a blanket, she didn't know where. Rana, cradled in one of the women's arms, emitted squeals whenever she was moved – into the X-ray room, out again, into the treatment room. Her face was ripped by shrapnel. Nada lay in a bed. The doctor lifted the blankets to reveal a bloody mess of open leg. She howled and screamed as they tried to clean it. Her head was heavily bandaged and one eye closed and swollen.

'Why did he do this to me Mum? Allah, why did he do this to me?'

'The skull also open,' the doctor said.

In the corridor, another doctor shook with anger as he demanded, 'Where is the UN?' The remaining UN staff had all left in convoy a few days before the bombing started and no humanitarian observers or war crimes inspectors had been sent in to replace them. As well as the young wife, Nahda, and little Zahra, Fatima and Khalid's sister Hana died. I tried to establish exactly where the missile had come from, which direction.

'From a plane,' they all said, pointing at the sky, their fingers describing a round-and-round motion. 'It circled above us for a couple of minutes,' Khalid's younger brother said. It fired three rockets, one of which demolished the entire upper storey of the house.

Khalid sat silently crying in the corridor, on the floor, body bent, head in his hands. A tiny boy cried and clapped his bandaged hands, calling out '*Ummi*' – Mummy –whenever he was left alone. Safe in the lap of an aunt, he drifted off into his own world, touching his fingertip to the still-damp blood on his sleeve, looking intently at it, putting the finger to his tongue, his ear torn, his face chequered with cuts. He was Mohammed and he was four.

His dad arrived, an army coat over his *dishdasha* (the traditional tunic worn by men), from their home near the air force officers' club – the rest of the family had left there, believing they would be safer in the agricultural area away from any possible targets.

Mohammed huddled on a bed, eyes glazed in shock, unresponsive to what went on around him. Shane, a great big kid from Philadelphia, sat on the floor without a word and started drawing a picture. Mohammed's eyes were drawn to its colours and he watched for a while.

Shane got out a pot of bubbles and started blowing. Mohammed's eyes followed them drifting to the ceiling, rainbowed and shiny. Slowly he reached for one, popping it with his finger, smiling as it burst, his eyes coming back to life as if a wall around him had started to crumble as well.

Of course his trauma would take more than a bubble to heal but the memory stayed with me. Months later, at a festival in England, but already planning to return to Iraq, I saw a man blowing giant bubbles with some simple device and resolved to take one back with me. I walked through to the Circus field and resolved to take one of those with me as well. Stubborn as I am, once I'd said it, it had to happen.

A friend set up a website called Circus2Iraq. I sent out an open email inviting circus performers to come to Iraq, warning that it was a dangerous place and travel insurance wouldn't cover it. I proposed a month-long trip, asked people to raise their own funds. Despite poor pay and conditions, I got a bunch of clowns: Amber, one of Shane's housemates from Philadelphia who did circus and theater work with poor kids from their neighborhood; Luis, a French street performer with a gnome face who first came to Iraq as a human shield; Sam, a former clown, turned roadie for the comedian Mark Thomas; and Peat, a professional fool from England, a former soldier who learned to juggle in a cell after a minor misdemeanor involving the theft of a tank. Peat used to be a biker, with a coffin for a sidecar, then got into working with traumatized children in war zones: Kosovo, Northern Ireland. He joked after a trip to Albania that it was getting too quiet and he'd have to go to Iraq next. Friends called his bluff and passed on my email.

I arrived back in Iraq two months before the circus started, working on various solidarity projects, helping out where people or groups needed an English-speaking advocate to speak on their behalf, making links between ordinary Iraqis – students, doctors, teachers – and their counterparts in Britain, keeping a weblog telling the stories of the ordinary people I met and whatever else seemed to need doing.

I hadn't planned to be part of the circus, only to organize and co-ordinate, but Amber arrived with two sets of stilts and taught me to walk on them in our living room. I got the tailor down the road to make me a pair of extra long trousers, Peat devised us a simple act and I became a stilt-walking clown.

The one-month tour became three months as the effectiveness of the circus egged us all on and money kept coming in from people who read our web reports. The rest of the clowns left at the beginning of April, coincidentally on the last day that the highway to Jordan was passable before the US troops sealed off the section around Falluja and besieged the city.

While the mainstream media increasingly confined itself to fortress-like hotel complexes and armored travel with gun-carrying security advisers, I went to Falluja taking in medical supplies and escorting ambulances which were being fired on by US troops.

I kept a weblog ('blog') throughout – it started before the war* with emails to a few people about the things I was seeing and the people I met, which were passed on and posted until they were being read and reprinted

Peat introduces Woodbine to children in Samawa, southern Iraq.

all over the world. When all the communications towers were destroyed and the internet was unavailable I carried on posting via a satellite modem borrowed from an anonymous lender and smuggled into Iraq with a small bribe to avert a thorough search of our luggage.

There was, after all, a real hunger for genuine information, for the voices of ordinary Iraqis and not just the political and military figures, not just the press conference soundbites that were served up by the mainstream media.

This book differs from the blog in that it's been rearranged for the sake of coherence and things have been taken out for the sake of space. I've updated only where it seemed imperative: the situation is always evolving

---

* I use the word 'war' essentially out of laziness: as Bill Hicks said, "War is when *two* armies are fighting."

and this is my picture of a particular time.

Being a clown, going into the squatter camps, the orphanages, the schools, being out on the streets, playing rather than aiding or reporting, going wherever people were rather than looking for 'stories', gave me a near-unique perspective, a very different experience from the journalists, filmmakers, NGO workers or soldiers in Iraq.

Being independent before and during the invasion – neither a journalist nor an NGO worker, not a member of any organization or human shield group – likewise allowed us an uncommon vantage point as it meant that Julia and I slipped through many of the surveillance and control nets. I won't pretend we were free to go wherever and talk to whomsoever we liked but we certainly had more leeway than most.* We did, though, have to hitch a ride on the permission of the Iraq Peace Team in order to enter the hospitals once bombing began, so we were 'minded' then.

The book is – as the blog was – about more than just the circus. It covers the time before and during the invasion, through to a couple of months after the other clowns left. It's a space for ordinary Iraqi people to tell their stories and experiences, in their own voices; it's a personal history of Iraq over the period from February 2003 to May 2004; it's an exploration of some of the context and causes and an indictment of British and US government actions.

It's also about empowerment, about what can be done with not much money, a bit of cheek, the determination to go where the UN and the news media will not, a laptop, a broom and a cardboard box.

---

* To begin with, the Shields were gloriously free of any idea that they were meant to be under surveillance and more or less did as they liked, but they were quickly reined in by the Government and sent either to officially selected sites like power stations and refineries or back to Jordan.

1

WAITING FOR WAR

February-March 2003

In August 2001 I went to Iraq for the first time. I went to talk to ordinary Iraqis and find out what was happening to them, breaking the sanctions by taking in goods without an export license, including CD-Roms for medical training. It was so hot I felt like the fluid in my eyeballs was boiling. The people were so desperate and the surveillance so intense that I felt like an alien from outer space.

I'm sorry to say I knew next to nothing about Iraq until 2000, when I went to a talk by Joanne Baker, an activist who had been to Iraq twice to break the sanctions. She talked about children dying for lack of safe water or of curable diseases for want of drugs which, though not strictly under embargo, were put on hold by the Sanctions Committee.

During the 1991 war, aged 17, I had assumed 'we' were right to evict the Iraqi army from Kuwait and to protect the Kurds from Saddam's troops. I was outraged by the stories Joanne now told of what had happened since then to people she had met, the things she had seen – the malnutrition, the death, the savage poverty, the petty and vicious deprivation of basic necessities – and each story was multiplied thousands of times over by the United Nations' statistics.

I started campaigning against the sanctions, started reading all I could about Iraq, Saddam, the embargo, its consequences, started trying to tell as many people as I could. I discovered a widespread perception that the Iraqi people somehow deserved it, that they were perceived as 25 million clones of Saddam. I discovered that the sanctions weren't news: if more than a hundred children a day were dying as a result of their impact, that was the day-before-yesterday's story, and probably hadn't been covered even then. The louder I shouted, the more journalists' fingers were stuffed into their ears. Finally one of them said to me, 'How do you know all this is happening?'

I realized it was time to go – time to go and listen to stories in streets and wards and shops in Iraq and tell them all over the world, time to defy the government order which prohibited me taking food and medicine to people who needed them.

The amount you could carry meant the goods themselves were token, although when there was no up-to-date medical information at all, a couple of pediatric medical textbooks on CD-Rom could make a real difference. It was difficult to get a visa for more than a 10-day visit in August 2001, which wasn't ideal but was the best I could do.

Although the interplay between dictatorship and sanctions was complicated, what I saw on the ground in Iraq confirmed what I'd heard at home. There could be no doubt that sanctions were devastating people. I put names and faces and individual stories to the numbers I was familiar with: 5,000 excess child deaths per month from malnutrition and curable diseases. I witnessed one of them, 11-year-old Abbas, fall into a terminal coma while his mother, screaming, tried to haul him back, to cling to him, pinching his cheek, slapping his face, calling to him as if her body which nurtured and delivered him into the world could somehow keep him from leaving.

Arriving home, his mother's distress, the doctors' helplessness to intervene and my own stayed with me. But so much else did too. I struggled to make sense of it. There was so much you couldn't ask people because you didn't have time to build up enough trust for them to open up. I felt like I'd started something by visiting Iraq but been unable to do anything meaningful to help.

Within a month of my return, New York and Washington were attacked on 11 September. As the media overflowed with material about these murders of civilians, the absence of such concern for the civilians of Iraq gnawed at me. Then Afghanistan was attacked and it became increasingly clear that Iraq would be next. In my head were vivid memories of students struggling to get degrees with no textbooks or journals, of people selling their books on the street to buy medicine but also of intricate sculptures from stories like Aladdin and Ali Baba and living legends like Babylon and Nineveh. The idea of war being waged against ordinary people who had already suffered so much – and of the world's view of that war being mediated only by the corporate press - was unbearable.

Iraq before the invasion

During the build-up to the invasion in 2003 I heard a lot on the news about political figures, military spokespeople, weapons inspectors and all manner of other people who weren't the ordinary Iraqis I'd met a year and a half earlier. I decided to go back, along with Julia Guest, an independent film-maker who lived near me in Easton, Bristol. I wanted to talk to people again and find out how they were feeling about the imminent invasion and, if they would tell me, about Saddam: I knew 'the news' wasn't going to tell me what was really happening.

The highway in from Jordan was liberally ornamented with the remains of tires. On my first visit I'd seen what those tire remnants meant. People couldn't afford new tires: 60 per cent of them had little or no income aside from the food ration. Bald tires blew out and drivers lost control of the cars, which careened across the road till they found something to crumple into. No flowers, just torn rubber marked the spot.

The Iraqi Government wasn't giving out tourist visas at the time and we had to sneak in by registering for a youth and student conference which we had no intention of attending. We succeeded in escaping all but the opening ceremony, which was predictably appalling, full of propaganda from the ruling Ba'athist Party. People planted in the audience leaped up at intervals to start pro-Saddam chants and all the Iraqis present had to join in for fear of looking disloyal. Several panic-stricken white doves emptied their bowels freely throughout the auditorium.*

At that time a foreigner couldn't get an apartment or stay with Iraqis in their home so I stayed in a hotel, the Al Fanar, close to the Palestine where almost all the international media eventually based itself. Visible from my window was a sculpture of a magic carpet, from the Aladdin story, with two people kneeling on it, leaning forward, looking up as they took to the air.

To the east there was a mosque with an ornate blue mosaic dome and minaret, behind which the sun rose, and from which the muezzin called five times a day. The summons blended in constant riotous noise with the ubiquitous car horns, the sirens, the horse-drawn gas carts whose drivers banged out a rhythm on the canisters to call people to bring out their empties and, after dusk, the wild drumbeats and trumpeting of bus-borne wedding parties. Everyone wanted to get married before the war, just in case.

To the south and west was the Tigris, calm, enormous and reflective, and beside it groups of boys playing football and packs of feral dogs. Palm trees grew along every street. The moon had waned to half, fading out across a diagonal. Baghdad was beautiful, stunning, alive, filled with generous people who plied you with tea and were eager to communicate and children who greeted you: 'Hey Mister. Welcome.' Mister was unisex, as in 'Mister Joanna'.

Over cardamom coffees and lemon teas in the Baghdad coffee shop where the 1958 revolution was plotted, amid the echoing clatter of the old men slamming down dominoes onto the tables and the fragrant smoke of *narghilas* (bubble pipes), we met two final-year medical students. They said that if bombing began they would go to the hospitals to do whatever they

---

* Before I went, several people suggested that the Ba'ath Party would try to use us for propaganda purposes. Of course they would try, just as the British and US governments tried to use Iraqi exiles for their propaganda purposes. That didn't mean we would let ourselves be used, or be of any use.

could to help – though they would still come to the coffee shop to smoke, chat and play dominoes and backgammon even if bombs were falling.

People in Baghdad seemed not to talk much about what they called 'the situation' but another acquaintance, Soulaf, talked about the bombing in 1991, when she was 13. Her four-year-old cousin had cried constantly throughout the bombardment, in terror for his life. Her voice quivered as she described it, fighting tears. She wiped her eyes, trying not to smudge the black eyeliner. The schools had closed and when they reopened she had studied by candlelight because there was no electricity.

Despite the visa difficulties there were peace campaigners in Baghdad from all over the world, from Chad and China, Syria and Sri Lanka, and even from the US, though it remained illegal under the US's sanctions for its citizens even to travel to Iraq except as journalists or UN personnel.

Denis, from DR Congo, came in solidarity with the Iraqi people because his student organization thought it was important to send someone over. The US had been doing much the same in his country for years, Denis said, agents coming in and arming, funding and training opposition fighters to destabilize the country and gain control of the minerals, especially coltan, used in mobile phones, computers and space technology.

Some of the students at the conference organized an anti-war march for 18 February with bi- or multi-lingual banners. I marched with a group of young Iraqi women who clapped their hands and chanted. The students we met in the colleges were roughly half-and-half men and women. Probably around two-thirds of the women covered their hair but many wore trousers and make-up. They were friendly and welcoming, keen to practise their English and eager to know what I thought of their city.

Over the noise we exchanged names and favorite English football teams – mainly Liverpool and Manchester United for them; Brighton and Hove Albion for me. Julia Roberts was popular with both men and women, as were boy-bands like Westlife, N-Sync and the Backstreet Boys but, even so, that wasn't an excuse for bombing these people.

A cluster of young men were jumping up and down, going round and round in a circle, chanting, one hand on the shoulder in front, the other punching the air. The rage against Bush was tangible as they shouted 'Down, Down Bush' and 'Down, Down USA'. Many of their slogans were the standard ones praising Saddam and there was a large banner saying 'Saddam is our Choice' but, like the pictures in every shop and office, it was almost certainly more a matter of expediency than political preference.

Minders and firewalls

When Julia was filming we were given 'minders', two women who worked at the language school at Baghdad University. Minders were part of the everyday surveillance of all aspects of life in Iraq, no matter who you were, but by then there were so many journalists in the country that there wasn't much supervision left for the likes of us. Mostly we were left unminded and spent time either with the local students or in the back of taxis or hidden in crowds.

Majid, a teenage student, and his brother Raed drove us out to a human-made lake, in which two palm trees stood improbably on island pedestals. Raed explained that they had been there before the lake was built. On mounds, between the lake and the engineering college opposite, an anti-aircraft gun and a radar emplacement had the look of museum pieces. Men in khaki fiddled about with them while passers-by ignored them as everyday sights. As we drove up to the tollbooth, just past the mounds, Raed muttered: 'Don't speak English now.'

Raed was an architect and had just come back from a spell working in Jordan. Their mother was Iraqi, their father Palestinian and they'd lived all over the Arab world. Raed used to work in an Iraqi satellite TV station while he was at university. Some 50 per cent of the programs had to be 'political' and a further 15 per cent news. What, we wondered, might a political program in Iraq consist of? Raed's description sounded more or less akin to religious TV show *Songs of Praise*. There wasn't, he said, much room for discussing politics. Julia suggested it might be quite scary to be a journalist in Iraq. The brothers laughed. 'It's quite scary to be an Iraqi.' But still, Majid said, life was better in Iraq than in Jordan.

On a lighter note, entertainment remained a problem, even for those who could afford it. In 1991 the Government decided to close the night-clubs, and since then young people had gone out to the theaters for dances. Alcoholic drinks were kept concealed under the seats, behind the drinker's legs until no-one was looking, or else disguised as some innocuous soft drink, but by 10 or 11 o'clock everyone was loud and silly and a bit unsteady on their feet because Iraqi beer was cheap and strong. Perched away from prying ears on a wall by the lake, Raed said he would like to see more freedom in Iraq. Yes, he said, that would include some American things, films, music.

He explained that it was illegal to have a satellite dish. If you were caught with one you were fined, roughly the equivalent of $100, or jailed for six months. Of course, rather than go to jail, people paid the fine if they could and two-thirds of the money went to the person who reported the illegal dish. The poverty caused by sanctions created a situation where people were desperate enough to sell their neighbors like that, created a fear of the people next door which stifled almost any dissent or uprising.

Out of fear, he said, a lot of people wouldn't tell you they wanted rid of Saddam but more or less everyone did. But, he said emphatically, 'We don't want America to come along and impose its system, its Pax

Americana. We don't want them to come and "rescue" us.'

As for their family's preparations, their house was stocked with food and water and guns but not to excess, as they said some families were doing. 'Every house is an independent state,' Majid laughed, equipped with all necessities. One family friend showed them the shopping list of provisions to be got in for the war, and the list included coffins.

'I said what do you want coffins for and he said in case someone gets killed. I don't know, what do they think they're going to do – bury them in the front garden and just carry on?'

Majid suggested going to a tower nearby for the view. Raed thought it a very bad idea. The tower overlooked one of the presidential palaces. Bringing two British people there wasn't likely to be good for your health. Instead, still giggling over the possibility of climbing up the tower with a telescope and peeping at Saddam in his bath, we went for Turkish coffees and a *narghila*. The mere joke, overheard on the street, could have been a beheading offence for an Iraqi.

There was a plume of thick black smoke over the city all day and on our way back the lads realized it was coming from an oil refinery on the south of the river. We all assumed it had caught fire accidentally but it was still burning the next morning. The air was no worse than usual: it always reeked of petroleum fumes because fuel was cheap and there were far too many cars, mainly clapped-out ones, often made out of two even more decrepit ones cannibalized and welded together across the middle. The fire turned out to be deliberate, testing different mixtures to create black clouds over the city so as to obscure it from aerial bombers and satellites.

Majid and Raed became frequent companions over the next days and weeks. Walking down the street one evening, crowded with people strolling, Raed and I talked quietly about my blog. 'I have a website too,' he muttered. 'It's political.' I asked for the address. 'Not here, it's not safe,' he said. It wasn't until I got back to England that I heard of the Baghdad Blogger, Salam Pax, whose writing was being read all over the world on a blog called 'Dear Raed', started because he said Raed never replied to his emails. 'We just wrote it and prayed the authorities wouldn't find us,' Raed said later.

Internet had been available in Iraq for about 18 months by then. A few had a dial-up connection at home and there were state-run internet cafes around Baghdad but access to a lot of sites was blocked by firewalls. Lamenting this to young Iraqis, you would often be told about programs or methods of getting behind the firewall: software you could download free, because you couldn't get a credit card to pay for anything, or a tunnel behind the firewall that you could access from another site. Majid would refer to a site and say with a shrug: 'You have to break a few firewalls.'

The firewall seemed to me to sum up life in Iraq. An array of things were officially inaccessible, either embargoed by the US and British governments or forbidden by the Iraqi one, but when you scratched the surface, there they were. Everything was bootlegged. A garden of illicit satellite dishes nestled under cover on rooftops and blossomed only at night. People hid their real opinions, talked with their eyes rather than their voices, got you to disguise your foreignness by telling you not to say anything in English just here. Smuggling of oil and surcharging brought cash into the country which was fueling an increase in public-sector wages and overall employment. Life was a maze of tunnels behind the firewall.

The very fact that we were at the edge of war showed that sanctions hadn't worked here. History suggests they are effective only where the sanctioned people have the capacity to change their leadership. In Iraq the sanctions had destroyed any such capacity. Nevertheless the spirit and defiance of ordinary Iraqis had enabled them, over time, to find ways of making do, of filling the gaps – and now it was about to be destroyed all over again.

Carel de Rooy, the head of UNICEF in Iraq, said that if the country's power stations were damaged or destroyed there would be severe knock-on effects on the entire civilian infrastructure. He told us the system was in a much worse position to withstand attack than it was in 1991 and the effects of any interruption to the already deficient electricity supply would quickly become critical. He said water was being stored in tankers, that emergency generators had been installed at water pumping plants, which would operate as long as fuel stores lasted, but these would not be adequate for the needs of the population.

Carel explained that 12 years of UN sanctions had left the population highly dependent on the state. The government food ration was distributed to every resident and other essential goods like electricity, water, fuel and some non-ration foodstuffs were so heavily subsidized as to be free or almost free. Many people were employed by the Government, which had created jobs to fill some of the gaps left by the collapse of private-sector industry. Again this dependence made the civilian population far less capable of withstanding attack than they had been in 1991.

According to the Fourth Geneva Convention on the protection of civilian persons in time of war, effects cease to be collateral and become intentional when they are inevitable and foreknown. It is prohibited to attack or destroy objects indispensable to the civilian population. The presence of military objectives within a population does not deprive it of its civilian character. There was already a 2,300 megawatt per day deficit in Iraq's electricity supply. Any attack on a power station would be a grave breach of international law. Any attack on a telecommunications tower next to a block of flats would be a grave breach.

The garden pump and Mr Blush

We watched as the preparation for the likely water shortage was played out in detail. In Ghazwan's garden three men were sinking a well. They worked with a metal pole that had a crossbar. Two of the men would walk this round in circles while the third would jump up on the bar, feet crossed for balance. They drove the pole ever deeper, adding sections as necessary, because the water got cleaner and more plentiful lower down, though it would take four or five days to flush through so that the water was clear.

A metal tool was used to make a screw thread on the end of the tube for the pump to be attached. It would have to be a manual pump, because if there was no electricity to power the normal water pumping system there would be none for the well either. It was right outside the kitchen and bathroom for convenience, as far from the sewage pipes as possible.

The well diggers were busy. This team had dug about 25 in the last week, for anyone who could raise the necessary $25. Elsewhere they were being made on street corners, in colleges, by mosques – anywhere there was a patch of ground.

'All my life,' said Ghazwan, 'I've turned on a tap and water has come out. Now I have to rely on this hole in my garden.

Ghazwan was a Ba'ath party member and, although not an official minder, was able to get away with associating fairly openly with foreigners. Much of his information about the world outside, though, came from an illegal satellite dish; he was periodically prosecuted for it and each time called on his brother in Britain to send the money to bail him out. He seemed always to put a positive spin on the Iraqi Government but, without overtly criticizing the regime, revealed more than most people dared to.

He referred to Bush and Blair as a single entity – Mr Blush. 'Blush' was pushing for war despite the objections of his people, he said. Both countries now locked people up indefinitely without trial, or even interview. Both governments were putting pressure on the Turkish Government to join the war, he pointed out, despite the overwhelming opposition of the Turkish people. They were subverting Turkey's democracy even as the European Union demanded greater democracy as a condition of Turkey's entry.

Ghazwan thought it a bit ironic that such countries called themselves democratic. 'We have a dictatorship,' he said, more frankly than most, perhaps because seeing nothing wrong with it. 'You're supposed to be a democracy. What kind of democracy is it you are going to bring us with your bombs?'

An NGO official who wanted to remain anonymous but who had lived in Iraq for many years wondered what would happen to the Kurdish people at the hands of Turkey. Turkey's treatment of the Kurds is no better than Iraq's: the languages and culture have been suppressed with even Kurdish names being banned by the Turkish authorities. Turkey made repeated incursions into Kurdish northern Iraq during the existence of the No-Fly Zones with the complicity of the British and US air-force commanders who policed them.

I met Roland, from the International Committee of the Red Cross, when he'd just been to Kirkuk, one of the largest cities in northern Iraq. In the north he'd met journalists training with the troops in camps preparing to follow the invasion and show the war to the world from the military perspective. He'd found the 'embedded' journalists dressing and increasingly talking like the military, boasting about what 'we', rather than 'they', the soldiers, were going to do. A lot of them were eager for 'something' to happen – for the war to start so they could get their story. He wondered if they'd ever seen a war. He grew up in a France destroyed by war, where people were still afraid.

The presence of international peace activists in Iraq, he felt, was positive because of the attention drawn to facilities like power stations and their importance to the civilian population for water, sewage, hospitals. 'People don't believe there have been power cuts here for 12 years,' Roland said. 'Yet when they come here, they see there are power cuts every day.' He felt the situation was already unacceptable from a humanitarian point of view. There were enough poor countries in the world without deliberately impoverishing rich ones.

Shop after shop was closed down, thick metal grilles across the front, bankrupted by high unemployment and low wages left after a decade and a quarter of sanctions. There was loads of stuff for sale, if people could afford it, laid out on tables in the street. Everything was made in China: buses, tractors, fire engines, clothes, shoes, fake designer belts, cosmetics, toys, household items. At a push, you'd find something made in Syria. There used to be a fleet of British Leyland buses, but the UK companies refused to supply the spare parts. By cannibalizing, they kept a dwindling fleet running for a while, but in the end the whole lot were scrapped and replaced with Chinese.

Entrepreneurial spirit was thriving. There was a little boy who begged by the Press Center whose shoes were almost entirely detached, top from sole, with the backs flattened and his heels hanging over the end. We tried to draw round his foot on a piece of paper but the muddy broken line was little help so we just picked a couple of pairs in different sizes, reasoning that there were plenty of other street kids needing them.

As it happened, they were both too big but it hardly mattered to him. When we next saw him he was wearing a smart new pair of shoes that did fit – someone else had thought the same as us. But the time after that he was back in the ragged pair, his feet almost bare again, banking on the fact that whoever bought him the last pair would have left the country and would never realize he was selling all the shoes the foreigners bought him.

There was Saif as well, who frequented Sa'adoon and Abu Nawas Streets. Some street kids begged, some shone shoes, others sold sweets or tissues. Saif dealt in hugs and kisses. The first time I met him, he reached up and kissed me on both cheeks, handed me a pink flower, took my hand

Saif – the street boy who dealt in kisses.

and strolled down the street with me until something else distracted him. The next time I saw him, I gave him a couple of pens. Another day he gave me a small fruit, apple-like in flavor, but with a stone in the middle.

One time we passed a pastry stall and I bought him one. Happily, he offered me a share, which I declined in view of the crowd of flies he'd blithely blown off it before taking the first bite. Another day I gave him a jumper and he took off his waistcoat and gave it to me to hold, putting the new one on over his ragged-sleeved sweatshirt and returning the waistcoat over the top. It must have been about 30°C (86°F) outside. He ran down the street when he saw you coming, arms outstretched, his face grubby and alight with his smile, and flung his arms around you. He was probably given more than all the other street kids put together.

Before the sanctions, education was free and compulsory up to secondary level and children were in school instead of having to fend for themselves and their families.

Prince Adnan's Emporium

We drank sweet tea with Prince Adnan in his rug-and-copper shop in the Baghdad copper market, opposite the Al Khalaf Mosque on Rasheed Street: 'Prince because I am from family of King.' He indicated the picture on the wall of the former King Faisal, installed by the British. "I met him one year, when I was seven years old and he was few years older.'

He showed us a photograph of himself as a young boy with his father, surrounded by rugs and copper. 'My father had shop in London. Old Curiosity Shop. Before 45 years. I like English people very much. You have good heart.'

He said he loved dancing. He was 62 and his wife 65. She wouldn't dance with him anymore, saying she was too old. He asked if it was the same in Britain. Did people still dance when they were 60? Did their wives dance with them? He was going to a party that night. He said people didn't go to public places to dance very much, but to parties in each other's homes. 'When I was young, always if anyone want party, then call Prince Adnan, but now, I am old, still dancing, but not stay out so late.'

Mr Kerim, a neighboring shopkeeper, was a teacher in the Institute of Technology, but he made better money in the *souk* (market), so he gave it up and took on the family business. On the wall, in a frame, was a license dated 1918, certifying that Kerim's grandfather had the formal approval of the British colonial authorities to run his shop. There was a black-and-white photograph on another wall of his father and grandfather sitting on the step of the shop, the grandfather in his mid-forties, as Kerim was now. He had three children aged 15, 13 and 10, two boys and a girl, all in school and hoped the oldest would take over the shop, then added, 'If still here.'

Mohammed and Hosam were Kurds from Sulemaniya, running an emporium of rugs, copperware and all manner of exotic kitchen implements: jeweled hammers for breaking up sugar, a cylindrical contraption with a handle at the top and holes in the bottom for squeezing lemons, flour pails engraved with the pictorial story of Sheherazade.

But the *pièce de resistance* was a helmet: one of those huge, heavy, old-style things with the bit that comes down between your eyes – to keep swords away from them, I suppose – and a mane of chain mail behind. With it was a chain mail vest and beside them, a photo of Mohammed, a decade or so younger, looking fierce in the full combo. I tried the helmet on and Hosam held up a mirror. 'Ha ha,' he said. 'Now ready for cruise missiles.'

I laughed but I had begun to wonder what it would look like when the first missile hit a city of five or six million people. What would it sound like? How would the air smell and taste on your tongue? What would it feel like: would the earth shake? Would the air? And if the skyline was collapsing, could you still find your way when all the familiar landmarks had been dismantled? Would there be any passers-by to stop for directions?

People were reluctant to go into the shelters – the mere mention of Al Ameriya, hit by two missiles in 1991, killing over 400, evoked a shudder. To stay in a house, upstairs or downstairs, would be to risk being crushed, so that left outdoors, as far as possible from a bridge, oil refinery, telecom tower or anything along those lines, but somehow that felt a little too exposed. Many talked about going to farms in the countryside.

There were premonitions in the air: one night we were shaken awake by a boom and a roaring sound and the earth seemed to wobble. We stumbled to the window but the street was normal. That time it was only thunder.

We met a man called Omar, a friend of a friend, who invited us to dinner in his home. There was always a delicate balancing act between self-censorship and putting other people in danger. If you talked to Iraqis, asked what they thought or went to their homes, it might cause suspicion to fall on them. If you didn't, then, like the mainstream media, you risked silencing them altogether.

Omar had four children. His daughter Alia had been married just over a fortnight before and I was shown the wedding photos. 'We have a happy life,' said Omar. 'Sometimes we are short of money, but we are better off than most.'

Jalal, the oldest son, fetched his graduation pictures. He had recently qualified as a doctor and now worked as a resident in the Saddam Teaching Hospital. Two of his friends, Marwan, a pharmacy student, and Odai, a medical student, seized the opportunity to tease me all evening about my bad Arabic pronunciation. They teased Sabah, the second youngest son, about eating too many falafels: 'They give you gas.' Sabah said that was where all the Middle Eastern legends about magic carpets came from: people eating falafels before bed, so their sheets ended up levitating on all the wind passed in the night.

The youngest son was born during the bombing in 1991. Omar explained how he took his wife to hospital. 'She had labor in the dark because there was no electricity, and then straight after I brought her home, but there were no windows in the house. They were all broken by the bombing, and I was afraid she would go into shock, so I took her to her father's house and that day we went out to the country.'

Now 12, the war baby insisted he wasn't scared. All of them did. Perhaps it was bravado: some even said they didn't believe the US and Britain would manage to conquer Baghdad, because everyone would resist them, but others shook their heads. They knew bombing would be intensive, maybe the most intensive bombing the world had ever seen and that they wouldn't have any defense against that, but Jinan, a doctor of physics from Dundee University, said she would pick up a gun to defend her home 'Of course. Everyone in Iraq has a gun. Everyone knows how to hold a gun.'

Someone asked what I would do if it was my home. Wouldn't I pick up a gun and fight anyone who tried to invade it? I thought about it, tried honestly to imagine anyone attempting to invade my home, and couldn't. Yet again the good fortune of my life hit me in the face: here was a child of 12, born in – literally – the darkness of war, who had already lived through the 1998 bombing and would soon have to move from his home because it was too near a telephone exchange to be safe, while I was contemplating for the first time whether I'd pick up a gun and fight off invaders.

'All we want is to live in peace.' I was hearing it a dozen times a day. Jalal said, 'If we want to change some things it's our business. It's not for America to come and tell us we have to change, we have to have a different government. We haven't got any mass destruction weapons. This one now they're making us dismantle [the Samoud 2] is not a mass destruction weapon. The countries around us all have weapons and we can't even defend ourselves, but we agree to dismantle it because we just want to live in peace, yet still they want to attack us.'

The tickle monster

One day, traveling with the journalist Felicity Arbuthnot and lawyer Akhtar Raja, we found ourselves in front of an accumulation of curious children. Felicity waved at a tiny one and he started to cry. 'I always have that effect on children,' she muttered. I knelt on the ground and said '*Marhaba*' (hello) and one or two replied, 'Hello.' The crowd grew so I did what I do best – I pulled a face. All the kids laughed, so I pulled another. Their mothers began to join them: stunning women with enormous dark eyes.

'*Ismi* Joanna,' I said – my name is Joanna.

'Shwanna,' the kids repeated, and went through all their names: Maha, Zaineb, Treibe, dozens and dozens of them, and this one is that one's sister and that one is this one's brother, and these two are cousins, and as the introductions went on the huddle grew closer. Assuming a fearsome look, I growled and made a tickle-monster grab for one. Shrieking gleefully they all jumped back and, giggling, advanced again.

'Rrrr,' I said, and they all squealed again.

Shortly a couple of guards were sent along to suggest we leave, so we waved to the kids, said '*Ma'assalama*' (goodbye) and walked away. The group which accompanied us grew and grew, though the guards told them to go back, and soon the whole party had reassembled by Zaid's taxi. Akhtar, a British-Pakistani lawyer investigating a fatal US/UK bombing in the northern no-fly-zone, had met Zaid first and made him his favourite taxi driver on account of his good English and fine sense of humor.

Where were we from, the kids wanted to know? England, Ireland and Pakistan, between us. There was a girl of maybe ten who was learning English at school. 'What's that?' she said, and 'Thank you'. *'Afwan,'* I replied: you're welcome. They asked for more faces and I pulled more, high on the kids' laughter. One started doing somersaults on the railing beside the road. I reached, monster-like, under the railing for their feet and the shrieking and giggling started again.

A tiny one with round cheeks, long black plaits and a face full of mischief blew a raspberry and doubled up with mirth. I blew kisses, with expansive arm gestures, and they blew kisses back, bright, chatty, laughing, a little girl all in black with the most melting smile, a taller one carrying her little brother, kissing and nuzzling his cheek, a young boy who tried to copy the faces I pulled, all of them with hearts wide open and full of laughter. I don't want this to sound sentimental. Civilian populations ought not to be bombed, children or adults, beautiful or otherwise. It was just that there was this tension of waiting and that unbearable contrast between the happy moment and what we adults knew was to come but the children, surely, did not.

Eventually we had to leave and they waved us off with more kisses blown after the taxi. I suddenly caught sight of the sharp, bright crescent of the new moon in the dusk sky. Then Felicity pointed out the Ministry of Defense building, just a minute or so away from those laughing children, their mothers and their homes, right in the firing line if the US and Britain decided the Ministry was a target. Driving back, we chatted about English football until Zaid asked me: 'What will you do if the war starts?'

'Zaid,' I said, honestly, 'I don't know. What will you do?'

'I'll be on my roof, getting the view. I've seen it all before. So if you find you need anything, just call me.'

Zaid was then 30, two years older than me, and all but two of the last 22 had been at war.

Talking to him the next day, we were interrupted by another man who came over and muttered something in Arabic. 'OK,' Zaid said to me, steering me away. 'I'll arrive you to the hotel.' The other man had told him we were being watched by an intelligence officer. If you poked your finger into the air in Baghdad you could feel the squelch and suction of fear, paranoia and suspicion.

Fragments of news formed a mosaic of possibilities: proposed changes to the wording of the draft UN resolution, resignations, speeches, arrivals, departures, dates, deadlines, potential uses of the veto by France, China, Russia, flashes of hope, chutes of fear, twists in the plot.

So Zaid and I went to the Medina Al-Abb – the City of Games, a dilapidated amusement park packed with Baghdad's kids, teenagers and adults queuing up to scare themselves silly on a rollercoaster with nothing to hold you in the cars but '*insha'Allah*' and your own knuckles. Behind the tangle of scaffolding and rails, three men rolled out their mats and began to pray amid the roar of the machinery and the screaming of the fair-goers.

A miniature train jingled in its enclosure, doing laps around a peeling polar bear whose head just peeped over the rampant vegetation. Kids stood between two horses on the carousel, one foot on the stirrup of each one, facing backwards, undulating side to side and up and down. The young women, many in long skirts, smart blazers, stack heels and headscarves – though there were also many in jeans and t-shirts – managed to look elegant even spinning around the anti-gravity machine.

Amid the crowds and the music and the clamor, whistles, hoots, I felt, for once, like no-one was watching, no-one was eavesdropping. Finally I understood why people seemed to talk so little about the war. They were heartily sick of the whole thing. It was beyond their control. There had been exams the previous week, but teachers and lecturers said it was impossible to give a lesson because the students couldn't concentrate. They talked not to discuss the war but to distract themselves from it.

An unbirthday

I had a birthday, which was a pleasant surprise, as I wasn't due another one for two months yet, but Asmaa and Israa brought out a huge cake when I went round, and decided the cake deserved a birthday to celebrate, so we went to the lake with a big bag of fruit and had a boat ride in the sunset. Asmaa gave me the knife to cut the cake with and told me to make a wish.

'What did you wish? Can you tell me?'

'I wish for peace Asmaa. What else could I wish?'

Mimi declared herself to be a '*shaadi*' – monkey – and Mimi-Monkey she became, squealing in glee as Zaid turned her upside down and I spun her round and round. She stuck her tongue out when she laughed, a full-bodied chortle that took over her entire being, one small finger pointing at the source of her amusement. For the first hour she hadn't said a word to me. By the time we got in the car to go to the lake she was chatting happily and we walked hand in hand along the wall beside the water. When Asmaa sang to her she started dancing and, as we walked back after watching the sunset, oblivious to our continued existence, she sang Spice Girls songs all the way to the car.

Amid the laughter it was possible to forget, for a while. 'Do you think the kids have any sense that something is wrong?' I asked.

'No,' Asmaa said. 'But I cry on my own because I'm so frightened for them. I don't know what's going to happen. I have to have faith that if God wants us to live then we will live.'

I asked Zaid if he would be called up to fight. 'I don't know. I don't know how to fight.' He did his 18 months' military service working with computers. Zaid and Asmaa confided in the days before the war that they were longing for the invasion. They wanted rid of the Iraqi Government, though they asked me not to attribute those opinions to them by name until it was all over. They'd been listening to Voice of America radio, to the messages broadcast by Bush and Rumsfeld, telling the Iraqi people they were praying for them, coming to liberate them. They wanted desperately to believe them.

Ever the optimist: Zaid.

'Zaid,' I said, in the car, 'the US is not coming to make things better. They encouraged Iraq to start a war with Iran because they wanted you to fight Iran for them and thousands of people died while they were helping both sides so the war would go on longer. You know that.'

'Yes, I know,' he agreed.

'And then they encouraged you to invade Kuwait because they wanted to get at the Kuwaiti ruling family.'

'I know that. They always use Iraq.'

'And then they imposed sanctions on you and caused even more death and suffering. Twelve and a half years of sanctions, while they continually moved the goalposts and they said it was worth the price of so many Iraqi children dying.'

'Yes.'

'And now they're coming to bomb you – again – and you think they're suddenly going to start acting in the Iraqi people's interests?'

'I don't know.'

'They're going to bring in a US general or a leader from the Iraqi National Congress and a lot of them are as bad as what you've got now. They were part of the program of killing the Kurds, they were part of all of it. Not all of them, but some of them.'

'No, we don't want that. We want someone from here.'

'Zaid, do you think they're going to let you choose? They kept Saddam in power, gave him weapons, gave him money, covered up his human rights abuses, blocked international condemnation of what he did; they kept him where he was all the time he's been oppressing you because he was their ally.'

'Yes, but now they're going to get rid of him.'

'And replace him with someone who does what they tell him. They don't care what happens to you. They never have.'

'Well, I don't know.'

I felt mean, pissing on his bonfire. 'Well, I just hope you're right and I'm wrong. I really do. But think about this Zaid. What do you think would happen if the Iraqi people decided they wanted to keep the oil industry nationalized?'

Sandbags and sticky tape

Each day there was a queue of boys outside the recruitment office, call-up papers in hand. Small sandbag dens, like a child might make, began sprouting out of the pavements, by way of some protection against shrapnel and flying debris: it was better than a poke in the eye with a sharp bit of metal, so to speak, but it wasn't much. They were on street corners and in little walls in front of some buildings, houses and shops. People had taped Xs on their windows to prevent them shattering. Sandbags. Sandbags and sticky tape against stealth bombers, cruise missiles, uranium bunker busters and all the other cutely named murderous hardware the US-UK had piled on the doorstep. Sandbags, all there was to shield soft human bodies from burning metal and explosives.

On 12 March the bulk of the remaining UN and embassy staff left Iraq. Ibrahim from Médecins Sans Frontières showed me their mission briefing, including diagnosis and treatment for a whole list of horrors:

sarin gas, chlorine gas, nuclear bunker busters, depleted uranium. Biological weapons, it said, cause more fear than real emergency, but bunker busters – Hard, Deeply Buried Target (HDBT) missiles – cause intensive radiation within a certain area, as opposed to normal nuclear weapons which detonate above the ground and send their radiation much further. The bunker buster fireball penetrates into the ground and sends out a fountain of debris.

There was also a book on surgical treatment of war wounds to limbs. I didn't look for long. I knew, of course, that war mangles bodies, but seeing the practical preparations for the effects of bullets, cluster bomblets, debris, landmines and so on made it all seem both hideously real and grotesquely unbelievable.

Kamil was a man of enormous dignity, quiet sadness and the elegance of the dancer he used to be, a lifetime ago. A few days before the war he stopped speaking. He would communicate only in signs. We understood well enough. There just weren't any words which would do.

The shops were all emptying, piling stock into sacks and taking it somewhere safer. The petrol stations were overflowing with cars. Even Husam now warned us there was a war coming. A few days ago he'd sworn blind there wasn't going to be an attack. It was only when we told him the UN were leaving in convoy, along with most of the embassy staff, that he rubbed his chin, frowned, and remarked that that was a bad sign. Now in his office, shaken out of complacency, they were putting everything into a back room with no windows: the photocopier, the TV, computers, all their files.

The office was in the tallest building in the area, a street away from a telephone exchange. In 1991 everything above the second floor collapsed and all the windows burst inwards when the telephone exchange was hit twice. Targets, Husam said, were always hit two, three, four times, from the top, from both sides, just to make sure.

CNN was on, broadcasting business news and adverts for Texaco, showing its shiny new pipeline, built by friendly smiling people to move the nice oil about and not a word about pollution of the planet, displacement of human beings and the uneven distribution of resources the pipeline really meant.

There was a report showing graphics and explanations of various military hardware and jargon. Here's an armored vehicle that has stinger weapons. It can carry four at a time. A British MP said he would vote against the war, but once it started he'd be '100 per cent behind our boys'. Where were their principles? Why did people who had been made irrelevant by the Prime Minister persist in upholding the pretence that there was some legitimacy to this process? Where was the vote of no confidence?

I pushed my chair to the window and looked at a street dotted with palm trees and cedars, a woman in a long dress walking hand in hand with a small boy in blue trousers and a stripy jumper, a pair of schoolgirls wearing the uniform long navy pinafores with white blouses and carrying shoulder bags, two old men shuffling, cars and buses hooting in the road. Beyond, lines of washing were strung between the balconies and the studio presenters counted the hours until it was all to be shattered. The midnight deadline. The 48-hour evacuation warning. The speech at 4am local time.

The day before the war

Undoubtedly there were those in the country who wanted war to begin, in the way you long for a thunderstorm on an unbearably humid day. People were as afraid of the Iraqi Government as they were of bombs. People's eyes said different things from their mouths and they talked when they knew no-one else could hear. Most wanted rid of the ruling clan but, even so, most rejected a US invasion as the means of change. That wasn't what people were supposed to say, so I was inclined to believe it.

Thawra, then known as Saddam City, was the poorest part of Baghdad and noticeably more run-down than anywhere else. It was a Shi'a district, touted then as the most likely starting point for civil unrest after bombing started. People told you not to go there: 'It's dangerous.' Around half of Baghdad's population of five or six million lived there. Shi'a from the rest of the country had moved into the dense slum where there was both more employment than elsewhere in Iraq and some sort of safety in numbers.

There was a big puddle in the doorway of the classroom at Thawra's Qataiba boys' school. A woman in black dragged rags across it by way of a mop, but made little impact. The room itself was bare, without resources or a full complement of windows. Wooden benches were framed with the remnants of seat covers. Outside, a fence surrounded a peeling statue of a schoolboy in a suit, gazing philosophically into the distance, his pedestal an island in a swamp. Behind him stood a crumbling building devoid of any windows at all. The principal's office was as battered as the rest, deprived of maintenance for 12-and-a-half years of sanctions.

Over 12 years of sanctions, of incalculable deprivation, and yet tomorrow was the day before the war.

There were 22 teachers taking mixed-age classes of 745 students. The students were aged anything between 16 and 23, because the boys tended to miss a lot of time: many of them had to work, some went to the army and then returned to school. A male teacher shouted amid the clamor of the classroom, 'We will not fight for Saddam Hussein, but we will fight for our land. I will accept any Arab as president but I will not accept a foreigner. If the Americans come, they will be very strong at first, but after some time they will see resistance. We will fight them. It doesn't matter about sects, Shi'a, Sunni, Kurd, Christian. I am Kurd. We will all fight together, not for the Government. For our land.'

It was the first time I'd seen anyone vent frustration so openly. Then he muttered: 'We need to change the Government, but I don't want America invasion. This not bring freedom. I can't talk here, because of security.'

Accompanied, unfortunately, by minders, we went to visit the home of Yasser, one of the students in Thawra, where 14 people lived: his parents, his brothers and sisters, his aunt and several cousins, nieces and nephews and his paralyzed grandmother.

Yasser shared a room with his cousin Mustapha, a physics student at Baghdad University. The boys had two posters on their wall: one of Manchester United Football Club and one from the film *Braveheart*. 'It's about freedom,' Mustapha explained. 'Mel Gibson, he is like us, he is a free man.' He gave me a fierce look as if to tell me I must read between the lines. *Braveheart* is a film about the Scots rising up against English occupation; Mel Gibson's character William Wallace leads a rebellion and is hanged for his trouble, so he's free only in the sense that he fights for freedom.

But did Mustapha mean freedom from Saddam or from occupation by foreigners? Or both? They had a Kalashnikov in the house for defense. I asked who they expected to need to defend themselves against

Yasser's sister Farah with her daughter Zainab.

– Americans, the Iraqi army, looters. A shrug. Anyone who threatened their home.

The boys said they would carry on studying during the war, though Yasser's school and Mustapha's college were already closed. Yasser's sister lived there with her husband, who was studying translation, and her daughter Zainab. The house was ramshackle from the outside, but within it was spacious and comfortable – sofas occupied one corner and two walls, while rugs and cushions framed another wall.

In Thawra the shops were still open, unlike most of Baghdad, because people there were too poor to buy in bulk in preparation. The market was busy with horses and carts and people among the stalls with tattered raffia shades over the goods. Traffic was light in Baghdad and a journey that would take 40 minutes on an ordinary day took only 15.

Like Yasser, Thoraya wasn't at school. She was 17, born in 1985, during the war with Iran. She was five years old in the first Gulf War. She and her brother Usama were terrified and crying during the bombing: the family used to sit in the bathroom, which had no windows, for fear of imploding glass. Thoraya's friend's house collapsed in the bombing, killing everyone except the father. The buildings now were in a worse state than they were in 1991, Thoraya's dad explained, even those that hadn't been weakened by bombing, because most people couldn't afford maintenance during the years under sanctions.

Faroukh's school was open, but only the teachers were inside, and Leila, the beautiful cleaner whose grey hair showed just at the front beneath her scarf. A crowd of Faroukh's mates were at the gate clowning, hugging each other, singing football chants and declaring AC Milan to be the greatest.

'We don't know when we will see each other again or if we will at all,' said Faroukh with a shrug.

Metal sheets sealed the windows of most of the non-food shops throughout the city; men were bricking up the entire front of one – against looters, apparently, rather than bombs. Pick-ups loaded with furniture, chandeliers, antiques, toys passed by. In the internet center the staff moved in mattresses and bedding so they could protect the equipment against theft. There were tents at the roadside with soldiers sitting around them. A boy in a uniform sat in his position in the street, head on his knees.

As if it was the city of Baghdad that was the problem. As if it wasn't the idea that the West could support and fund and arm Saddam Hussein, knowing that he minced his political opponents and destroyed whole towns full of people. As if it wasn't the idea that once he was beyond control the people of the entire country could be besieged, denying them adequate food. As if it wasn't the idea that after 12-and-a-half years of suffering and death, you could flatten their country, 'shock and awe' them into surrendering with Cruise missiles.

The 48-hour deadline would run out at 4am. Ahmed came and knocked on the door of our apartment close to midnight and told us the bombers were coming. He shook my hand, held my shoulder and told me he was sorry. *He* was sorry? It was his country and they were my bombers.

A siren sounded and my heart flipped, but then followed the familiar horn sound of a Red Crescent ambulance. Going where, I wondered? What accident, what illness could possibly befall you in the hour before the war? It was 3.30am.

2

WAR: 'SHOCK AND AWE'

20-31 March 2003

Low thundering booms drew us out onto the balcony, where I could feel the pulsation through the air and see the sky sparkling with anti-aircraft fire until the showers of tiny meteors faded out into the daylight and the explosions stopped. The feral dogs that lived on the riverside ran down the middle of the road, which was wiped clear of cars, trying to escape the noise, which was in stereo.

It was 20 March. The streets stayed empty all day. Nothing was open to travel to. There was nothing in the shops and the metal or brick frontages were staying where they were until it was all over. The invasion had started and yet not started. Bush said that morning was only an 'opportunistic strike'. The full weight of 'shock and awe' hadn't yet begun.

That morning the manager of our hotel was arrested, seized by two men in uniforms and dragged, screaming and struggling in obvious panic, to a vehicle. Apparently this was because some ignorant journalists were filming the bombing from the roof of the hotel, even though they were all supposed to be staying in the Palestine Hotel across the road. The men wouldn't tell us where they were taking him and we couldn't do a thing to help him. We hardly expected to see him back, but within the hour he was escorted through the door. The edifice wasn't crumbling just yet.

We were still in limbo.

That night's bombing started around 8pm. It was closer than before – the windows were rattling and we saw something hit the far side of the river. There was speculation that it was the press center but in fact it was part of the complex where Tariq Aziz, the foreign minister, had his headquarters. Three of the buildings were mashed and smoking; the tall red one was apparently unscathed.

Zaid would call for me in the mornings pretending to be my driver, ask the hotel staff to ring me and then wait outside and we would drive around the city unnoticed, seeing what had changed. We used to sing, every song we knew, as we traveled around Baghdad. 'It is war,' he said, 'and we are singing!' But what else could we do? We talked about running through the streets with Asmaa and the kids tearing down Saddam portraits and, for me, letting down the tires of US tanks.

Thoraya said she slept with her mum the first night of the bombing because she was scared. The second night she started having dreams: she was running down the road, all the memories from last time were coming back.

Wandering around our part of town, most things were still closed, but in New Baghdad – perversely one of the oldest parts – the marketplace was bustling. There were more cars on the road than in the previous couple of days, though it was still quiet, even for a Friday, and the litter which had strewn the streets since Wednesday had been swept into the gutters and piled up.

The 'guards' at Mosfa Daura, the oil refinery, didn't bother stopping anyone – they just waved you through. If you didn't know the way to the place you wanted they'd hop in the back of the taxi and direct the driver. The soldiers dutifully sat by their trenches all day but they disappeared at night.

I doubted whether anyone was really going to fight the US and UK military. Some people would tell you the US couldn't win, would never take Baghdad. One man told me to tell the British that the Iraqi people would all stand and fight to the death because they loved Saddam Hussein. I tried to tell him that there was really no need to say that; that I knew a lot of people wanted rid of Saddam. We were alone in his car – he could say what he liked, but he wouldn't have it.

I don't know. Maybe he was right. Maybe some people really loved Saddam. Maybe. But not, I thought, the young conscripts in army uniforms. Certainly not Waleed, who was avoiding going home to escape being drafted into the army.

On the 21st a journalist rang from Britain and said the B52 bombers had left Fairford airbase several hours ago and were coming for us. All my information was coming from journalists in Britain and Australia ringing for interviews. The port of Um Qasr in the south had apparently been taken and ground troops were inside northern Iraq. I thought something was hit in the Daura complex, where the refinery and the power plant were. There was a crater and smoke in the area of the bright orange oil flare that you could see from miles around, rumors of civilian casualties but you couldn't find out anything.

By 8pm it was dark and I knew the bombers would have reached Iraq. I knew they were in the sky above us and I knew there were ships in the Gulf which could fire Cruise missiles this far. As I sat in the internet center typing a blog entry the explosions began. The floor shook, as did I. Was this the full onslaught, this third night of bombing, or just another 'precision strike'? My heart thumped as I quickly signed off, wanting to send the message before the electricity went.

Directly across the river, one, two, three impacts flung us backwards, jets of flame shooting up. Car alarms howled, prayer calls sounded and all the while the sky went on sparkling as if the stars were burning out and dying. The horizon glowed with flame in some directions and from time to time the roar of a plane reached the ground, though long after the thing had passed.

Asmaa said in the morning: 'Mimi was so scared, she cried and screamed. At last we gave her Valium, a small piece, to sleep.'

Firas, from the hotel, said he too gave Valium to his kids, five and six years old. The bombing was much more intensive: 320 missiles, compared with 75 the previous night and 40 in the first wave. The official figure was 207 civilian casualties that night (according to Iraqi state radio) and 14 the night before: one man dead; three men, nine women and a child injured.

It was more or less impossible those first few days to go to the bomb sites or to talk to the victims. Journalists were given a mass tour of the hospital that morning and saw what one of them said were horrific injuries but they were for the most part unable to talk properly with the injured. Iraq, for some reason, was determined to play down the harm to civilians. Paranoia reigned and it was hard to do anything. We used to meet friends away from prying eyes or wander over to the Palestine Hotel to use the internet.

In the evenings I sat setting the world to rights over tea and cake with the hotel staff round the desk on the ground floor or leaning against a post on the roof with Ahmed, the bear-like man who'd come to tell us the bombers were coming, looking out at the city lights, or sometimes the lack of them, and the flashes and the jets of flame.

Shockwaves and cluster bombs

Samir took me to see his shop. I'd met him at the internet center and he had some simple books in both Arabic and English for language learning which he wanted to lend to me. It was in a row underneath the roundabout on our side of Jumhuriya (Republic) Bridge. It was closed with a heavy metal shutter and multiple chunky padlocks and, distracted by the struggle to unlock them all, Samir didn't notice till I pointed out that there were great shards of glass poking through the shutter.

One of the padlocks was warped and he couldn't get it open. In the end Abu Ahmed, whose shop was a few doors down, brought a big metal bar and Samir hammered it off. He pulled up the shutter to the clatter of falling glass and unlocked the door. It wouldn't open. He had to reach through the jagged window and release it from the partially slumped doorframe. Nothing hit this part of town, but the shockwaves were enough to cause serious damage. Three other shops in the row had lost windows as well – those whose doors had been left open behind the shutters had escaped. I helped him sweep it away while he apologized repeatedly for the state of his shop.

A couple of palaces had been hit and a state security building – no-one was crying over those. There was also a hit in a residential street – it wasn't clear what they were aiming for and we weren't able to go close enough to it to get much information, but there were houses either side and no obvious targets around.

Faadi, one of the students we'd met, saw from his roof an explosion in mid-air, followed by several explosions on the ground. The account indicated a cluster bomb. Cluster bombs caused a lot of deaths in Afghanistan when people, especially children, picked up or walked too close to unexploded segments.

Kelly Campbell, whose brother-in-law was killed in the US on 11 September 2001, went to Afghanistan as part of a peace group to meet families affected by the bombing there. She met a boy who had seen his friend explode when he picked up a bomblet. She said he'd lost the power to speak.

Here in Baghdad the kids still played outside on bikes in the day and crowds of youngsters kicked footballs, freed from school until all this was over. Carloads of cabbages seemed to be traveling all over the city, coming in from the farms. The third day of bombing was the first time I heard explosions before dark: something had gone up in smoke fairly close by, but you couldn't get out of a vehicle near the bombing sites so I didn't know what it was. It wasn't clear whether most of them were unexploded bombs being detonated or whether there were continuing attacks.

The word was that there were a further 1,500 missiles coming in the next two days or so but you never really knew where the word was coming from. The BBC reported that the house of Chemical Ali – Ali Hassan Rajid, who organized the Anfal campaign against the Kurds – had been destroyed and its owner killed during the first night of bombings. Zaid and I drove past trying to look like we weren't looking and it seemed unscathed. Who knows? Maybe he had a holiday home.

The Iraqi authorities announced two enemy planes had been shot down over Baghdad. Jumhuriya Bridge was clogged with traffic and a crowd hanging over the side. Boats darted up and down hunting pilots in the reeds. Something was burning on the far side of the river, too small to be a whole plane – maybe a piece of wreckage, maybe an attempt to flush out anyone hiding.

The accounts conflicted as to whether two pilots were captured then or only one or none at all, but around 11pm there was gunfire on Abu Nawas Street, sirens, screeching brakes and everyone running down to the river. Some said a plane had come down, others said a parachute, though I couldn't find anyone who claimed to have actually seen either. One said he'd seen a man running and then everyone else chasing him. Fires were lit again in the reeds, guns were loaded and cocked and bystanders were ushered off the street.

In truth it's unlikely that any planes were shot down at all. The bombers flew too high and too fast for Iraq's ancient anti-aircraft guns even to tickle them but feverish rumors spread, heedless of possibility.

Heba at Amal's birthday party.

Each day it looked more and less like a country at war: more, because the smoking buildings were increasingly common; less, because the streets became busier. Still nothing was open but the street stalls went on trading and food was cooked on barbecues outside the takeaways. The sunsets were stunning, but with them came the knowledge that, at any moment, the strikes might start. Everyone phoned friends afterwards to check up on each other: are you OK, how close was it to you?

On 23 March we held a birthday party because Amal, the daughter of a friend of a friend, was 13. We started with the birthday cake, because there were explosions in the distance in all directions and, if we were going to be forced to abandon the party, we weren't going to risk having to abandon the cake. Mohammed, my Kurdish taxi-driver friend from my first trip to Iraq, was grinning broadly, crumbs and sugar all over his moustache. Amal, at the head of the table, was queen of the garden behind the riverside teashop.

The twins, Heba and Dua, posed for photos, fiddling with their headscarves before presenting dazzling smiles, heads on an angle to make sure you got their best sides. Anyone tall enough to reach was co-opted to shake the tree in the garden to make the little red stoned fruits fall off that the kids loved. As explosions wracked the sky they ran back from the tree to the table, then carried on as soon as the burst turned out to be anywhere but in our party.

The twins made us all spin them around till the ground was strewn with dizzy people, exhausted after too many games involving chasing one another round tables, headscarves hanging round the girls' necks. Fadma and Majdi galloped about the garden in ballroom style and Mahmoud clambered on everyone until his ticklishness was discovered and then he had to hide.

Visiting the victims

The sky was black with smoke all around, looking ready to roar with a huge storm, but above it was bright blue. The explosions happened all day now, though not frequently. Though in the middle-class areas everything was still closed, in the poorer parts of town the streets were as busy as ever.

Close to buildings which were hit, a lot of houses lost windows. In some, where the upper parts jutted out above the ground floor, the top parts were sagging, hanging loosely from the main structure. Trenches of oil were burning furiously, the black clouds enveloping clusters of houses and turning the road to night as you passed through.

Finally we and a group from Iraq Peace Team were permitted to speak to people in a street where a missile struck a house on Saturday evening. Eight people lived there and were eating together in a downstairs room when the missile hit. It didn't land directly on the house – it was, they said, a glancing blow. The roof had collapsed, as had the ceiling between lower and upper floors. Bent steel reinforcing bars and broken concrete slouched into the downstairs room and rubble filled the garden.

A poster was still on the remaining wall of what had once been the single women's room. All the family had glass wounds to their legs. The houses either side were damaged – in the one to the right, as you looked from the street, there was a hole in the side at the back of the house and a crack so that the back wall was slumping away from the rest of the building.

The kids from the other houses in the street said they heard and felt the blast. Another neighbor from opposite told us how shaken his 80-year-old mother was. All their windows were smashed. The Civil Defense

Force had been to the site straight away and taken the wreckage of the weapon. No-one knew whether the missile missed its intended target or the bombers thought it was a target.

In the Kindi hospital, just before we met the people from the farmhouse mentioned in the Introduction, we interviewed people who were hurt when a bomb hit their house: a young boy with a shrapnel wound to his abdomen, who had had to have part of his intestine removed and a colostomy bag installed; a young man who had multiple glass and shrapnel wounds to his arms and legs and a severe leg fracture – he could remember nothing of what had happened except that he was in his house at the time.

Another woman, Suad, cried quietly beside us, waiting to speak. Like the family from the farmhouse, like many others, she had decided to leave Baghdad for an outlying family farm when a missile struck a college of the Mustansariyah University. The force of the blast overturned the car. Her legs were broken. She was holding her two-year-old daughter when it happened. The child had glass in her head. Suad's sister had a serious abdominal wound and hadn't been seen since they arrived at the hospital.

Ahmed, who worked in the internet center, mentioned the same blast to me earlier in the day – it was near his home and his windows were all broken. He thought it caught a primary school as well, but only destroyed the fence. The stories started to come together, to form a more complete picture of the effects of just a single weapon.

Asked to take a statement from another casualty, we found him already dying, his family around him, so we didn't go into the room. As we walked away one of the men came after us with a tin of sweets to offer us. 'Thank you for coming,' he said in English.

On 23 March a ferocious sandstorm enveloped Baghdad. It and the bombings both beat at the windows and thundered through the city but, after a missile exploded, flocks of birds filled the sky, dislodged by the shock waves. After a gust, they were replaced by a cornucopia of rubbish, drifting in the smog of sand and dust and smoke which had turned the air a dirty orange so thick it blotted out the sun and everything went dark in the middle of the day. Even the rain was filthy: the cleansing, healing drops filled with grime on the way down and splattered you with streaks of toxic mud.

It went on for a couple of days. The Iraqis called it orange weather; some said it was on their side. It wasn't even five o'clock and the sun wouldn't set till nearly seven but it was dark outside. I half imagined the war being like this, the sky staying dark all the time, but without the orange. It stank as well, of smoke and oil and I don't know what else. The darkness and the grime and the fierce cold wind lent an unnecessary sense of apocalypse to the flooded craters, broken trees, gaping windows and wrecked houses where the bombs had hit.

Still the stories came from the south. Nasariyah had fallen, there was still fighting in Nasariyah; Basra had been taken, Basra hadn't been taken; they'd decided to come for Baghdad, leaving Basra surrounded, and rely on the assumption that Basra would capitulate once Baghdad was captured.

Essa Jassim Najim, a 28-year-old first-year engineering student from a farming family near Babylon, couldn't speak because of shrapnel wounds to his head and neck but his father explained that three days ago they were attacked by two groups of Apache helicopters. The first group attempted to land and the farmers resisted them with guns, aided by the Civil Defense Force. The second group of helicopters attacked the house, destroying it with a missile.

Another farming community in Ad-Doraa also reported an attack by Apache helicopters at 4pm on Saturday. Atta Jassim died when a missile hit his house. Moen, his eight-year-old son, had multiple bowel and intestinal injuries from shrapnel; part of his intestine had been removed. His six-year-old brother Ali and mother Hana were also injured by shrapnel.

Saad Shalash Aday was another farmer, from Al-Mahmoodia in south Baghdad. He had a fractured leg and multiple shrapnel wounds, including a ruptured spleen, perforated caecum, colon and small bowel, abdominal and leg wounds. Two of his brothers, Mohammed and Mobden, were also injured and ten-year-old twin boys Ahmed and Daha Assan were killed inside the same house when a bomb exploded two or three meters from the building. The doctor, Ahmed Abdullah, said two other men had been killed in the same attack: Kherifa Mohammed Jebur, a 35-year-old farmer, and another man whose name nobody present knew.

Eight houses and four cars were destroyed and cows, sheep and dogs were killed. The eyewitnesses described two bombs, each causing an explosion in the air, and cylindrical containers – cluster bombs, some of which exploded on the ground.* Others did not explode. The two explosions were about 300 meters apart, with a few minutes between them. From first hearing the plane overhead until the second explosion, they estimated, took about 10 minutes.

'Is this democracy?' the men demanded to know, gathered by Saad's bed. 'Is this what America is bringing to Iraq?'

At nine in the morning a group of caravans was hit with cluster bombs, according to the doctors. A tiny boy lay in terrible pain in the hospital, a tube draining blood from his chest, which was pierced by shrapnel. They

---

* CBU-87 and RBL755 bomblets are bright orange/yellow soda-can sized objects; ATACMS bomblets are bright baseball-sized spheres (Human Rights Watch).

said he was eight, but he looked no older than five. The doctors were testing for abdominal damage as well. I'm not sure whether he knew yet, or could understand, that his mother had been killed instantly and his five sisters and two brothers had not yet been found. His father had gone to bring blood for him and his uncle, Dia, was beside him.

Rusol Ammar, a skinny ten-year-old girl with startling eyes, flinched occasionally when breathing hurt her – she had multiple injuries from glass and shrapnel, as well as a fractured hand. Her dad said something had hit their street and exploded. They were in their house and tried to close the door against the fireball but the windows blew in and the glass and shrapnel flew everywhere. Dr Ahmed explained that, at the velocity caused by an explosion, even a grain of sand could cause injury to a child Rusol's size. They weren't yet sure what was in her chest.

'Is this democracy?' Rusol's dad asked.

Farms are not a legitimate target, even if you do want to land your helicopter on them. From the legal perspective, the presence of a military objective within a civilian area or population does not deprive the population of its civilian character, even if you can call landing a helicopter a military objective. You cannot bomb an area of civilian houses knowing that people in the vicinity are likely to be hurt by flying glass and shrapnel.

More than that though, more than the illegality of it, it was wrong. It was desperately, horrifyingly, achingly wrong.

The bombing of the market

The internet connection was down and phone lines were unreliable even within Baghdad. The Iraqi TV station was hit during the night. Friends in the south of the city said there was no water or electricity when they woke up. By morning, though, the sky had cleared: a mixed blessing because while we could see again so could the bombers.

In Al-Shaab market, bombed the previous day, Mohammed Al-Zubaidi told us he had a shop where he made and sold cushions for car seats. It was the second unit from the left as you looked at the remains of the building. It was burned out but you could still see his small compartment. His assistant, Faris Al-Bawi, was crushed in the blast and his body incinerated in the fire that followed, along with his 11-year-old son Saif who was helping him, because his school was closed for the war.

Mohammed was out of the shop and saw two rockets dropped, about five seconds apart at 11.30am. He couldn't see the plane because of the thick air, but said he heard it. There was a crater in the middle strip of the road – not deep – and the buildings either side of the road were wrecked and burned out. The US tried to claim the Iraqis bombed the marketplace themselves but Iraq had no aircraft flying.

Hisham Hussein said he was about 200 meters away, indicating a set of traffic lights, when it happened. He saw the missile hit the front of the building where Mohammed's shop used to be. It wasn't a huge missile, he said, which fitted with the relatively small size of the crater. He said a lot of people were injured in the flats above the shops. The shops were all open and the market was busy. He thought 25 people were killed. Someone else said 45-50 people had gone to hospital. No-one could think of a military target nearby.

Mohammed said five people died in the restaurant near his shop. Abu Hassan, a 45-year-old father of five, 17-year-old Malik Hamoud and Sabah Nouri, 28, were all working there. Two customers also died but no-one we met knew their names. The crowd of men told of women in cars which caught fire, burning to death because no one could get to them. Safa Isam and his brother Marwan, 17 and 12 respectively, were injured in a car driven by their father, who died.

Family after family had been torn apart: mothers, fathers, children, wives and husbands, and it had only been a week.

Within the same district a missile hit a home next door to Balqis Secondary School for Girls on Tuesday night. The school was damaged: most of the neighbors thought that was the intended target. The bomb plowed through the wall of number 74 next door, bursting into square fragments about half a centimeter long, pocking the walls in all directions with what looked like a rash of bulletholes: small pits about five centimeters in diameter at the surface.

The television exploded and a metal bar on the window was bent. The mattress on which the family was sleeping was covered with blood. Munib Abid Hamid managed to shield his wife and child with his body. His wife Sahar Taha had chest injuries but had been discharged from the An-Naman surgical hospital. Their six-year-old son Khaiser Munib had two broken legs. Munib's parents were downstairs with the rest of the family, all unhurt.

Munib was a solid-looking man. The doctor said he'd only survived this far because he was so strong. His mother told us in gestures that he was cut from his chest to the bottom of his torso. His body was peppered with the metal squares. The doctor said he had multiple injuries to his abdomen: they had removed bits from his intestines and liver, both legs and feet, but some had had to be left where they were.

The bandages which encased his legs were yellowed and foul-looking – he was fighting gas gangrene and still in danger of losing his legs. 'How can I work in future?' he asked. 'I am a car mechanic. I think I am finished.' Another livelihood destroyed. The question, as in previous days, echoed like the after-rumbles of the bombs: 'Is this democracy? Is this freedom?'

Because people weren't going to work or school, they were mostly at home in the middle of the day and six died when a missile demolished five homes in Adamiya at lunchtime. It landed vertically on number 13, killing the grandmother, Khowla Sherkhli, the father, Ahmed Munier, and the daughter, Maha Ahmed. Three survived with injuries. Another three died in the street whose houses backed onto that one. In number 11, 65-year-old Wadha Mukhlif and her husband Abid survived despite being crushed and lacerated, as did 10-year-old Hamsa Waleed and her mother at number 15.

It all seemed so casual. Daily I saw mangled homes and bodies, only a corner of the picture, and that was only the most dramatic aspect. Zaid had been without electricity for three days and the water supply was intermittent. Majid said his and Raed's house had only an occasional power supply and all their windows upstairs were shattered.

He was worried because their house was near the airport and one of the theories was that forces would land there and advance into town, taking them right past his house. His mates had all left, mostly to the countryside but, from time spent in the hospitals, I knew the farms were being viciously attacked. Home wasn't safe, the farms weren't safe, the market wasn't safe. Nowhere, nowhere was safe.

And why and why and why, like a sigh, like a mantra, beside every hospital bed, every bombed and burned-out house: why did they do this to us? Why did they kill my child? Why are we a target? Why can't my mum come back? Why destroy my shop and my living? Why can't anyone stop them?

And why? Why did the human species ever bother with the creation of language only to dream up and carry through ideas so monstrous as to wither all the words we ever thought of, to strip them of meaning in the face of that intent?

And why is it considered a legitimate way to live, for a person to get up in the morning, kiss his or her kids goodbye and go and spend the working day experimenting and discussing and planning and building novel and ever-more efficient ways of severing soft, beautiful, living human bodies?

And why is there no way of physically preventing someone from getting in a plane and flying over schools and homes and firing rockets which burst through the wall and into a million fragments in the middle of the night, splintering a family's sleep and driving vicious metal squares into their flesh and vital organs?

And how? How did it ever come to this? How did we surrender our power so completely that an entire world of people screaming 'No' is not enough to stop a few from bringing about all of this? How did we forget that they were supposed to carry out our will? How did we lose sight of our responsibilities to each other, and continue to pay taxes and commit our labor to the people who harness it all towards death and their own power?

And when are we going to put an end to it? They have to go. These politicians have to go. This whole system has to go. If we can think of ways to kill, in their homes, people we can't even see, render non-existent whole buildings by remote control, we must be able to imagine and bring into being a better way to run our world, to conduct ourselves without these corporate-controlled governments, or perhaps without any governments. They've failed us, whatever their ideology: now it's time for the people.

The missile by the mosque

The night of 27-28 March the bombs were so immense that I could see the flashes from inside a room with the curtains drawn and my eyes closed. The building swayed like a treehouse in the wind, rocking long after the sound had died away and the soothing voice of the prayer call was singing out, as if from a machine activated by the sudden shaking of the minaret. In fact it wasn't the buildings that rocked in the aftershock of the explosions but the whole earth. It felt exactly the same on the ground floor as on the fifth.

The communications towers were hit during the night and next day, and from then there were no phone lines, even for emergency calls: people had to make their own way to hospital in private cars. There was no internet either; caught between the two warring sides, the Iraqis were now locked out of all communication with the outside world. Even the carrier pigeons had dirtied the pavement and deserted.

There was no way of telling the US/UK governments' bomb fires from the Iraqi Government's oil trench fires: as ever, both sides at once were choking the Iraqi people, poisoning and darkening the air they breathed. People were running desperately low on money because they weren't able to go to work. My silent dancer friend Kamil's house was wrecked – it was on Ash-Shaab street, near the ruined market.

Friday prayers on 29 March and a rally went on outside the mosque, people crowding into the circle opposite, among the fountains. A thick crust of sand had mummified the streets and buildings with a monotone yellowish-grey, clogging the drains so that the blood of two sheep, butchered on the pavement, provided an almost welcome splash of colour.

Across the city a missile hit the middle of the street outside the Omar Al-Faroukh mosque on Palestine Street at about 4.15, just as people were leaving after prayers. Ahmed was walking out behind his friend Omar when he heard an explosion and saw his friend fall. Omar was a student at Rafidain College. He had fragments of shrapnel about 3 centimeters long removed from his liver and abdomen. His lower ribs were fractured and his left hand had shrapnel wounds. His grandfather, Fuad Taher, demanded that Bush and Blair be charged and brought to court.

Firas Hamid was the last of the victims to come out of surgery, having had two fragments removed from his liver and one from his kidney. His right arm had a compound fracture beneath an open wound. He was 16 and, like Omar and Ahmed, was leaving the mosque when the explosion happened.

Another missile hit, close by, three minutes later. It wasn't clear from the friends and relatives in the hospital whether it hit the other side of the road or hit a building, but it was near.

Akael Zuhair was standing in front of his house opposite the mosque. Shrapnel from one of the missiles hit him. He was 20. The doctor said his condition was critical, with shrapnel wounds to his left shoulder, left chest, right forearm and forehead, possibly lodged in the frontal lobe of his brain. There was no brain-scanning equipment. The doctors were waiting for a skull x-ray to show whether the piercing was superficial or deep. There were no intensive care units either: after 12-and-a-half years of sanctions, most hospitals didn't have enough working units, if any at all, many of the parts being embargoed on the pretext that they had dual military and civilian uses.

Akael began to regain consciousness while we were there, thrashing his limbs about while his family and friends tried to hold him still and comfort him, in the absence of painkillers, and his mum's tears overflowed.

'I am his mother,' she whispered. Nothing else. I held her without a word.

His dad heard the explosion in the street and said the kids came running in to tell him Akael was hit. 'Help us,' he said, 'because we are attacked in homes and streets and markets. We are not something to be squeezed. We are thank to people in all the world, but especially in America and England. More than a million people in England say no to war. There is not a problem between people. There is a problem with governments.'

'Humbling' is too small a word for the experience of being offered forgiveness at such a moment.

Again, no-one could guess what the intended target was. All of the clusters of friends and family we took statements from said there was nothing military in the area, nor even a communications tower.

Less than three kilometers north of the mosque and just 15 minutes earlier, a couple in their fifties, fleeing Baghdad for a farm in the countryside, had all their possessions with them when another missile flattened them; they didn't know yet whether they'd lost everything or someone had salvaged their things for them. Fawzia showed us what little money they had left, dyed red with Najah's blood.

And about 9am on Thursday 27 March, 35 kilometers or so south of Baghdad on the main road to Wasit, Haitham Abid was driving a lorry when a missile landed close to a grain silo by the Grain Board building. The lorry crashed and the back part caught fire. He wasn't sure whether he jumped from the cab or was pulled clear, but his right thigh was badly broken.

Forced to leave

I was in the Palestine Hotel looking for a friend when the frisson of excitement spread through the journalists that a hospital had been hit. A palpable wave of disappointment followed when it turned out to be only a second market, at Al-Shuala: Dr Tariq said there were over 50 deaths and lots of injuries. Another market was nowhere near as good a story. The war, apparently, was starting to drag. Nothing was happening. 'House destroyed by bomb' was a story. 'Second house destroyed by bomb' was still at least half a story. Another and another and yet another house destroyed by a bomb was not. Whole packs of reporters were starting to leave.

Other foreigners were being expelled from the country, the activists and independents who were too hard to keep under control. Eventually it was my turn: the man from the Foreign Ministry said simply: 'Leave this hotel. Leave this country.' There wasn't any way round it, nor any shame in it that such a government didn't want me around, but I was desperate about leaving all my Iraqi friends, desperate about having to go when there were so few independent witnesses to all the crimes.

Someone emailed to tell me I wasn't giving the US enough credit for its efforts to avoid civilian casualties. It seemed those efforts were visible only with the help of a television and a reporter willing to ignore the bodies piling up, to say they weren't news and turn the camera the other way. There were too many civilian casualties, too far from military targets, for all of them to be mistakes.

The convoy we were supposed to go with left without us so I got to say goodbye to Zaid, at least. He looked tired. He hadn't been sleeping, because there was nothing to do all day to tire him out: no work, no money, nowhere open to go to, not even the kids to play with because they were staying somewhere else.

I wasn't able to go and see the people we met the day before in the hospital: Akael's mother rebounded in my thoughts. The bombing was a constant background noise all day, a rhythm in stereo with no visible source. Ali at the internet center was playing a game on the computer involving tanks firing missiles at things in a city. Wasn't that a bit too close for comfort, I asked, or was it simulator practice in case he needed those skills in the coming weeks. He thought that was funny.

The kids in the Fanar Hotel were playing Risk, a war board game in which players invade each other's countries and try to take over the entire world with small plastic pieces. War is deeply strange.

Meanwhile the actual soldiers used to share warm bread with us, standing round a wooden sand-box which did the job of a table, pouring glasses of sugary *chai* from a metal flask, every one of them giggling like a schoolgirl, guns across their shoulders, while Sabah clowned in the face of it all, making jokes in mime about bombs falling, about peeling off his uniform and running away, hugging the pillar behind him in half-mock terror, telling us his huge burly mate got his hair cut by his mum, snorting with uncontrollable laughter. I hope they did run away, rather than face those overwhelming weapons and armor with only a hard hat and an old rifle.

As I left, down the highway to the border, my eyes overflowed with all the unbelievable, intolerable, uncontainable sadness in that place. Talib, an Iraqi man whom I trusted absolutely, drove us as far as the border with Jordan. From there the only transport was a bus to the refugee camp at Al-Ruwayshid, populated by nationals of Sudan, Palestine and other places who had nowhere safe to go.

Two years later some of them would still be there, trapped in a desert no-man's-land but we lucky few, Jordanian students and foreign activists, shared a minibus into Amman and went home, home to a gorgeous sunny day, to bright green English countryside at RAF/USAF Fairford. This was where someone loaded the bombs on to the B-52 planes. I never even saw the B-52s when I was so far underneath them in Baghdad, great ugly sinister things. This was where someone climbed into the cockpit, amid the birdsong and the daffodils, and set off to drop bombs on people going about their daily lives.

People had consistently been stopped when they had arrived at Fairford to protest against the use of British bases for the bombing of Iraq and had been refused access to the peace camp. They had repeatedly been stopped and searched under Section 44 of the Terrorism Act 2000, which allows the police to stop and search anyone within a designated zone, for no other reason than being there – though being there is not in itself illegal, let alone terrorist. Protests at the base had been heavily interfered with throughout.

I know, of course, that in Iraq the freedom to protest would be considerably more restricted. But that's not the point. The lack of civil and political freedom allowed to the Iraqi people is not a reason to bomb them, especially given that the lack of freedom is in part a result of CIA assistance to the Iraqi Government when it was an ally. In any case, there is little triumph in comparing ourselves with one of the worst systems and concluding that we come out better.

Where is our democracy, as people in Iraq kept asking me; where is our legitimacy to impose change on others with bombs when we use terrorist legislation to prevent ordinary, democratic, peaceful protest? Where is our moral high ground when we create a Human Rights Act which allows freedom 'within the law' and then uses the law to take away that freedom? Freedom of assembly within the law becomes a mere placebo when, within the law, as amended to deal with the Human Rights Act, the freedom to assemble can be taken away at the whim of a few police officers.

The Berlin Wall moment on room service

Meanwhile, in Iraq, Ibrahim from Médecins Sans Frontières (MSF) went missing, along with François, the head of mission. They were arrested for spying by the Iraqi authorities because they were using a satellite modem (identical to the one Julia and I had borrowed for the trip and smuggled in) following a tip-off to the police. As the days went on and the news claimed that the Iraqi authorities were no longer in control, it seemed more and more likely that they'd been killed, but in fact they were moved from prison to prison, incredibly crowded, until the guards could no longer get any orders and dumped all the inmates on to the streets in Ramadi.

On the day that Baghdad fell to US troops Nicolas de Torrente, MSF US's Executive Director, testified to the UN Security Council that: 'In Iraq... the conflict is essentially being carried out in a vacuum. The political agendas and military strategies of the warring parties have resulted in nearly completely shutting out independent humanitarian assistance.'

He warned: 'The US Government has also made efforts to enlist aid organizations in support of its agenda. US-based humanitarian organizations have been prohibited from accessing southern and central Iraq by US sanctions. Our concern is that [the] highly visible "hearts and minds" strategy may fuel dangerous suspicions that all humanitarian activities, and international aid personnel, are identified to the US/UK coalition and working on its behalf.

'The situation in Afghanistan gives us reasons to be worried. After the demise of the Taliban, fighting and tensions have persisted. The perceived association between Western military forces and humanitarian aid organizations has become a serious security liability, not only restricting access to many areas of the south and southeast of the country, but also jeopardizing their safety.'

On that day, 9 April, the world's media showed a joyous crowd battering the prone statue of Saddam with shoes and cheering. The zoomed-out version of the picture, widely seen only later, showed a crowd of maybe 150-200 people, many of them press and soldiers, and a few dozen Iraqis, surrounding the statue in an otherwise empty square whose entrances are all blocked by tanks.

Another photo, this one much closer in, showed the face of one jubilant young man who, in another photo, stands beside Ahmed Chalabi, the US's preferred new leader, among his group of exiles, trained and drafted in with CIA help.

What that means is that it was very much an invited audience, at an event played out right outside the journalists' home in the Palestine Hotel. Pre-war, whenever the Iraqi Ministry of Information wanted the international reporters to notice a demonstration they would thoughtfully arrange for it to take place right outside the Press Center, just to save them a journey.

Here we had the roving Ministry of Information bringing you the required Berlin Wall Moment on room service. No need to leave your balcony.

What it means is that the Iraqi people were cheated, yet again, by the US and UK. That moment belonged to them, just as the chipping and hammering and climbing of the Berlin Wall – that mighty, inspiring, overwhelming night – belonged to the divided Berliners. Instead it was stolen, cheapened, deflated, CNN-ized.

Day after day, following this, I received satellite emails from two Belgian doctors I met in Baghdad, talking about how US soldiers stood by when the hospitals were looted, about how their ambulances were routinely shot at when they tried to move around the city.

One, leaving with three injured civilians in the back, returned minutes later with a rash of bullet holes, the driver and front seat medic injured. One of the patients had a new bullet wound to the chest. Dr Geert Van Moorter, from the Belgian organization Medicine for the Third World, said he took a white flag and went to confront the soldiers. Their reply was that the ambulance could have been carrying explosives.

Let's be clear about this. That risk belongs to the soldiers. They are military personnel, protected with the best body armor there is. If there is any doubt as to whether something is or is not a legitimate military target, then it is not. It's not a risk for the injured civilians to take, for their wanton ambulance riding.

Challenged over the willingness of his soldiers to shoot at ambulances, the commanding officer stated that they were only young and they got nervous, and reacted by shooting at things. Well, that's all right then.

The legitimizing of existing power-brokers began early. The British in the south said they had invited an unnamed local sheikh with influence to form an interim 'presence of leadership'. It wasn't clear how he came by his power and influence, but he came by them within the context of the old regime. In the south, it was reported, people were being given water.

In fact they were not. Water was being sold to them. The soldiers were giving water to people with tankers, because they were afraid of being mobbed by desperate crowds if they distributed it in person. The people with tankers were being allowed to sell it to people who needed it. Who owned the tankers? The people who had attained power, influence and wealth under the old regime.

Maybe it was intellectual laziness, or feebleness, that prevented some commentators seeing past the Saddam-or-War dichotomy that was thrust across the debate by the US and UK governments, stopped them questioning the storyline of Iraq War Live, the soap opera. Yet, as a result, most people might never know that the bids for the contract to set up Iraq's mobile phone network after the war were invited before the attack even started. That might have cast more light on what we were really fighting for. It was never a choice of either war or the status quo. It never should have been.

What if Saddam had been indicted for war crimes back in the early 1980s when he used poison gas against Iran – or the late 1980s when he used it against the Kurds? Would he have managed to keep the firm grip on power he was then consolidating? Might he have lost his immunity and been arrested and put on trial? What if at that point, his allies Rumsfeld and Reagan hadn't given him any more money and weapons? What if they, too, had been indicted for complicity in his crimes?

What if there hadn't been a ceasefire called just at that crucial moment in the Gulf War of 1991, specifically to allow Saddam to use his helicopter gunships and Republican Guard to put down the rebellions? What if we had given the rebels help then to overthrow Saddam themselves?

But all wars are disastrous for all people. The idea that, in the face of humankind's great problems, the solution is to send out young, poor and working-class people to kill one another and the general public is outdated and ridiculous. In all wars the majority of casualties are civilians. It is not *this* war but all wars which are wrong.

3

'WE HAVE NOTHING':
THE REBUILDING OF IRAQ

November 2003

Returning to Iraq in November 2003 I was more afraid than I had been when the war was starting. Many of the things we had been afraid of then were now coming true. Two friends had escaped attempts to kidnap them; Michael Birmingham had been visiting inside the UN headquarters when it was bombed. Crime was beyond control, violent crime, and everyone was armed, even some of the street children: that final-straw rumor which had convinced us before the war that people were getting hysterical.

But in a way that was all the more reason to go back. The governments were trying to tell us everything was better now. Most of the media were going along with it. Columnists in Britain were changing their minds, saying the untold casualties they'd feared hadn't occurred and it was obviously better now Saddam was gone, so they were no longer opposed to the war. According to this version, the Iraqis, suitably grateful, were apparently getting on with watching satellite TV, reading thousands of newspapers, even enjoying the freedom to be prostitutes. That wasn't the same story I was hearing from those friends in Iraq that I could still get in touch with.

There was a real energy among the people I'd met, professionals, students, children, mothers, to connect with their Iraqi counterparts, to communicate, to help, person to person, where they could. But introductions were needed, someone who could put them in touch, to make it happen, otherwise the energy would peter out.

The circus would arrive in two months and I needed to prepare for that, to find an apartment, translators, drivers, to make sure we had all the official documents and permissions we needed. And I'd sworn to Zaid I'd be back, to make sure the promises he'd believed in were being kept.

Tearing down the desert highway at first light, the driver and I both alert for the ubiquitous bandits, I found my previous homes, the Al-Fanar and Andalus Hotels, absorbed into the 'Green Zone' fortress

around the Palestine and Sheraton and the closure of a stretch of Abu
Nawas, beside the river.

The most obvious difference was not the rubble – the years of sanctions
had seen to that, nor even the tanks and humvees which roared about, but
the razor wire and blast walls outside schools and banks and hotels that
announced that this was a chaotic and unstable place to be. That and the
explosion that woke me up in the morning, launched from a donkey-cart
towards the Palestine Hotel.

Raed Jarrar (right), founder of Emaar, or 'Rebuilding'

After about a week I tracked down Raed and moved in with him and
Waleed, sharing a house, a Kalashnikov and a security guard named
Abu Hassan with Raed's organization, Emaar. There was a fast internet
center about five minutes' walk away which had a generator and we all
congregated there in the evenings, writing our weblogs, when the power
to the house went off.

When he was in a cantankerous mood Abu Hassan would refuse to
let me in the door, saying Mr Raed was not home. He also insisted on
locking the metal cage door behind me after I went in, which meant I
couldn't let myself out of the house again without yelling to him across
the road where he sat in a little hut, music blaring, the far side of the

roaring neighborhood generator from me, eyes anywhere but on our front door. Had anyone come to blow us up or kidnap us it's unlikely he'd have noticed. In fairness, though, he had a dangerous, tedious job and no-one did come to blow us up or kidnap us so I oughtn't to grumble.

After the invasion, Raed started Emaar to involve Iraqi people in their own civil society and the reconstruction of the country; the name means something like 'Rebuilding'. The message, Raed said, was no to foreign companies, Iraqis can do it themselves. Mass leafleting yielded around 1,000 volunteers who were interviewed for teams of 10-12, at least a third of them women, in Baghdad and nine southern cities.

These teams identified needs, worked out plans and tried to make them happen. For example the Baghdad group, which met in our living room, painted the support pillars white for visibility on an unlit piece of road which had become an accident black spot.

Emaar implemented around 150 micro-projects at around US$100 each and a dozen mid-scale projects, including building three schools in the Marshlands, each school costing around $2,500.

A village near Nasariya

Driving down to Nasariya with Raed to see one of the schools we were forced off the road by a US military lorry in a slow-moving convoy. Bored, I suppose, the driver just shoved us sideways into the dirt and carried on. US troops were already unpopular in our house after Raed and Waleed had been stopped at a checkpoint on their way home the night before, shoved, shouted at and accused of filming pornography because there was a video camera in the car.

In any case we arrived at the Nasariya office, which had been damaged by the explosion at the nearby Italian Carabinieri headquarters. The doors were blown off and were found inside the building. Every window was shattered and glass fragments were embedded in the plaster. The walls and ceilings were badly cracked. The volunteers were all unhurt but people had been killed in buildings the far side of the Emaar house. They were still cleaning and repairing.

Just after it got dark some of the volunteers came back with food and the information that there was to be an *infijar* – an explosion, within the next few minutes, of some unexploded item nearby. *Infijar*, *dababa* (tank) and *rashasha* (machine gun): these were among the first Arabic words a foreigner learned in the New Iraq, taught by any child you met. We all trooped up to the roof to watch – everyone always did. Even though we were expecting it, it still made us all jump. Abbas was involved in the armed uprising against Saddam in 1991 and said it was the same then – even when you were expecting a blast, they never stopped making you jump.

Armed rebellions aside, Abbas wasn't active in local civil society before

Emaar, but now he devoted all his spare time and energy to it. He ran a restaurant that his father and grandfather ran before him, specializing in the traditional sheep's head and feet, skinned, but with the brain and eyes still there.

Emaar's freedom from political and religious affiliations was what first attracted him. Decision-making was decentralized, by consensus within each local group with no hierarchy. Raed provided co-ordination, support and funding but everything was up to the teams. Individuals had the space to develop their own projects and the Nasariya group had decided to take the project out of town into the marshes.

On the way to a village where Emaar was working, our vehicles skated through mud, over earth bridges across streams and rivers, between palms, vegetable plots, reed or mud houses and tribes of small children. The area was controlled by the politico-religious Supreme Council of the Islamic Revolution in Iraq (SCIRI) and we were obliged to take two of their members with us. Raed made me cover my hair and told me not to smile at them.

The marshes had offered a safe haven for anti-Saddam fighters and activists because they were difficult for troops to get into. This village wasn't drained, as many were, but the diversion of water did, overall, have the desired effect of crushing the resistance.

Made of mud bricks, covered with mud-and-straw plaster and roofed with woven straw, the almost-finished schoolrooms would incorporate children aged from 6 to 14 in the first grade because none of them had ever been to school. The boys and volunteers proudly showed me around, telling me the headteacher was from the village and teachers would come from other schools to teach in shifts.

Girls passed by a little way off carrying water and bundles of reeds. It wasn't clear how many families would allow their daughters to go to the school. A stampede of shrieking boys fled the courtyard of a house, chased by a woman throwing clods of earth at them. She invited us in. Girls in bright clothes and patterned headscarves were leaning on the walls and looking after the youngest children.

Abbas summed up the contrast between Emaar's projects and the contracts given out by the occupying powers. Contracts for school rehabilitation were commonly worth between $60,000 and $100,000. US corporations Bechtel and Halliburton were the main beneficiaries. 'They immediately sub-contract the work for about $20,000 or $30,000 to a company which sub-sub-contracts for around $10,000 or $5,000. And then the work is poor. The school ends up having some new paint, but low quality paint and brushes, new glass for the windows and sometimes new bathrooms. Thousands of dollars of our money is spent for nothing.' He got his information directly from a friend who worked

The village school near Nasariya.

as an engineer in the Ministry of Education but it was corroborated by published figures as well.

Ammar was a recent graduate from the technical institute, currently unemployed. He was feeling dismal because he'd just got married, on paper, to Safa, but before the marriage ceremony could take place their mothers had fallen out, followed by their entire families. The two were not even allowed to see each other any more.

Some of the volunteers were students at Nasariya University. Bassim was studying computing and Ali was a mathematician. They were keen to make links with universities outside Iraq who would work with them to rehabilitate their library. Part of Emaar's aim was to start open student discussions between the different ethnic, religious and political groups to increase understanding and reduce violence, then to widen the forum to include the whole community. The task of rebuilding civil society after dictatorship was as great as that of repairing the physical infrastructure after war.

There was a special department for new Iraqi NGOs in the Coalition Provisional Authority's (CPA) headquarters where 'capacity building' meetings were held by well-meaning soldiers. Millions of dollars were spent on promoting pro-occupation NGOs but ironically, inevitably, it was the individuals with the best English, PR skills and finance who were empowered to take control of civil society: the former Ba'athists. Later it was made overwhelmingly difficult to set up an NGO, with exacting requirements, constantly shifting goalposts and intensifying control.

Within a couple of months, USAID stopped funding Emaar, perhaps when they realized it was intended as a direct challenge to the occupation. The Nasariya branch carried on as an independent organization but none of the other teams survived as autonomous groups.

The police demonstration

Driving home from Nasariya, crawling through the flooded streets of Najaf, traffic lights changed, unheeded, from red to green and back while drivers hooted, all of them jammed in the middle of a junction trying to wriggle and shunt a way through until someone jumped out and started directing traffic. If you went the wrong way, you reversed around the roundabout till you got back to the turning you wanted. Women in *abayas* splashed across the road, black tights splattered with mud. Men hitched up their *dishdashas* around their knees and waded. A car got stuck on the side of a lorry after they drove too close together, closing two-thirds of the road.

Every car was plastered with grime so thick the registration plates were illegible and the back windscreens were blacked out. The drains were irrelevant in the face of real rain. It seemed impossible that anything would ever be clean again, like it did after the sandstorm during the war.

But at least there was light when we got home. Over the next months, US failure to sort out electricity, water, hospitals, security and so on, as they had promised to do, drove even the moderates and the pro-Americans to fury. Eight US government audits on Halliburton contracts were kept classified; another, published, found $212 million in 'questionable costs'. George W Bush's uncle Bucky made half a million dollars out of Engineered Support Systems Inc, which was paid $100 million for contracts in Iraq and on whose board of directors he sat.[1] Halliburton and Bechtel provided illicitly recruited workers from outside Iraq and the US with substandard food and accommodation and no body protection.

The police, meanwhile, had not been paid for three months and, along with security staff, one day in November 2003 besieged the building where young boys and old men used to queue with their call-up papers before the invasion. *Kull ishi maaku*, they all said, brushing one hand against the other repeatedly, as if dusting them off. *Kull ishi maaku*. Literally, everything is not available. We have nothing.

Police weren't even properly uniformed – they had shirts and armbands and provided the rest themselves. It made it hard to tell the genuine roadblocks from the Ali Baba (fake) ones. They were outgunned by the criminal gangs, having only pistols. They traveled in groups, powerless to prevent attacks on themselves or anyone else, hoping only not to be a target, but were increasingly under fire as collaborators. All that and no pay.

The officers said they'd had enough of the Americans. Some said that an American company was being paid $50,000 per school for repainting buildings. I'll do it for a thousand, an Iraqi friend said, just a throwaway comment. Then she thought about it: 'I'll get a load of paint and a load of cake and juice and we'll get everyone to come and do it together. It would make us feel involved and then they could save the money for giving people jobs.'

A security guard burned his badge in token of his frustration, making several attempts to get the laminated card to catch. One of the young police officers took off his armband and wrapped it round his head like a pirate's hat in good-natured silliness. My friend Imad was with me, a TV producer and activist from Beirut who arrived in Baghdad a week or so before I did. He had come to support the recently founded Baghdad Indymedia group Al-Muajaha (The Witness) and to find out from Iraqi people what Lebanese activists could do to help them.

'Amreeki,' people started calling: Americans. Two tanks had pulled up to the far end of the demonstration and the police and security guards, some still wearing their police armbands, ID cards hanging around their necks, ran to face the soldiers, who shouted and swore, issued orders in English, pushed people with their guns, threatened to arrest the police if they didn't go away.

'What are you doing here?' Imad asked the US soldiers.

'Supporting the Iraqi Police,' one said.

'But the Iraqi Police are on *this* side of the razor wire.'

'No comment,' said the lieutenant on his man's behalf.

Provoked, the police went into revolt, laying rubble carefully in the road, pulling razor-wire coils across from the central reservation and the sidewalk and turning rusting junk from the roadside piles into a barricade. Cars were surrounded and made to turn back and a man who tried to escape the siege with armfuls of files was sent scurrying back into the building. A loyalist police van attempting to get to the building was set upon by shouting men and screeched off.

Eventually an Interior Ministry representative turned up. He was allowed to cross the razor wire. The men crouched and sat in a crowd so that everyone could see and hear and he promised to meet them at ten o'clock the following morning. Always they promise to pay us in three days' time, then three more days, some muttered, but they tidied up and went back to work.

The Ministry representative admitted to Imad and me that the problem had arisen because men had been hired before authority had been given and that he couldn't guarantee that they would be paid. Eventually he accepted that, having worked for three months as employees, it was their right to be paid. But no, he still couldn't guarantee that they would be paid.

Kimadia and Jim Haveman

The next day though, instead of a meeting between the police and the ministry, there were huge concrete blast walls around the building to keep those inside safe from the workers. It was becoming commonplace in the New Iraq, to separate the people from the decision-makers. The Convention Center, for example, where much of the political business went on, was the middle of a fortress in whose grounds a maze had been constructed out of razor wire, concrete wall pieces, barrels, tents and checkpoints. For Iraqis, unaccompanied by foreigners, it was hard to gain admittance at all, never mind get any answers.

There were five checkpoints to get through between the last passable bit of road and the front door. At each one you were frisked and metal detected lest you had found a rocket-propelled grenade launcher or similar item in the few meters since someone last checked. The place swarmed with soldiers, mercenaries, security guards, bodyguards standing about with phones, curly wires coming out of their ears, big guns in their hands and small ones strapped to their legs.

There were posters everywhere for things like the internet bazaar – 'don't walk the streets, order online...' Some of the international staff even slept there, in the corridors, a short distance from their desks, afraid to leave the compound, meeting only those Iraqis who had jobs on the premises. Other signs indicated the whereabouts of various offices, the Bechtel Corporation's Baghdad bureau right next to the Ministry of Planning.

In the same area there was a welcome desk for 'Human Rights and Transitional Justice'. It was unattended but for a sign stating 'This office handles only the following cases: 1. Past human rights abuse under the former regime: killing, missing cases, torture and rape; 2. NGO education.' The actual Ministry of Human Rights, incidentally, was based in the Ministry of Oil, the two being indivisible.

So it was that, around this time, Imad and I met Sami and Abbas,* workers from Kimadia, the state-run medical supplies company, who asked us to help. They asked us not because we had any special expertise but because our faces were white – I had come back to a New Iraq where people still felt a need for advocates from other countries to assert their rights to the authorities. Often they weren't let into the buildings where the authorities were and in any case Sami and Abbas were afraid of being targeted if they made a fuss.

Since about 1997, Kimadia, like a lot of state enterprises, had been run essentially as follows. First, the Government gave a subsidy to the company. Workers then received a small monthly salary, treated as an 'advance' on their annual payment. It was between 45,000 and 60,000 dinars a month,

---

* Their names have been changed.

the latter equivalent to $30 a month in November 2003. The rest of the money was kept back for the running of the company and distributed at the end of the financial year. It wasn't ideal, because it meant the workers incurred debts for several months against the promise of the end-of-year payment, but at least they could borrow enough to live on.

The problem, Sami said, was that the money for 2002 hadn't been paid to them. It had been due to be distributed shortly after the invasion. It had been brought in sacks to the warehouse with a list: 'We saw with our eyes,' one woman said, 'how much money we were each owed, but we never quite held it in our hands.'

According to the old system, the money was apportioned according to rank not only within the company but also within the Ba'ath Party. After the invasion the same managing directors remained in place and, though the Party was ostensibly gone, the same distribution policy had been followed. When the workers started demanding a fairer division of the funds, they said, the accountant's son who was holding the money got out a gun and started shooting. US soldiers arrived and seized the money. That was the last the workers saw of it.

At the warehouse that morning a pick-up sat idle, with a Red Crescent and 'Medical Supplies' stenciled on the side. Freelancers had been hired to take supplies around the country, so the company's drivers had no work: already labor was being casualized, which meant that costs were reduced, secure jobs were lost and workers had less negotiating power. Warehouse workers crowded to tell us their stories and vent their anger at Jim Haveman, the US senior advisor at the Ministry of Health.

Sami pointed out a colleague who had six children and a wife to support. He couldn't pay his rent any more and had moved into one of the many squatted former government buildings. Most had borrowed money for basic essentials, secured on the annual payment, then couldn't repay the loans.

Rent and food were more expensive now than before the war and the sunken cheeks, creased eyes and crumpled foreheads of many of the workers testified that the wages had been painfully meager for a while before that. Sami and Abbas were 31, only two years older than I was, but looked easily 15 years my senior. *Kull ishi maaku*, they all said. We have nothing.

A letter from Jim Haveman to the workers stated that the matter had been 'dealt with' in the spring. Kimadia was a corrupt organization, it said. There could be no profits for distribution because it was a state-subsidized company. The intention of the accountant and his son, he declared, had been to give the money to the managers and a selected few, not to all the employees, and the billions of dinars seized by the soldiers now formed part of 'the general funds of Iraq'.

The women who crowded into one of the offices said they were ready for strikes and demonstrations. Some 90 per cent of the workers had signed a petition calling on Haveman to release the funds. Khalida, the managing director's secretary, originally said she wanted to be the first signatory. When it was brought for her to sign she advised them to drop it or they might lose their jobs altogether. She refused to tell us anything, saying she wasn't authorized.

Sami said: 'They told us to forget the whole thing because Mr Jim Haveman is worse than Saddam.' According to many of them, the heads of the Profit Boards, Abu Assen and Ahmed, passed on a threat that those making a fuss would be viewed as working against the coalition forces and arrested. 'We said to them: "They might arrest a couple of representatives but could they arrest all 4,000 workers if we all stood together?" They said Mr Jim Haveman will scatter you to the stars. You will never see each other again.'[2]

So Imad and I went to the Ministry of Health. We handed in our passports in exchange for visitors' passes. In the old Iraq we would have had to tramp up and down between levels 1, 2 and 5 chasing pieces of paper from one person which would permit us to ask another for an appointment to ask a third for a piece of paper to grant us passage into the office of the secretary of the assistant of the person we wanted to see, to ask a single, simple question. In the New Iraq it was the same.

We didn't find Jim Haveman, who, we were told, took his weekends on Sunday instead of on Friday like the rest of the country. Returning another day, we were able to speak to his assistant, who said she would discuss with him whether our questions were the kind he wanted to answer.

I was even able to speak to the Iraqi head of the Ministry, who was familiar with the case and agreed that the workers should be paid but had no authority. For weeks I called them, dropped in, sent emails, but all they would say – and I never did communicate with Jim Haveman in person – was that the matter was closed. The workers were never paid their wages. The money seized by the soldiers was subsumed.

The economic invasion

Looking around for context, I learned that the Coalition Provisional Authority had introduced a number of new laws imposing a wage scale, privatization of state-owned companies, utilities, the banking system and natural resources, foreign ownership of land and the perpetuation of its own orders. One Ba'athist law it kept in place was that which banned trade unions, despite international labor law protecting workers' right to organize.

In addition, the International Monetary Fund (IMF) compelled Iraq to accept a structural adjustment program involving privatization of resources, trade liberalization, foreign ownership and rollback of public services in exchange for debt relief. By the time of the invasion, Iraq had the highest debt to export ratio in the world. Loans to Saddam, many of them linked to arms deals for the wars against Iran and Kuwait, had accrued a vast amount of interest even before the sanctions, which the oil revenues were insufficient to cover. Under the sanctions Iraq couldn't pay back any of its debt at all, but compound interest kept building.

Debt relief ought, then, to have been complete and unconditional, if the Iraqi people were truly to be liberated from Saddam. It wasn't their debt. Instead the erasing of a large proportion of the debt was made dependent on a review of Iraq's implementation of the IMF program. It meant the new government, regardless of any mandate it might be elected on, was already bound.

From then on, economic control secured, a series of 'Iraq Procurement Conferences' were organized by the British-based company Windrush Communications to facilitate multinational takeovers. It was only the pervading chaos in Iraq that held up this project, though it was unjustified by military necessity, falling squarely within the definition of pillage, outlawed by both the Hague laws and Geneva Conventions. An occupying power is not allowed to change the legal or economic structure of an occupied territory nor to extract its natural resources.

In fact, it appears the British Government knew this beforehand: a leaked memo from Attorney-General Peter Goldsmith to the Prime Minister stated that 'major structural economic reform' proposed for Iraq may 'not be authorized under international law'.

Economic justice is central to any kind of social justice, just as economic independence is central to any true political independence. Iraq's domestic dictator had been replaced by a global one: the IMF and its own 21st-century rod of iron. Only now you could buy a battery-operated plastic dancing Saddam on the street outside.

A few months later, less than two years after the invasion, and the promises of reconstruction were abandoned altogether as Bush announced he would ask for no new funds for the reconstruction of Iraq. Large amounts of the $18.4 billion pledged for rebuilding had been spent on fighting, preparations for Saddam Hussein's trial, elections and four changes of government.

It's straightforward enough. Rebuilding in Iraq has to happen, physical and civil, but Iraqi people are capable of doing it themselves, with a little international solidarity. It has to be a reparation, not an investment.

1 Eliot Weinberger, What I Heard about Iraq in 2005, *London Review of Books* vol 28, no 1, 5 January 2006.
2 It is of course possible that the threats actually came from those claiming to pass them on and not from Jim Haveman.

4

TO KURDISTAN

18-21 November 2003

The first section of the road north from Baghdad was the same flat brown expanse as almost the entire highway west towards Jordan. The hills started suddenly as if stopped dead on their march south, the first few rows stunted, trampled by those behind. Green hills softened the horizon against the bright blue sky, giving way to rugged mountains, grayish now as winter came.

Kids ran about in fields while grown-ups picked leaves, bright green leaves that seemed beyond imagining after Baghdad. True enough, if you stood on a high roof, Baghdad was a carpet of green, with blue, gold and white domes poking through, but the green of the palms was coated with grime, dust, glued on by oily residues that thickened the air. It wasn't this kind of green.

Arriving with Salam and Imad in the Kurdish zone in northern Iraq was like arriving in another country. Some said it was, or ought to be; others were adamant that it was Iraqi. The language was different. Most young to middle-aged adults spoke at least some Arabic, though many of the old men understood Kurdish dialects, Farsi, Turkish and no Arabic at all.

A lot of the men wore the traditional Kurdish outfit of enormously baggy trousers, gathered in at the ankles, with a loose collarless jacket in the same fabric. The jacket tucks into the trousers, with a waist sash around the join so it looks like a single garment, generally in a fairly dull color. There's a shirt underneath, whose collar is worn outside the jacket. The music was different and there were no tanks on the streets. The last US soldiers I'd seen were at a checkpoint, hours before. Instead there were occasional Mine Action Group vehicles.

Even the sweets were different, as was the currency, the economy having been separate from the rest of Iraq since 1991. The old dinar, prior to the devaluation under sanctions, was still in circulation here in Suleimania and a single dinar still existed whereas, in Baghdad, your smallest note was likely to be 100, with 250s more common.

As we dithered on the pavement Salam announced that he would acquire a guide and translator. He stepped into a barber's shop, seemingly at random, and a young man flung his arms around him. Heyman, whom Salam had met once before, took it upon himself to make us welcome. His family's house was warm and busy with four sisters, two brothers, Heyman and his parents. The beloved youngest brother, Rawish, was three. A fourth son was in Britain and photos of him were all over the house.

The girls dressed me up in Kurdish costume, as worn on special occasions. Underneath were loose trousers and a sleeveless smock which came just below the hips, in a bright red, sequined fabric, with a sheer, flowing gown over the top, black with deep red leaf and flower patterns. A short waistcoat went over that, black with a jangling fringe and a jeweled collar which fastened at the throat.

In my Kurdish finery with Rawish.

The sleeves on the gown were way longer than arm length, widening at the ends and they were tied and draped around the back, but loose enough not to restrict your movement at all. On the head was a sort of skullcap, also fringed, with a sash tied around and hanging down the back, which made me look like I had a fancy plant pot on my head, but the rest was good. Rawish joined in with his own costume, hugging the bits in glee as they were brought out of their bag and strutting like a king in his finery.

Bitter history

In the 1920s, when Heyman's grandfather was two years old, his mother and uncle were killed by bombs dropped by British planes, under the political command of then-minister Winston Churchill, supporting the Arab regimes' war against the Kurds.

Heyman's dad, now 55, described how, throughout his childhood: 'Every once in a while we had to escape and take refuge up in the mountains. They used to arrest a lot of us all the time. Some families got buried in a place called Hamia which is now a high school. They were buried alive and then they threw dirt on top.

'In the mountains it was very cold and we didn't have any food or any of our things but we wouldn't care because the enemy was far away. The Kurds are very active people. We are not lazy. We used to work a lot, eat plants and fruits, some of us even went to other states for work and provided for the family.'

Heyman added his own memories: 'When I was about 12 and started wanting to move around, my mum and dad would tell me no, you can't go there, this street is dangerous, this area is not safe – they were scared of the Ba'athists. We couldn't say anything, even as children. I remember my friend's friend who was 11 when he got arrested by the Ba'athists and even today we still know nothing of him. It was terrifying.

'In the 1980s my dad ran away from military service and we had to flee up north to our village. Life up there was much better than here. I also remember when we fled Suleimania in 1991 and we went up to the Iraqi-Iranian border. It was very hard. I was about 12, 13 years old. We were better off than other families – we had a car, while most of the families did not. I saw an old man walking with no shoes and falling down on the way. We were able to stay in a friend's house but some families had no shelter.'

Abu (father) Heyman went on: 'The Ba'athists were totally nasty to the people, they were criminals, beasts. This war was in the best interests of the US but Saddam gave them an excuse to attack Iraq. He launched a war on Iran and then on Kuwait. He spent 35 years in power without doing anything good for Iraq. He was supported by the US, Britain, France, Germany and Russia. All the chemical weapons were from those countries.

'Then under the sanctions a kilo of flour was worth ten dinars while now it's a quarter dinar. Everything was very expensive.

'The Kurds own land that contains loads of oil and Saddam didn't want us to be in control of that and didn't allow us to have our own government nor any kind of freedom or liberties. They would send a Kurdish man to do military service far in the south. This is all because of greed. Why would anybody take somebody's freedom?

'But still there is no freedom. It's better than when Saddam was in charge but it's not freedom. Saddam didn't even give freedom to the Arabs: they had to hang his pictures and sing about him, all singers sang about him. Even architects had to praise Saddam. In Iraq under Saddam no-one had freedom. It wasn't only the Kurds.

'If the Kurds living in Iraq got their freedom, Turkey, Iran or Syria would be afraid that Kurds in their states would demand their freedom as well. The Kurds are oppressed by Turkey, which has a very strong army, supported by other countries.

'If Britain had our interests in mind they never would have created such differences between Arabs and Kurds under the British mandate. It would have been Arabs, Turkmen* and Kurds all living together, but making difficulties among us makes it easier to control us. Now America is the ruler of the world and if we were united – the Kurds, the Turkmen, the Arabs, all living together in Iraq – we would never have allowed the US to interfere.'

Heyman (far left) and friends in Suleimania's town square.

Heyman quoted a Kurdish saying to the effect that if two fish were fighting in the sea, it would be because Britain fueled the conflict between them. 'They are the origin of the problem. They don't solve the problem. In the first place they were the ones who created the problem, so how can they claim to have solved it now? They need this problem in the region to justify their presence.'

But he went on to talk about Gandhi. In looking for his enemy, Gandhi realized that it was not the civil servant in the administrative buildings of India, nor the British soldier on the Indian streets, nor the British man or woman on the streets in the UK. To find his enemy he would have to look within himself: likewise the Kurds, the Turkmen, the

---

* 'There are some 3.5 million Turkmen in Iraq, generally concentrated in northern Iraq near the oil city of Kirkuk. They are the third-largest ethnic minority in Iraq behind the Arabs and Kurds, and just ahead of the Assyrians.' (from David Nissman, 'The Southern Azeri-Iraqi Turkmen Connection').

Arabs and other Iraqis needed to look within themselves, unite against the divide-and-rule tactics of successive powers.

'We want a separate state, an independent state with the Kurds of Syria, Turkey and Iran, but our best interest nowadays is being with the Iraqi people due to our economic and political situation. All we need is stability, peace and freedom.'

The political prisoner

We'd gone to Suleimania because Imad wanted to interview former political prisoners and now we met Ashti. Her name means 'peace' in Kurdish. She was born in 1966 and joined the Communist Party in 1988. All political activity had to be carried out in secret, which is why there was little, if any, non-party-based activism. Opposition was mainly either Communist or Islamist.

At about 1.30am on 1 June 1989 a group of men burst into her family's home. One of them was called Abu Hadil. She knew they'd come for her because, as far as she knew, no-one else in the family was politically active, though her parents didn't know she was a Communist Party member.

'They asked, "Who is Ashti?" I said, "I am Ashti" and they took me.

'They didn't hit me when they first arrested me but they took me to the security police headquarters in Suleimania and the beatings started the minute I arrived there. I was a girl, only young, about 22 and used to the comfort of my parents' home. I was a teacher then in Darhandikhan. I was wearing jeans. Jeans were seen as a symbol of capitalist America. They started beating me really hard and asking me "are you a Communist, you can't be a Communist, how can you be a Communist and be wearing jeans?"

'I denied any knowledge of or connection with Communism. I said I had no idea why I'd been arrested, so they started beating me again. They threw me in a big room with other women, not from the Communist Party, but from other Kurdish parties.'

After one year in the National Security HQ in Baghdad she was sentenced to 15 years in prison. She was interrogated and tortured throughout that first year. She hinted at rape but could not say the word.

'The manager of the prison was a woman named San'a but the security guards were men. They were not men, they were wolves. They treated us the way the national security forces did. They were really rough. We are a people with traditions and a woman is to be respected, she must have her privacy. They used to do things to us that were very... hard.

'The Government didn't give us food – it was provided by our friends and families. We were allowed two hours' visiting time per month, during which our parents would bring food. I don't know why they were so tough on us. I saw my parents from 9 till 11 once a month. They would bring me food but sometimes this only lasted 15 days and I wouldn't be able to see them till the next monthly visit.

'When a woman was giving birth in the jail, the other women were not allowed to go and help her. If another woman went to help her she was shot. The woman in labor couldn't scream or cry out – if she made any sound, sometimes they would stitch her lips to make her silent.

'Because of the torture I have constant pain. They hung me by my arms, behind my back, which affected my spine.

'We were not allowed to have pens, paper, even cardboard from detergent cartons. I heard a male comrade saying they allowed the men a radio at one stage but this was never allowed in the women's prison. For us it was beatings sometimes and solitary confinement. For example, on Nawroz, the Kurdish New Year, the men were allowed to celebrate with music and folk dancing. I danced the Kurdish folk dance and they put me in solitary confinement for three days in a very small room, one meter wide, and gave me no food.

'I was the only Communist activist in the jail among 45 women from the Daawa party [an Islamist party] so it was hard for me. I wasn't only sentenced for 15 years. I was also sentenced within the jail for being a Communist among the other prisoners. At the beginning they were not nice to me, they wouldn't allow me to eat with them or talk to them, they told me I was dirty, they wouldn't have anything to do with me.

'I thought to myself I was destined to be here 15 years so I have to learn to live with them, made an effort and they realized I was nice and not rude. Deep down inside they were all nice and they changed their treatment of me, but still I was kept in a room alone while they shared rooms. Would you be able to live in a room alone inside a prison and a prison owned by Saddam himself? Would you be able to eat alone, sleep alone?

'After three years I was released. When I left prison and saw the sanctions outside I felt sad – these sanctions were not on the Government, the Ba'athists. These sanctions were imposed on the people. The poor didn't have food in the first place and the sanctions made it worse for them. The sanctions were horrible – food, medicines and stuff that the people needed.

'If they gave us the right of self determination the Iraqi people are good enough to not need soldiers to protect them. We are capable of ruling ourselves. We are ready to do this. It's not one person from one party who is going to rule Iraq, it's a group. If this group unites we can make it. In prison the problems between different groups were fueled by the Ba'athist regime in order to divide and control us. Without deliberate provocation of conflicts we can work together.

'I will be a Communist until I die. I joined the Party in 1988. Those days were very difficult – the Ba'ath party was very cruel. Many people were tortured and I was one of them, but I understood that I could not tolerate capitalism. I knew these things might happen but resistance to oppression is like your blood – could you leave it?'

Then, left to her thoughts, silent tears overwhelmed her.

The torture chambers

The national security building in Suleimania where Ashti's torture started was now a museum and memorial. Damaged in a firefight, parts of it were crumbling. On the way in there were photographs of whole families who had been arrested and killed, walls with names scratched on, dates.

An old man looked at the photographs along with us. He had been held in the other jail in Suleimania, arrested with 32 members of his extended family because his daughter and her husband were Peshmerga [the traditional Kurdish term for a rebel] fighters. He stood, hands behind his back, showing how they had been forced to stand.

A sculpture was part-built in the yard, made of bullet casings, in the overlarge figure of a man, arms crossed in front of his face – the Ba'athist, ashamed. In one of the torture areas a local artist had tiled the walls with a crazy paving of broken mirrors so that everywhere you looked you were surrounded by fragments of yourself, mingled with the reflections of thousands of tiny lights all over the ceiling. In a courtyard in the middle of the complex was a white stone relief of a group of people, adults and children, tied together. 'This commemorates a family killed all together.'

Heyman indicated a bare, square, gray room about six meters wide, a single hole-in-the-ground toilet in the corner shielded on three sides but open

Never forget: a statue in the torture chambers.

on the fourth. 'The women's room. Ninety-six women were kept here at a time.' They wouldn't have been able to sit, let alone lie down. Then, a corridor or so away, a similar cell: 'This was the children's room.'

The solitary cells were no more than a meter square and the shared ones only a little bigger. Names, dates and pictures were engraved on the walls. 'They came in the night and took us all.' 'I have not seen my daughter for 25 days.' A tree. A flower with leaves growing towards the sun.

Here and there were statues to illustrate what happened in a given place. On a flight of stairs was a blindfolded prisoner, handcuffed to the rail so he couldn't stand straight. 'Every person who passed would hit him. This was for new prisoners.' Another figure stood alone in a solitary cell.

A mannequin hung by the wrists, tied behind the back so the head was forward and the shoulders wrenched back. The museum guard showed how the interrogators would pull down on the legs to increase the pain. 'Men and women were hung here naked.' This must have been what Ashti tried to describe. Electrodes were attached to the figure, wires running to the power source. A tear in the armpit of the figure: 'Even the statue is broken, so how could a human being bear it?' The floor linoleum stained black with blood: real, not replica, in irregular patterns.

Tears ran and ran: how would you ever close your eyes again, or smile, or speak? How had Ashti ever stopped crying?

Saddam but not only Saddam

Ali Hamid Qadis and Mohammed Arif were both arrested the night before Ashti. Members of any party other than the Ba'ath were viewed as traitors. The military *Anfal* [destruction of Kurdish villages], Ali explained, was followed by a political one.

All the former prisoners I spoke to were clear that Saddam was responsible for what happened to them. But Ali explained that it was more complex than just one man: 'The US and Britain and Europe in general all helped the Ba'athist regime to overthrow Abdul Kerim Khassim. They replaced a democratic regime with a dictatorship. When Britain took over Iraq after World War One they or France could have formed a Kurdish state. Still today they are reluctant to form a Kurdish state but they use the Kurdish cause for their own interests.

'When the US ambassador [April Glaspie] met with Saddam before the invasion of Kuwait and stated that the problem between Arabs was for them to solve and not for the US, this was like a green light for Saddam to invade Kuwait, which paved the way for the US to invade Iraq. The presence of foreign troops in Iraq is an occupation. It was the duty of the people of Iraq and the national parties to carry out change and not for the foreign troops to invade under the title of liberation.

'The sanctions were nasty and they affected us in prison because they wouldn't give us enough food any more. We didn't have electricity or water and prisoners were eating cats; they would even eat a dog. It only affected the Iraqi people. We knew it would not affect the regime. The sanctions did not contribute to the fall of the regime.'

He told his own story: 'We were interrogated, beaten up and tortured in Suleimania and Baghdad. We were flogged, electrocuted. When we got to Baghdad it was a month before the interrogation was repeated all over again and of course accompanied by beatings and torture. I lost my sight as a result of a beating on the night of 13 September 1989. The effect of the beating on my head and my body and my back affected my sight so that bit by bit I went totally blind. I was denied treatment.'

Mohammed Arif looked after Ali in the jail after he lost his sight. He took up the account: 'At midnight they would call out someone's name and would take him to interrogation. The people who guarded our rooms had nothing to do with us except for keeping us in place. At night different people from the interrogation committee would come and question us.

'They used to take us one by one for interrogation and torture, sometimes for two hours, sometimes for three, sometimes four. When it was over they would put you on a blanket, carry you and throw you in the air, back into the room. They didn't care whether you would die or not.'

And you come out, back into the light, and all around are mountains, dark blue against a bright sky, and trees and cool air and warm sun and the man you just met is in darkness forever. You stand there, amid the walls inside, among the mountains outside, and the screams haven't died down. But torture is designed to isolate. People go through it utterly alone and, as loudly as they might scream, nobody who can help hears. Or nobody who can hear helps. How many people tonight will be tortured in the darkness in countries which our governments still support, fund, arm, supply with torture instruments? And what will it take for us to stand up and stop them?

5

SADDAM'S ARREST

14 December 2003

A man in the road crossed his wrists to signify handcuffs and called out *'Saddam kelabach'* through the window. Kerim, a taxi driver I knew from my first visit, asked did I think it was true? Saddam was *'kelabach'*?

The woman begging with her six-year-old daughter flung her arms around me: *'Saddam kelaboutch'*. The watch seller came over to try to kiss me as well but I'm not sure that was anything to do with the capture of Saddam. An old woman in a raincoat and a floppy hat stood on the island in the middle of the road twirling a plastic mop.

Every café had a TV on and every station was showing pictures of an old, grubby, bearded man being pulled from a hole and having his beard inspected. My friend Khalid, Raed's brother, said it was definitely him. 'He has been on television for 12 hours a day for 35 years. I am sure it is him.' Marwan said it was all a trick. 'It's not the real Saddam.' Firas, who ran the internet café, was grinning enormously, taking photos of everyone and everything. 'My brother died in Saddam's war with Iran. Now they have caught him.'

Soon people started to remark on the presence of dates on the trees in the background of the footage of Saddam being hauled from the hole. This meant, they said, that the events couldn't have only just taken place, as claimed, and must instead have been in late summer when the dates ripened. It probably meant the new authorities had held off announcing the capture to see who else turned up, who knew where Saddam was and was still working with him. It meant, though, that having decided it was time to inform the Iraqis of his arrest, those authorities chose to lie about when it happened and assume the Iraqi people wouldn't notice.

There was more than the usual amount of gunfire in the air as word spread, but nothing like the night the Iraqi football team won an Olympic qualifying match. There was ambivalence. Even as some people put up newspaper clippings and posters showing Saddam's beard and teeth being investigated, for others a shift was under way.

I went out with some friends to see what was happening. In Kadhmiya, a mainly Shi'a* district, we met Sa'ad, who lived near the old secret police HQ, now occupied by US soldiers. The resistance, he said, was not from Kadhmiya but he added: 'We weren't as happy as when we heard that Uday and Qusay [Saddam's sons] were killed. It's not because we love Saddam but because he was captured by Americans, not by Iraqis. They're not here for the benefit of Iraqis but for their own benefit.

'Between us, he deserves what he's getting because he caused the deaths of lots of people but I would defend Saddam against foreigners. We have a saying: "Me and my brother against my cousin, but me and my cousin against the foreigners." I was not a Ba'athist. Saddam didn't hurt me but he took us into wars we weren't meant to be in. He spent money on stupid things and didn't give enough to the people.'

As for the gunfire, he added: 'Some of the shooting was celebration but in truth after a while it's just because there are lots of weapons, so mostly people are just trying their guns. I bought a new gun quite recently and I fired it just because it's new and I wanted to fire it.'

The neighboring Sunni district, Adamiya, was in open revolt. A shopkeeper called Ammar told us: 'The resistance had very good luck yesterday, about 10am. They hit three American humvees† in front of the big Abu Hanifa mosque and two in Anter Square and three in Al-Saleya, nine altogether. There were at least five men in each car and I don't think any survived. Twelve Iraqis were killed. Two of them were mujahedin and ten were civilians.

'If you have time, if you want to see something, stay here until four o'clock. Something is going to happen. If you like you can watch from my roof. The rumor goes around telling people who have shops to stay indoors at certain times. It won't start dead on four but we will stay indoors after that time and not go out walking.'

Even in Adamiya, though, he said: 'Those operations have nothing to do with Saddam. We don't love him – he's killed and tortured people, but because they are invaders, because they have occupied our country, they don't deserve to stay here. It's not really right for him to be judged by the US. The Interim Council is not much better than Saddam because they came from outside the country and they didn't live the suffering.

'I think resistance will increase now. A lot of people didn't fight before because they did not want to be called pro-Saddam, but now he is gone, it's pure jihad, and there is no reason not to fight.'

Jinan, a teacher in Al-Jaam'a, set out the counter-theory: 'I think resistance will decrease because most of them were with Saddam and

---

* The Shi'a people were more victimized under Saddam, a Sunni, though there was no open conflict between the groups within Iraq during his rule and intermarriage was common.
† High-Mobility Multipurpose Wheeled Vehicle – effectively an armored car.

now Saddam is captured they will fade away. I think things will get better because they announced there will be more focus on reconstruction now they are not distracted trying to find Saddam.' She added: 'We are celebrating because the slayer is gone that was torturing the people for 35 years.'

Ghanim Al-Khayoun agreed: 'I wouldn't call those people 'resistance' and they will fade away now Saddam is gone. I think Saddam surrendered and begged the Americans not to kill him. Really he was not even a dictator but a thief. I don't just blame Saddam but the Iraqi people as well who supported him through fear or love or greed.'

Saddam the poker player

The youngest son of the leader of *Beni Ased* [Tribe of the Lions], a Marsh Arab people from near Nasariya whose marsh was drained, Ghanim was a history writer and an intellectual. Many members of his family and his people were killed. As part of the family he would be a supervisor to whoever ruled in Nasariya where, he said, people went out on demonstrations to celebrate the arrest.

'Saddam was a poker player. He gave an interview in 1990 or 1991 talking about how you have to use your cards even if they are not strong. You fake it and pretend you have strong cards. It was said about a person from ancient times who was like Saddam that he acts like a lion on me but in wartime he acts like an ostrich. In Iraq in general, we have the habit of showing our muscles, trying to prove we are strong, but whoever shows off will lose from the first fist. His children died with more honor than him.

'I once beat Uday playing billiards in the hunting club. I saw all my friends whispering, because whenever they play with Uday, they will lose, they are scared, but what people saw of Uday was just a media thing of him being strong, evil and brave. Really he was just a coward. Qusay was much cleverer. He was planning to be in charge one day.

'To me Saddam's trial is not important. I would judge him by the laws of the Qur'an. If he committed one crime, he would have to be killed. How many times should we kill him? Some people think knowledge is over religion, which is why Saddam started showing religious interest in the last ten years to try and regain points.'

Others though, of all groups, opposed execution, favoring life imprisonment. A man with a biscuit flagged us down to ask about fuel and chat about Saddam: 'I want him to be jailed for life, not executed, because I want him to see how things will improve. But,' he added, 'I also want America to keep its promises because we had hope when they came in and so far they haven't done anything.'

Hamsa's friends in Fallujah described demonstrations and fighting.

Rafah, whose husband was a prisoner of war for 17 years in Iran, said: 'It's not just resistance and mujahedin now, it's everyone. The mujahedin were holding their RPGs* openly in the street, not even bothering to hide them, not hiding their faces. Everybody is in the street demonstrating so there are thousands, you wouldn't recognize individuals.'

'The Americans are using some kind of weapon, sort of small globes of white light that split into smaller lights and as they get nearer the ground it turns to gas. They're thrown out by aircraft, a fighter plane rather than a helicopter. We don't know what it is.† The aircraft has a very loud voice which is working on people's nerves, it's like sound bombs or something.

'They lost control of Fallujah and Ramadi yesterday. The people took over the mayor's office [where US troops were based] and looted everything. On Tuesday at midday they hit the train. It was full of equipment and food for the Americans, and they took all of that, so then the Americans started going into the town today to try and take control.

'They only have troops in the mayor's office normally and the rest of the troops are outside, because they were always being attacked. Now they've taken a school as a base, near the main street, and they took over the mayor's office again, a youth center, the train station and the police station, so those are now occupied by the Americans and lots of soldiers and tanks are in the streets, lots of checkpoints.

'The next few days are going to be hell. I sent my two girls to school today and they were sent back. There was no school because they were afraid for security, so they haven't been to school for two days. We've had no electricity for two days and we can't go shopping because everything has been burned, even vegetables, everything that was in the way was burned. Whoever captured Saddam is not better than him.'

In the mud streets of Abu Ghraib village, where haystacks lean on the houses and horse carts outnumber cars, the clattering of metal gates was interspersed with explosions. The ones on the top of the hour were usually controlled explosions of munitions collected and brought in to the airport. On the north side of Abu Ghraib there were rivers and bushes where people could hide and fire at planes when they came in.

Hamsa's uncle Hikmet summed up the two-fronted battle against the old regime and the occupiers: 'Every day in Abu Ghraib there are people killing ex-Ba'athists and people killing any person who works with the Americans. They warn Iraqis to stop working with Americans or get killed. Abu Ghraib is like a beehive. If you touch it at all it will be very angry.

---

* Rocket-Propelled Grenade launchers.
† It is likely she was describing magnesium flares which are dropped by aircraft and split into bright spheres of light to give a short-lived view of the area.

SADDAM'S ARREST   81

'People are fighting because they are comparing now with Saddam's time. We have so much oil and yet there is none in the filling stations. The Iraqi army left weapons abandoned on the streets so people collected them. If I knew where Saddam was I would go and release him. I hate him but he is like the flag I used to hold.'

Hamsa wanted to talk to some soldiers as we were passing but they all said they were under strict new orders not to talk to anybody. Fernandez of 41FA (he didn't tell us that, his helmet did) let slip 'I think they did a good job' but told us we'd have to go to the base for signed permission if we wanted to write that down. I don't suppose Saddam's arrest looked such an own goal from Fernandez's perspective.

Soldiers versus schoolchildren

Sheikh Adnan Al-Ani, Imam of the Al Hasanein [Sunni] Mosque in the Ameriya district of Baghdad, described how troops' actions only exacerbated the situation: 'Here in Ameriya the schoolchildren went out and demonstrated, lots of young people. The Americans tried to get rid of the crowd, which then sat in front of tanks and started cheering "Long live Saddam!" It wasn't really for Saddam himself but for Iraq, because people know that chanting his name will provoke the occupiers.'

A day later, Ahmed, an English teacher, picked up the story: 'There was a demonstration the day before yesterday after school finished, against the coalition and for Saddam. Yesterday the American army came and surrounded the whole block. They just crashed into the school – 6, 7, 8 into every classroom with their guns. They took the name of every student and matched the names to the photos they got from the day before and then arrested the students. They actually dragged them by their shirts on to the floor and out of the class.'

The children at Adnan Kheiralla Boys' School in Ameriya were still scared, still seething with rage. They wouldn't give their names. Another boy, Hakim Hamid Naji, was arrested that day. 'They were kicking him,' one of the pupils said.

The headteacher was reluctant to speak. No, he said, dissembling, looking down at the desk, there were no guns. The soldiers who raided the school did not have guns. But Ahmed followed the soldiers on the raid. 'The translators had masks or scarves to cover their faces because maybe they are from this area and they don't want to be recognized. They came and chose several students and they took them.

'The demonstration started after school on Tuesday. I advised them not to do it because I am their teacher and the Americans don't care. The children had pictures of Saddam Hussein from their textbooks and that's all, so they demonstrated and just said we want Saddam Hussein.

'The American soldiers came with tanks and stopped the demonstration and afterwards took pictures of the students. I begged the soldiers to leave them alone because they are naïve, they just believed this was a civilian demonstration. They didn't believe they were doing anything wrong, but the soldiers were very rude to the students and treated them like soldiers. "They are kids, they are teenagers," I begged the officer, but he didn't care.

'Yesterday I went with some of my friends to some Iraqi soldiers and they promised to help the students. There were no leaders, this wasn't an arranged demonstration. It came honestly, some of the students said, because we love Saddam Hussein. Some of the students said no, we hate Saddam Hussein. I told them, it's OK, let some love him and let some hate him; we can all express our opinions.

'There were no weapons, there was no bombing, but the Americans came in the classes with their weapons. I told them, just calm down, but they said no, these are not just kids: in Abu Ghraib we have 16-year-olds shooting at us. I said yes, but these are in school. They have books, not weapons.

'And they took pictures of us, what is your name, stand here. I am not a criminal; I am a teacher. They took pictures of most of the teachers. I told them you have to educate people, not punish them, but they brought tanks and helicopters, surrounded the school, came in with weapons everywhere, used teargas on the students and fired guns above their heads to scare them.

'They had some sticks, electric sticks and they hit the students. Some of them were vomiting, some of them were crying and they were very afraid. The soldiers told me Saddam Hussein is a danger and you are with Saddam Hussein.'

Another teacher, previously a lawyer, backed Ahmed up: the soldiers had definitely had guns when they went into the classrooms. The students said the same. The teacher said the boys arrested were aged 13 and up, taken from their classrooms and put into a truck. It was believed that they were taken to the prison camp at Baghdad airport. One student had his arm broken because of the beating.

The boys, frightened and suspicious, wouldn't let anyone film them or tape-record their voices, would only speak with their faces covered, refusing to give their names or even ages. They'd seen schoolmates pointed out by a masked translator with the troops. 'Only 40 kids out of all of us were on the first demonstration,' one said, 'but after the raid, we will all go out on Saturday after school and demonstrate against the occupation. It has turned us all against the Americans.'

'We don't care about their tanks, we don't care about their machine guns, we don't care about their prisons,' another declared defiantly.

One of the children who was arrested agreed to talk about what happened: 'The soldiers pointed at me and I was grabbed by about eight of them and dragged out by my clothes and my collar. They threw me on the ground and searched me and cocked their guns on me.

'We were held in chicken cages, about two meters by a meter and a half with criss-cross wire. They were swearing at us a lot. They didn't beat us but they accused us of having relations with Saddam Hussein, asking who organized the demonstration, telling us anyone who is against American interests will be arrested.

'They offered us some food but more curses. They didn't inform our parents at all. The headteacher came with three of the fathers. Most of us were held between seven and ten hours but one student is not Iraqi and he was held for much longer. They questioned him for two hours and then made him stand outside from 10pm till 2am in the freezing cold. We were mostly about 17. The youngest was 13.'

Adnan Kheiralla, after whom the school was named, was a brother-in-law of Saddam's, popular with both Sunni and Shi'a. Saddam killed him, apparently because of his popularity. When statues of former regime figures were being destroyed after the invasion, people protected his, one in Baghdad and the other in Basra. Kids had painted over the school's name to make it 'Saddam's School'.

None of this was considered 'News'. A scattering of Iraqis and a couple of freelancers were all that went to listen to the children. One told me later that he'd sent out the story on a couple of newswires and received just a single response, from an editor angrily informing him that this was 'Not News'. What US soldiers did to those children for demonstrating nonviolently was 'Not News'.

Trying Saddam – and his accomplices

A final word on Saddam's trial, because it is something I care passionately about. If legal systems, domestic and international, belonged to the people they would be different. The prospect of a guilty verdict on a token charge, however appalling, to justify execution is a travesty. Although the normal role of a criminal defense lawyer in an adversarial system like that of Britain or the US is not to ensure that the truth comes out, in the case of a national leader, a dictatorship, multiple crimes, it is essential that the truth is heard so that the country can begin to heal.

In most modern legal systems it is a crime to aid and abet an offender. It is a crime to supply an item which the supplier knows is for use in an armed robbery, for example, or a knife, knowing it is intended for use in a murder. If using chemical weapons is a crime, then supplying them is too. If using helicopter gunships against civilian populations is a crime, so is selling them to a man with a known history of doing so. In English law the accessory is as guilty as the actual perpetrator and liable to the same sentence.

That's why the truth, the whole truth and nothing but the truth about Saddam's rule will never be allowed out. Ronald Reagan, Donald Rumsfeld, Margaret Thatcher et al, the executives of BAe Systems (formerly British Aerospace) and many other sellers of armaments and torture instruments are all criminally implicated as aiders and abettors of murder, genocide, forced displacement. To date only Holland has arrested an arms dealer – one arms dealer – on charges relating to Iraq.

Saddam deserves criminal punishment, no argument. I look forward to seeing all those arms peddlers on trial too.

6

HEALTH IN A SHATTERED STATE

December 2003

Before the circus got started I had another concern. From my previous visits I knew that not only the hospitals were in a terrible state but also public health. Sanctions went a long way towards explaining both but environmental factors were implicated as well. My background, before I went into law, was in Health Science, and geographical patterns of illness and health. I did some research on cancer treatment for a journalist writing for *The Lancet* medical journal in Britain and helped my friend Husni set up an environmental NGO. But it was meeting Hamsa's uncle Hikmet which really sparked my curiosity.

Hikmet lived in the village of Abu Ghraib, close to the infamous prison and bordered on one side by Baghdad airport, a key battle zone during the invasion. Immediately after the bombing of the airport, Hikmet said, thousands of trucks started removing the soil from the complex. The locals didn't know where it was dumped but other trucks brought fresh soil to replace it and tarmac trucks came in to cover it over. The process is called 'landscaping', which makes it sound pleasantly aesthetic.

About a month after the bombing, the trucks started leaving their loads closer to the fence, tipping rubble, metal, broken crockery and general debris in the 1st June sector. Kids played and men, including Hikmet, foraged in the heaps between the houses. Someone else explained: 'There are no jobs. Sometimes useful things are dumped and we can find them and sell them.' Later some of the kids told us about sweets, ready meals and mineral water being thrown out. They went and ate the sweets and brought home the rest. 'No you don't,' scolded one of the mothers. 'I do, I do,' her child said with a gleeful grin. She went red and said: 'Well... sometimes.'

Hikmet showed us white patches on his neck, shoulders and back. They itched ferociously and had been spreading since they first appeared, after he started going scavenging in the piles of soil and junk. Had he stopped going there, Hamsa demanded. He grinned triumphantly: no he hadn't. Under her glare, the grin turned sheepish. There was no work. You

Hikmet and his wife Khadije.

couldn't pass up useful stuff dropped on your doorstep.

I scoured the internet for any clue as to what might be causing Hikmet's problem and came up with a November 2003 study by the Uranium Medical Research Committee: 'Witnesses living next to the airport report 3,000 civilians were incinerated by one morning's attack from aerial bursts of thermobaric and fuel air bombs. Since the cessation of the main phase of battle, several of the Baghdad area battlefields... [were] landscaped by the US forces and Iraqi contractors, thus preventing a thorough examination.'

It meant that nobody could take soil or water samples and people could only guess at the type of weaponry that was used there; they couldn't prove anything. Depleted uranium was a possibility – the radioactive waste product of uranium enrichment for nuclear fuel and weapons, itself used as a weapon for piercing tank armor and bunkers. Other suspects included napalm, white phosphorus or other chemical or toxic weapons or cocktail thereof.*

---

* It appears similar 'landscaping' was undertaken in Falluja after the November 2004 attack where white phosphorus had been used. 'In the centre of the Jolan quarter they were removing entire homes which have been bombed, meanwhile most of the homes that were bombed are left as they were.' A doctor said he saw bulldozers push soil into piles and load it on to trucks to carry away. In certain areas where the military used "special munitions" he said 200 square meters of soil were being removed from each blast site'. From Dahr Jamail, 'I treated people who had their skin melted', *The Independent*, 15 November 2005.

Gathering evidence

Hamsa and I went to the small Abu Ghraib hospital to talk to the doctors. Dr Jinan, at the outpatient clinic within the hospital, said there were patients coming in with illnesses that she and her colleagues couldn't diagnose. Patients were referred to the main hospital complex at Baghdad Medical City but were returning with still no diagnosis and having had no treatment. In particular, patients had been presenting with bubbles on the skin which 'become hot, like burning coals, get hard and spread.' She said they didn't understand it.

There had been an enormous increase in allergenic respiratory and skin problems with no apparent trigger. In particular there had been a rise in three conditions – alopeicia (hair loss), psoriasis and viteligo (skin problems). These were not infections spreading through the community but auto-immune conditions, caused by the body attacking itself, to put it simply. They were related to nerves, so fear and stress were relevant, but environmental factors were also believed to be important.

Health statistics were few and basic. I could get the monthly incidence of skin and breathing problems for in-patients at the hospital. I could get the rate per year of cancers, all types and all ages, again for in-patients (zero or one per year from 1991 to 1996, 7 in 1997, 3 in 1998 and then 11, 16, 15, 19 and 20 respectively for the last five years).

I could get nothing about outpatients treated in the clinic, nothing to compare the monthly data for this year with previous years, nothing about the geographical distribution of sufferers, let alone any details of the majority who never went for diagnosis or treatment because they couldn't afford it.

No-one knew what the occupying military authorities were hiding by removing the soil from the airport, or where they were hiding it. The chances were that the full effects wouldn't be visible for years and by then memories, pollutants and people would have dispersed, with the result that the effects would go on and the chance to monitor them would be lost. So Hamsa and I agreed to go door to door and ask the women of the community about illnesses and health in their families before and since the invasion. It was no use asking the men – they didn't know and without fail they said there were no problems.

In the row of houses closest to the airport fence, within the 1st June sector, every single household reported some kind of skin or breathing problem. Probably the most common was white patches on the skin like Hikmet's, which started, for most people, between April and July, the span of three months from the bombing. Or spots on the skin, which turned black and then the skin peeled off. Or blisters or bubbles on the skin, with or without fluid.

Women brought us inside, away from the men, took off their *hijabs* and showed us bald patches on their heads. The water was contaminated and, to combat that, it was filled with chemicals. It protected you from diarrhea but wrecked your skin. One of the women showed us her small son, whose scalp was like a toadstool of red skin and white pustules under the hair, insanely itchy but too painful to touch.

One family living near the fence told us that all their chickens died on the day of the bombing. 'There was no harm to their bodies, they were still complete, but they were dead.' The grandmother's eye ruptured during the bombing.

A five-year-old boy watched us with one eye as his mother told us: 'On the day of the bombing the smoke went in his eye and it ran for a week and then stopped. The doctor said he can't operate because the nerves are already destroyed.' His 22-year-old sister, deaf and mute from birth, had her first fit during the airport bombing and one every week or ten days since then. The mother was one of the women who had had several miscarriages in recent years.

Zakia's life

Zakia Ibrahim was 62 and surrounded by grandchildren. She wore an *abaya* (a garment covering the whole body) and had a huge mole under one eye; the contour lines on her face mapped her life. There were 23 grandchildren from her five sons, still more from the six daughters. At the end of the first day we stopped surveying and had Zakia tell us stories. 'I was harvesting wheat in my village when my first son was born. I cut the cord with something I had with me and carried on working, not like women today, lying on their backs for days.' It was 1958 and she was 17, already three years married.

They kept sheep, cows and donkeys. In those days you could live wherever you pleased and you went wherever there was land that you could use. 'But when the King came [in 1958], people were taken to places like Thawra* where there were authorities.' Boys and girls used to swim together in the villages, not like now, she said, when they are all separated. In 1963, when Iraq changed from monarchy to republic and urbanization increased, those things started to change as well.

Her husband was 13 years older. 'We used to be afraid we would be beaten by our husbands. We were not allowed to wear make-up. I was married in a small hut. When you looked up at the ceiling you saw the sky. We had no car – they took me to my husband's house on the back of a donkey and I sat on a tin can at my wedding. But then at least we had animals to raise for food, for eggs and milk. Now we have not even an egg. There is no gas, no fuel, no electricity.

---

* The building of Thawra was completed two years after the 1958 revolution.

Zakia Ibrahim: 'If I were President...'

'The Americans promised us first aid and humanitarian assistance but they have given nothing. Under the sanctions we would eat whatever we could – there was no variety. We couldn't even change our clothes. Under Saddam and the sanctions it was the same as now under Bush. It is not a pleasant life.'

Of Saddam's arrest the previous week, she said it was fate. He was caught because it was meant to be. 'Under Saddam, we could not even open our mouths.' But still she had sympathy for him: 'He has Muslim blood.' Her son was jailed, in 2000, for a year. He was avoiding the army, bribing an officer to overlook his absence so he could carry on supporting his family. He was beaten and tortured. 'They did not give them food. They were treated like dogs, herded, and I used to tell him, remember, they are Muslims like you.'

She was allowed a two-hour visit every three weeks, which meant a whole day traveling to get to Mosul, because he was jailed where his unit was based. 'But at least under Saddam we had security. I could travel back from Mosul after dark but now we can't go anywhere. I have told my sons' wives not to get pregnant because if the birth started at night we could not even take them to the hospital.'

Two of her sons were conscripted into the war with Iran. One was injured. 'No-one could say he wouldn't go. He would have been executed

Zakia and her family outside their home.

in front of his family. The year you went into the army depended on the
year you were born and then you stayed until the end – your end or the
war's end. But there was always food then. It was good living but so many
men died. There were always big funerals for the men who were killed.'
Things were better then, she said, because of the nationalization of the oil
industry. 'We had opportunities, better jobs, a higher standard of living.'

Another son was called up for the 1991 war but went into hiding. 'He
hid here, beside me,' Zakia laughed. 'So many wars. It's amazing we still
have flesh and blood on us.' They left Abu Ghraib village when the US
soldiers entered the airport, taking the kids to the tribal leaders nearby
and distributing them around the homes. She and some of the others
stayed in the house until things got really bad: 'It was like fire on top of
our heads.'

After the war, cleaning the house up, Fadhil, her 16-year-old grandson,
went to the roof to call the younger kids indoors and was shot dead by
US troops firing from a helicopter. 'Lots of people died in Iraq. It would
have been better to lose the house or have everything looted. It is better
to die than to live like this, to live with deaths every day.'

Two of her sons now supported the extended family. Her youngest son
was 21, married for three years with a child. He used to work in one of
the palaces, earning good money. Now there was no money. 'If I could, I

would work and let him sit, because he's still only a child.'

We appointed Zakia the president of the new Iraq. First, she said, she would bring law and order and then she would give to the poor. 'The rich already have thick bones. I have suffered with the poor. I met a woman who had never even tasted dates. Imagine that, in Iraq, where we grow the best dates in the world.' Then she asked us, 'Why don't you tell them to tarmac the road?'

And then we had to go because it was half past four and the ground was already rocking with sporadic explosions and the air thudding with helicopters so low you could almost flick mud at them. By dark, everyone said, Abu Ghraib was a war zone. Grandchildren danced after us to the car, between the swamps and the rubbish and the ducks and geese and cockerels poking about in them.

The swamp of suspicion

Over several days working within 1st June sector we found that the frequency of problems decreased with distance from the airport fence. The Dairy Buildings, the blocks of apartments on the other side of Baghdad airport, were a little further from the fence, the Dairy itself providing a buffer. Again, residents reported fewer illnesses: the same conditions but less concentrated than in the homes right by the fence.

The previous week US troops had raided three of the Dairy Buildings. We let them in, the women said, we didn't argue, but they turned everything upside down and still didn't find any weapons. Three US humvees drove past and the boys ran after them shouting 'Ali Baba' – thief – and throwing mud.

We were in and out of the hospital throughout and Sura, a receptionist we'd become friendly with, wanted us to meet her friend, Hassan, one of the guards. On 8 December at about 11pm he had been asleep, off duty, in the guardroom at the hospital entrance. A car arrived with a patient inside and his colleague went out to search the car, because all vehicles entering the hospital have to be searched.

A humvee of US soldiers came and started shooting at random with the gun on top of the vehicle. They all ran back into the guardroom. His two friends were injured by glass from the window. A bullet hit Hassan in his abdomen. Another went through the window of the delivery room while women were giving birth in there.

Just before Hassan went into the operating theater, the commander, a major, came and told him he was sorry, it had been a mistake. Hassan had had two operations in the 12 days since then, to cut away the infected tissue. He shuffled, with help, from the corridor back to his bed. It took two men to help him sit because he couldn't bend at the waist.

A friend filled in the compensation claim forms on his behalf but as yet they'd heard nothing. He was married with two kids; but his mother and several siblings were also dependent on him. His 37-year-old sister had breast cancer, which had appeared in May. She had epilepsy, which was aggravated by the chemotherapy, so now she was having no treatment for the cancer.

Back outside in the mud, a woman cautiously opened a heavy metal gate to us. She'd had five miscarriages in the five years since 1998. Her two girls were born in 1991 and 1994 and since then she'd lost each one at between three and five months of pregnancy. After the last one the hospital told her they knew of about 100 women who were having repeated miscarriages.

Another woman lost six babies in ten years, five girls and a boy, each one born prematurely at about eight months. They were born alive but died within the first day. Yet another had lost her baby just three weeks before, after eight months of pregnancy. She said she got a fever, lost all her water and the baby died. She saw him, she said. He was perfect and complete. These ones, at least, were longer-term problems not caused by the most recent bombing at the airport.

The talk of miscarriages reminded me of Bassima. I met her on the first day of the survey and she said she hadn't been able to feel her baby moving lately so she was going for a scan the next day. Before we finished for the day we went to find out how it had gone. It turned out the local hospital's equipment was broken and she couldn't afford the private clinic's fee of 9,000 dinars ($4.50).

Bassima's husband used to be a schoolteacher in Nasariya. Unable to find teaching work, until recently he worked as a security guard at a school in Baghdad. His colleague was shot for 'working for the Americans' and threats were made against him too so now he was off on leave. He didn't know whether to go back and risk being shot or to quit and be without money for Bassima, the two kids and the new baby.

We arranged to take her for a scan the next day but when we went to pick her up some men came to the house. Was she going to be a spy for the Americans? What were we going to pay her? Surely she didn't believe that this was about health? A woman came in and sat down. Who were we? What were we doing? Why were we taking Bassima for a scan? Why were we asking about health? What was in it for us?

Bassima's baby was fine – heartbeat, movement and fluid all normal. But that was the end of the survey. Men went to Hikmet's son's house that night and said his father was working as a spy for the Americans and they were sure he knew what happened to people who did that. As if we would have gained any information about the resistance by discussing health, baldness and blisters with the women of the community; certainly nothing that the American troops couldn't find out with door-to-door raids.

In Abu Ghraib the swamp of suspicion was just like the old days: too many of their people were in the prison, too many dead, too many houses raided. I wrote up the study thus far the next day and sent it out to the people in the village. Finally they believed that it was exactly what we'd said and Hikmet was welcomed back but still, it felt like that had to be the end of it.

A toxic land

Because of the threats, we weren't able to test water, soil and air to map the environmental contaminants which might be responsible but we did achieve a general picture of health conditions and some of the clean-up work that might be needed. But even without the bombing, poison came from the air, the soil, the water. During the sanctions period it was impossible to repair the country's sewage and water systems, damaged by both war and old age. The sanctions committee placed pipes on hold for a long time, lest anyone should attempt to fire anything unusual out of them – the infamous effluent supergun. Pipes were corroded, causing leaching of heavy metals.

My friend Husni, a professor of Environmental Pollution, said there hadn't yet been any testing of Iraq's tap water or sewage but, when he worked in Libya, water from similarly corroded pipes was contaminated with lead, cobalt, zinc, magnesium and manganese. Most heavy metals cause damage to the brain, liver, kidneys and other internal organs.

The Tigris and Euphrates in the Baghdad area were running low because of dams up-river: there were 28 in Turkey alone. The discharge (total amount of water) of the Tigris fell from around 40 billion cubic meters in the 1960s to around 16 billion in 2003. This means that pollutants are more concentrated. If the water had already been used for irrigation further up the river it was contaminated with pesticides and fertilizers before it reached Iraq.

By 2003 half a million tons of raw sewage (plus heavy metals) were being dumped into the Tigris, Euphrates and their tributaries every day. Some was used as fertilizer, so the heavy metals passed into the soil and from there to the plants, into the animals, concentrating in the people who ate them. Seepage of groundwater into the river brought more pesticides and fertilizers from the irrigation water, as well as salt.

Husni explained that under Saddam no-one could mention environmental pollution, as it would imply criticism of his policies, and since Saddam no-one cared. There weren't even effective road laws, let alone environmental or health and safety ones, so industrial waste, chemicals and petrol also ended up in the river. Instead of environmental legislation, he said, now there were companies wanting easy money.

The road to the airport used to be like a wood, Husni said, but the

Americans cut down all the trees along it, for their safety. 'It takes years for a palm tree to grow and only a few seconds to chop it down. Baghdad needs some green cover.'

Less dramatically, there was rubbish everywhere, including the rivers – rat-infested and toxic, and no-one to remove it. Nobody was employed as a refuse collector, at the municipal tip or the incinerator.

Apart from all that, the *Christian Science Monitor* had recently surveyed a few areas with a geiger counter and found four with extremely high radiation levels. There were no warning signs; kids played and people lived among the contamination.

Along the road from Hilla to Baghdad, burned-out tanks marked the kilometers, some tucked in among the palm trees, some stark at the roadside, for some reason not thrown into the tank cemetery at Al-Dora, a huge expanse of wasteground where defeated tanks and vehicles were piled. Aala went there daily to cut bits of metal off the tanks to sell; Kurdish men came to buy from the people who scavenged a precarious living there. It was divided into territories within which a particular group or family had the salvage rights. Aala's mum died when he was still in nappies. His dad had left them for a new wife and the older brothers and sisters took care of the younger.

Now 16, he was fairly independent but, tiny and powerless, he was only paid 1,000 dinars – about 50 cents, for a day's worth of metal. His older brothers got a better rate. He mustered a small smile. The oldest brother provided food for them, so sometimes he had enough money to go and play billiards. He would play till his money ran out and then come back to the wasteground. There were five families living in the houses immediately bordering the cemetery on their side.

I asked him if anyone had warned him it was dangerous to cut metal from burned-out tanks. No, he said. It used to be that a lot of people died from explosions there, but there were not so many now. A memory caught him: there were some journalists who came with a machine and they said there was a reading on it, that it was dangerous to climb on the tanks and take the metal, there was something, what was it called? Radiation. But he didn't know anything about that. Like Hikmet in Abu Ghraib, the risks of illness later were less than those of present destitution in a country with unemployment running between 60 and 80 per cent.

Depleted uranium and cancer

Professor A Hadi Khalili, vice-chair of the Iraqi Cancer Board and head of the Department of Neurosurgery at Baghdad University College of Medicine, explained: 'We do not know whether there is a statistically significant link between depleted uranium (DU) and cancer. We were planning to do a proper study with the World Health Organization starting in March 2003 with six projects but it was delayed by the war and now it is on hold. So there is no solid evidence of a link, only presumptive evidence, because the biggest increases have been in the areas where the greatest amount of DU was used.'

Professor Khalili thinks the most urgent need is for experts in epidemiology and statistics. 'We can do our own analysis but we know there is more to be done. We need to have experts analyze our data and help with planning strategies, to stay for two or three months and go into depth with our figures. One of the problems used to be that the Government would not release any census information – it was forbidden for anyone to know how many people were living here. I don't know why. So the two WHO experts who came could not do proper statistical analysis.'

Cancer prevalence in the country was always underestimated, he said, because not all cases were reported. Some patients couldn't afford to get to the hospital, others were never diagnosed. Some were clinically too advanced for effective treatment, so were never admitted as in-patients and never recorded. The registry team had careful procedures to prevent duplication, for example, if a patient was diagnosed in Basra and then came to Baghdad for treatment.

Nonetheless Dr Ahmed, a cancer epidemiologist working with Professor Khalili, said they were currently reviewing all of the information registered since the computerization in 2000. They moved into the Shahid Adnan hospital in the first days after the war when no-one else was working, and managed to save all their data. Everything was on files which were kept safe from the fires and looting.

In the meantime they believed that both the number and behavior of cancers had changed since the early-to-mid-1990s. Leukaemias had shown the biggest increase. Breast cancer had overtaken bronchial and urinary cancers as the most common tumor. Brain, colloidal and colo-rectal cancers had also increased five- to sevenfold up to 1999. The biggest increases in patients presenting with cancers had been in the south of the country, up to 1999. The statistical predictions for increases by 2008 were massive based on that data.

Professor Khalili opened pictures on his computer, one of the few in the hospital, and showed me pictures of eye tumors and, with pride, the after picture, the eye saved. He explained that the increasing aggression of cancers over the last 10 years meant they were seeing many 'museum cases' that would not be seen elsewhere, clinically advanced in a short time.

Why? 'Cancer is increasing throughout the world. Here the environment is full of carcinogens, in the air, the water, the soil. There have been three toxic wars using all kinds of weapons, including uranium weapons, and there have been explosions in weapons factories and dumps. There is also excessive use of canned food and the introduction of genetically modified food. Malnutrition increases susceptibility.'

In any case there was a wait of two to three months for radiotherapy when you were diagnosed with a brain tumor. Dr Ali in the Taba Al Nawawi Center for Nuclear Medicine explained that cancer treatment had long been neglected in Iraq because there had been few cases and it wasn't a priority. After the huge increase of the last few years there was an urgent need for radiotherapy machines and specialist teachers.

There were only two cobalt machines and no linear accelerators for radiotherapy in the hospital, the main cancer treatment center in the city. The assistant chief of the hospital, Dr Mahdi, explained that this was down to a combination of the restrictions imposed under the sanctions, political issues with the companies that manufacture the machinery and bureaucracy within the Iraqi Government. Since the war, it was international organizations rather than the Ministry of Health which were supplying a lot of their needs.

Dr Bashar from Mosul in the north, whom I met in a lift at the Ministry of Health, said his region hadn't seen the increases in cancers experienced in the south and center of the country. He put this down to patterns of pollution. The north was not contaminated with depleted uranium and experienced much less water pollution from irrigation. In addition the north has other water sources like rainwater and streams from the mountains while the south has only the Tigris and Euphrates.

By contrast, infectious diseases, mainly tuberculosis and malaria, were endemic in the north. Statistics from 1997, the most recent available, indicated 150,000 people in the province were infected with one of the two conditions: Dr Bashar suspected it was getting worse.

He put the high prevalence down to three things: first, lack of medical services, including doctors and vaccination; second, poverty, particularly the poor nutritional state of the majority of people; and, third, tradition – in some areas, particularly those where people are not Muslim or Christian but Yazidi, the women are afraid of needles going under the skin and so refuse vaccinations.

That evening Raed's uncle rang to say that US planes were bombing his district, Ad-Dora, with cluster bombs, littering another residential area with delayed-action explosives. We had electricity for quite a few hours, for a pleasant change, so we put the music on loud and turned up the bass to drown out the constant racket of fighter planes overhead.

Doctors in despair

'When Saddam was here,' Dr Faris half-joked, 'we knew who to blame for everything. We just cursed Saddam for whatever went wrong. Now we don't know who to blame – Bush, Blair, Bremer, the Governing Council,

Aznar [then Spain's prime minister], the people who are fighting. This is our democracy. Nothing has changed but now we have a choice of people to blame.'

Faris's former colleague, A'ala, who brought me there, explained: 'You know, we don't even have any senior doctors. We are still training, Faris and me. We are qualified anaesthetists but we are still under training for intensive care. The Ministry of Health would be responsible for employing a senior doctor. When I need an opinion I have to call to another hospital to talk to the senior to give me a telephone opinion, without their seeing the patient.'

A'ala and two friends, Drs Yasseen and Laith, had been seeking out foreigners to offer their services as drivers and translators to make ends meet. A mutual friend introduced us and we started talking about the healthcare system. The doctors' account differed from the official line that 'Today, all 240 Iraqi hospitals and 1,200 primary health care clinics are operating.'[1]

In Faris's paediatric intensive care department there were only two working units. Of those, only one had a spirometer to measure the gases given to the patient and the monitors didn't connect to the units any more, so the patients had to be monitored manually. That was less of a problem now there were only two beds in use. The other two units were broken and the companies, Drager and Tema, would not repair them.

When desperate they resorted to manual pumps, blue bubbles with valves. 'We ask the mother, we say to her, the life of your child depends on this, so she squeezes until morning, but you know, it's not right. Every squeeze is different from each other and with the machines everything is measured, it's controlled ventilation. This is not controlled ventilation and then things go wrong and the patient will die from another cause.

'There is no mixing either. The ventilator will do both, mixing and control, but here we have only industrial oxygen, not medical, so it's too pure and some of the patients die from toxicity. We do the best we can to save the patients but we know that what we do might kill them. When a patient is on a ventilator for a long time, I need to wean him off. I need to measure the gases to withdraw them gradually but I can't. That can cause barotrauma. If he vomits he will die because I have no oral suckers. We know it is all wrong but we have no facilities to put it right and no-one trying to solve it.'

At frequent intervals both men would shake their heads and, in unison, sigh: 'Nothing has changed.' Doctors' wages were still not enough to live on. They all had second jobs in private hospitals, drove taxis after work, sold vegetables or depended on relatives. A'ala was concerned that the effort and energy needed to improve things in the hospitals wouldn't be available when people were working in other jobs to sustain themselves.

'They promised more ventilators but I still don't have them, and from where are you going to get the nursing staff, from where are you going to get the senior doctors? Only the Ministry can put the money into this and, if they don't, this ward will go down and down until they close it and let the children die.'

The Ministry had not consistently provided even disinfectant – A'ala mentioned that the nursing staff at times bought the cleaning materials themselves. The wards were never fully cleaned for germ cultures. There was only one cleaner. A'ala wielded a phial of ineffectual drugs bearing the stamp of the old Ministry of Health, which had still not been replaced by new imports: 'Did we go through this war to carry on using these things from India and Turkey? Nothing has changed.'

'I am so fed up, I don't know how I can continue. Nothing changed when the Americans came except the money increased by little and the prices increased by much. Really it's not our country.

'People who used only to hate, now take action. People who were in the middle, started to hate. People who were for them, now are in the middle. That's what happened with Britain in the 1920s – they push, push, push, until 2,800 English soldiers were killed. That's not counting all the Indian soldiers who died. Their graveyard is nearby.'

Salam, one of the children playing in debris in Abu Ghraib village.

Faris smiled. 'They fixed it before the war, they put up a new fence. I don't know, maybe they decided to make it ready for the foreign soldiers again.'

Faris recalled government-subsidized chickens, raised by the Ministry of Agriculture and sold cheaply for several months of the year. Nothing has changed, they agreed, except now there are no more cheap chickens.

There could be no mistaking their reminiscences and current complaints for a longing for Saddam. Dr Yasseen had a place to study for a Masters degree in anaesthaesia in Cardiff (UK) but doctors were not allowed out of the country under Saddam. If they traveled, it was with false documents that said they were merchants or general workers. There was a joke about crossing the land border out of Iraq: someone collapsed and, instead of asking whether there was a doctor in the place, they would ask if there was a merchant or general worker who could assist.

They laughed as they talked about the tongue-loosening effects of ketamine, a horse tranquillizer used as a sedative when it was impossible or undesirable to use full anaesthesia. 'People didn't care what they said, they just said whatever was in their heads because it removes all the inhibitions, so they would shout and curse Saddam.'

Yasseen tried to leave by 'the northern route', via Suleimania, but the 'smugglers' turned out to be government agents. He was arrested and taken to the security building in Suleimania. He was blindfolded and seated, then told, 'But you're a doctor, we must treat you with respect.' One guard told another to give him a pepsi. He was clubbed across the back. A sinalco (lemonade) was a blow to the face, a mirinda (fizzy orange) one across the knees. You knew where you would be hit next but not the direction the assault would come from or when.

After two months he was sentenced to a year in jail and all his assets were seized – about 12 million dinars' worth ($6,000). After six months his family were allowed to buy him out for a million dinars. A'ala said everyone could see the changes in Yasseen, how he had aged in those eight months. A'ala too was arrested once and clearly appreciated his good fortune at having spent only a week there, during which his family paid $1,000 to protect him from beatings.

The gospel according to Jim Haveman

On the way to meet Salma Al-Hadad, the head of Paediatric Oncology [child cancer], we stopped to help two people handling a wheelchair with only two wheels left, occupied by a limp child with a tube in her nose, over the ridges in the pavement. There were no orderlies, let alone medical staff to supervise. I was meeting Salma to talk about how doctors in Britain could support their Iraqi colleagues.

She summarized the department's needs as 'everything'. She was just back from London where a group of Iraqi doctors had been hosted by hospitals in the British capital. She was very keen on twinning links between hospitals in the UK and Iraq, to boost Iraqis' skills after nearly 13 years in which even paediatric medical information was embargoed. Iraqi medical education was based on the British model and they used mainly British treatment protocols so they felt there were already strong links.

It wasn't hard to see the effects of the demolition by sanctions of the healthcare system, starkly exposed against the carnage of armed occupation and rampant crime. In fact, in an attempt to obscure it, the Ministry of Health – under the command of US advisor Jim Haveman – banned the giving of casualty statistics to journalists in December 2003 and stopped the Ministry from continuing to count those statistics, even denying that they had ever been counted, despite the fact journalists had been given figures up till then.[2]

Haveman, you might recall from chapter three, was the man who insisted that the Kimadia pharmaceutical company workers had no right to be paid. In an online 'Ask the White House' Q and A he disingenuously informed readers that: 'The [health] system suffered from decades of neglect of maintenance' and that 'Basic radiological services are available, but advanced equipment and digital radiology is a dream to the Iraqi people.'[3]

He failed to mention that the so-called 661 Committee of the UN Security Council, which oversaw the Oil For Food programme, was holding up so many contracts that spare parts and essential maintenance equipment were largely unavailable. He failed to mention that radiological equipment was held up by the 661 Committee as having dual military and civilian uses.

It was left to *The Economist*[4] to point out that Khudair Abbas, the Iraqi Minister of Health, 'has five telephones on his desk but none can call outside the Ministry. With no landline access to hospitals, the centralized distribution of medicines is faltering, and drugs are in short supply... Mr Abbas says emergency stocks worth $15 million are on the way, but, despite the corruption that undermined the UN's oil-for-food program under the old dictatorship, Iraq did get medicine worth some $250m a year.'

And it was left to Knight-Ridder[5] to observe that: 'Basics such as pain pills or latex gloves are often unavailable. Doctors routinely are threatened or attacked. "We don't have ointments," said Dr Muhammad Hihad, standing in Yarmuk's crowded emergency room. "We don't have bandages." Yet there are those who wonder why, for example, a $26.3 million renovation of Iraq's Umm Qasr naval base near Basra, which is under way, took precedence over fixing the sewage system at the country's biggest children's hospital, al-Iskan, where toilets sometimes overflow into the leukaemia ward.'

The position in international law is simple: the Occupying Power takes over the main responsibilities of the displaced national government, including provision of public services. Articles 55 and 56 of the Fourth Geneva Convention set out the obligation to ensure adequate medical supplies for the civilian population. Under no circumstances can relief operations be seen as alleviating the Occupying Power's responsibilities. They may delegate part of it to national authorities – and did so, with the early return in March 2004 of the Ministry of Health to Iraqi sovereignty – but the ultimate responsibility remains with the Occupying Power.[6]

Failing to fulfil that, failing to get medicines into Iraq's hospitals, allowing people to die for want of them, was and is a war crime.

1 Jim Haveman, 'Ask the White House' Q and A online
2 Associated Press, 10 December 2003.
3 Ibid.
4 *The Economist*, 1 April 2004.
5 Ken Dilanian, 'Iraqi Hospitals Remain Bleak Without US Aid', 3 March 2004.
6 Program on Humanitarian Policy and Conflict Research, Harvard University, www.ihlresearch.org

7

INCOMMUNICADO:
PRISONERS IN ABU GHRAIB

December 2003

Ahmed volunteered as an ambulance driver for the last 15 days of the war. He started out using his car, then he and his friend Ali started driving one of the hospital's ambulances.

'I brought 500 bodies and many injured people. I brought all of them to Saddam Children's Hospital [part of Baghdad Medical City] because it was the only one that was still functioning. I never even saw a dead body before and they took me to the morgue and there were 80 bodies there.'

He had no medical training – he used to be a university lecturer in applied physics. After the war, for three months, Ahmed and Ali carried on their ambulance work at night when people with cars wouldn't drive for fear of being shot by the soldiers. They got permission from the US authorities to move about after dark and, said Ahmed, after work they would start collecting patients and bringing them to hospital, sometimes held up by armed gangs, sometimes by US soldiers.

They kept the ambulance running as long as they could but eventually it – and their work – sputtered to a halt. Ahmed quit the science college because he couldn't live on the salary and then worked for an organization which cleared away mines and cluster bombs. At the college, he said, there was no structure after the war. People took freedom to mean doing exactly as they pleased, there was no co-operation and it became impossible to do anything.

By early December the ambulance hadn't worked for three months, yet, said Ahmed: 'One week ago the American soldiers raided Ali's home. They said they had been given "information" that he uses the ambulance to carry guns and ammunition around at night. They found nothing in his home, not even one gun, although you are allowed to have one gun.

'Now he is a fugitive. He cannot go home because they are looking for him; they will arrest him even though they found nothing in his home. He cannot go to the Americans and say he has nothing to do with moving guns, because they will arrest him as soon as they see him and he will be in prison for at least six months. That is what happens.

'They give $2,500 reward to people who give information so people tell stories about someone they don't like, or they make something up just for the money, and they take the prize. For three months Ali did not sleep, just worked and then came home and drove the ambulance and now he cannot go home.'

The signs promising these rewards were on huge billboards all around Baghdad. On one of the roundabouts the posters had been bloodied with red paint. Tale-telling had been a means of survival under the old government. Promising a couple of years' worth of wages to a population of which more than two-thirds is unemployed buys unreliable information but perpetuates one of the cornerstones of dictatorship: surveillance of the people by the people.

Ali was not alone in falling victim to false information: there were numerous cases of US troops acting on tip-offs without corroboration, arresting and imprisoning all the men in a house despite having found nothing in their raid.

On the second of two days of protests for the rights of people detained without charge by the occupying powers, people stood waiting quietly, holding pieces of paper, queuing to talk to activists, NGO workers, journalists, anyone who would hear their story, anyone who might perhaps be able to help.

Hamdia and Sahib Jum'a showed me a picture of their son Hayder Sahib Jum'a Obaid, who lived with them in Al-Habibia. 'My son was taken six months ago by the Americans and I don't have any information about him,' Hamdia said. 'I came here to ask about him and they told me to get a lawyer but the lawyer is asking for 250,000 dinars. I don't have money to pay, so what can I do? I don't know if he's charged with anything. He was just a taxi driver, he had a Brazili car and that was it.'

A Brazili car is, essentially, a lemon. They were imported from Brazil and sold cheaply and the streets were soon blocked with breakdowns because they were the most useless cars ever built.

'I am his mother and I went to a lot of places, to Basra, to Amara, to a lot of places, a lot of prisons. Some Iraqi people at the jail eventually told me you should get a lawyer for him, and then we will see if he is here or not. I asked them to take his picture in with them and make sure if he is here or not – I don't want to spend all the money if he is not here so I have nothing left to pay for a lawyer when I find him.'

Her husband took up the story. 'First I went to a lot of hospitals and to the morgue and I did not find him, so I went to the American base. After that I went to the computer office and they told me your son is in Abu Ghraib and gave me a paper with his name and a number on. I came here but no-one gave me any answers and the man inside, the translator, just told us to go and get a lawyer.'

Hamdia went on: 'Under the old regime he escaped from the army and even when they caught him they let his mother see him but now, no. Just let me see him. They should at least tell us where he is. His daughter is crying all the time for her father. Before, we were hiding our son from the old regime because we were afraid, we didn't know what they would do, maybe they would kill him, maybe they would take him to jail, maybe they would take him to the army, but right now it's the same thing.

'We thought that the Americans would do something good for us but they did not. They did the worst. Even under the old regime if you had someone in jail you could go and see him. When he was arrested before we paid money, 15,000 dinars and they let him go. Now we don't have any information about our son.'

Echoes of Kafka

In Franz Kafka's *The Trial* a man wakes one morning to find he has been arrested in his sleep; his home is occupied by warders and he is under investigation for something; he is never told what. He has to attend interrogations at unmarked courts in labyrinthine buildings during which he is not actually questioned at all. His case drags on interminably as a prominent lawyer 'works' on his behalf at a system into which he is

Sahib Jum'a.

allowed no insight whatsoever other than to know that it depends on one's advocate's influence and the officials' whims. Someone, for reasons of jealousy or dislike, calls down an investigation on another and from then they are trapped under indeterminate suspicion.

The bureaucracies and rules of the New Iraq threw up many references to Kafka but nowhere more so than in the prison system. Like Hamdia, people harked back to the old days when, in most cases, a simple bribe would see you reunited with your loved one or, at the very least, would protect them from beatings. Some families had apparently managed to retrieve individuals with bribes to people working with the coalition forces. Others said they would gladly pay if they could find someone reliable to give money to.

Abdul Rahman Abd Al-Khaliq told me: 'The soldiers came and put bags over our heads and I was put in the prison here. They took six people from my house. My father and I were released after 103 days. My four brothers are still inside. I was arrested in August at 3am. They destroyed two doors and everything between the two doors. Luckily no-one was in that room. They took everything: computers, telephones, even the pictures on the walls. They stole from my home 11 million dinars [about $5,500 – people keep all their money in their homes because the banks are unstable]. They hid the money inside their clothes.

'They just put me in one room and gave me ration food. I was wearing only shorts, because it was night when they came. I wasn't wearing anything on my chest. I wasn't even wearing shoes. I was asking them please, just give me something to wear and no-one would give me anything when they took me from the house. When I went into the jail, I asked the soldier, just give me a t-shirt but no-one would give me a t-shirt. Only when they moved me from that prison one of them gave me a t-shirt but still no-one would give me any shoes: they said no shoes.

'They took me first to the republican palace in Karrada and then here to Abu Ghraib. They did really silly things at first, like tying our hands and putting bags on our heads when they took us to the bathroom. On the first day they kept a bag on my head and my hands tied the whole day. After that it was only when they moved us from one cell to another.

'They will keep you there for three months and after that they will decide if they will release you or not. I was questioned only on one day and the rest of three months I was just in a cell. We had six cars, that's what they said, that was the first reason they gave for arresting us, we were Fedayeen,* that was the second one, and we tried to kill Paul Bremer. That's what they said.

'When they questioned me they asked: "Do you know why you are

---

* Saddam Hussein's élite soldiers – literally 'the Prepared'.

here?" I said no. They asked me: "Why do you have a lot of cars in your home?" I said we are a rich family, we have a lot of things, we are five brothers and my father. They told me: "No, there are a lot of people meeting in your home." I said of course. My father is the oldest one of the family, all the family gatherings happen in our home. They said: "No, you are trying to make a new party now, trying to resist us." They came for me at four in the morning and questioned me until ten at night.

'I said I will kill myself if you don't release me. I'm a student in college and I need to be in college. I was studying business in Ma'amun College. After that they brought a lot of pictures and started asking me, even about children, do you know this one, do you know that one, about every picture. All the rest of the days for three months. I was just in the cell on my own.

'The Americans are just like Saddam because anyone who gives them information, they give him money, just like Saddam's regime. They would give you money if you went and told them this person is against Saddam and now it's the same. The Americans are paying money to anyone who tells them that this is information about the resistance. They are cheap people, trying to get money for CDs and satellite TV.'

Another man said his brother was arrested when a police officer called Mohammed Saddam came to their home with US troops. The police officer had come to the family before to ask to marry one of their daughters and they had said: 'No, you have no honor.' In revenge, they said, he returned with soldiers, accusing the brother of being part of the resistance.

A woman told of a fight between her family and some neighbors. The other family told the troops that her sons were with the resistance. They were arrested in June and, as yet, she hadn't been allowed to see them. She heard from one of the other detainees, who had since been released, that an army dog bit her son while he was in the jail and he had to have 12 injections. Released prisoners were the only source of news.

It was testimony to the low quality of the 'information' bought by the Americans that so many were freed without any charges or evidence being brought against them. Unfortunately, because the review board met so irregularly, it could take many months before the release without charge was effected.

Worse, interrogation was privatized, carried out by employees of private firms who were neither covered by military law (because they weren't officially military personnel) nor by civilian law (because there wasn't any). People were arrested so randomly and copiously that most of them had nothing to confess under interrogation. The inquisitors took them to be the hard cases and tortured them all the more. In some cases the wrong house was raided and the soldiers, despite realizing the mistake, nonetheless arrested the men in the house.

Some of the arrests were trumpeted as victories against the resistance. Sattar Mahmoud Alwan told his brother's story: 'You remember when there was looting? The kids found something, not gold but it looked like gold, some shiny thing, and they picked it up in the road and brought it home. Then you remember on the television, they put a picture and they said it has been announced that they found a big general of the Fedayeen and the suiciders?

'It was my brother. His name is Khalid Mahmoud Alwan but he had no relationship with the Fedayeen. After a while they put him in the jail and that's it, we hear nothing about him. There has been no court hearing. He's just a normal civilian. He had a small shop for chocolates and sweets. They should make sure.

'If they want to fight the resistance, the resistance is out there. All they are doing is throwing innocent people in jail and saying oh, we captured the resistance. The fact is the resistance is outside and they are killing your soldiers. It's not freedom, it's like they are taking some revenge on our people.'

Qasim Hadi, the leader of the Union of Unemployed Iraqis (UUI), and Adil Salih, from the Union's leadership committee, were arrested in Baghdad on 23 November 2003 and held for some days despite the hypothetical new rights to freedom of association and organization. Qasim had already been arrested along with 54 of his union's members during the 45-day protest at the CPA headquarters in the summer of 2003, demanding either jobs or social security for millions of unemployed people. Islamist parties had also attacked the Union and its protests – another coincidence of views between occupiers and politico-religious groups.

Others were scooped up in mass arrests. There was Ahmed Berdi Shermouk from Habania, whose brother Abed was arrested driving home from the barber's to his village, which had been surrounded by US troops while he was gone. There was Abdul Khattan Mohammed, who had a letter from a lawyer stating that the Governor of Diwaniya had ordered the release of his son Tha'ir, subject to bail, because no charges had been made against him. Another man carried a list of 20 names of young men arrested from two villages near Ramad. Sayid Ghazi Shahaf, too, had a list of more than 20 names from Diyala.

'They surrounded the area,' he said, 'entered the villages and started choosing people. They took all of those people with them and we just don't know why they did that. They came on four occasions with a few days in between, one-and-a-half to two months ago. Nobody knows any information about any of them, even whether they are alive. I have come as a representative of the village. They are all farmers.'

Majida Hassan took out a clear plastic bag, unrolled it and withdrew

Sayid Ghazi Shahaf.

a scrap of paper with her son Tahin's name written in English and his tag number – 18751. Everyone there had one of these scraps, kept safe somewhere, from the computer office where, if you gave them a name, they might tell you the whereabouts of the person you're looking for, as long as their spelling of the full name, transliterated from Arabic to English without any common system, was the same as yours, otherwise there would be no trace.

They all had two A4 pieces of paper as well – one headed 'Request for Information' and the other 'Request for Visitation.' Each contained the name of the prisoner. The former stated that the bearer would like some information about the prisoner and the latter recorded a wish to be allowed to visit them. And that was it. They had pieces of paper.

Majida had been more than 50 times to the prison trying to visit Tahin. The guards always refused, told her to come back in four months' time. No appointment, just come back in four months. That's what the pieces of paper were worth.

It was no different for lawyers: Thabat worked for one of the several human rights organizations in a building, near derelict from the bombing, on Old Rasheed Street, near the Jumhuriya Bridge. They looted relevant buildings after the war to get the information which would help them to record what happened to prisoners under the old regime.

Now they tried to find out what was happening to prisoners under the coalition, where they were being held, for what and when they might be tried or released. Thabat was a lawyer but that was almost irrelevant. Where is the court, he demanded; where is the process, where is the justice? The officials at the CPA and Civil-Military Operations Center told him to come next week, come in two weeks, and never gave him anything.

A couple of days earlier I'd received an email entitled 'The good news' from someone in the US. Each sentence began 'Since President Bush declared major combat over on 1 May...' and purported to show some benefit to the Iraqis as a result of the war, some item of progress in rebuilding the civil and physical infrastructure. Apparently all the courts were now functioning. At least that gave Thabat something to laugh at.

Outside the prison gates

Outside Abu Ghraib prison a man put a hand, for balance, on the coil of razor wire that separated the protesters and families from the soldiers. 'Don't touch my wire,' the major bellowed. 'Ah, it is his wire,' said an Iraqi man next to me, 'but his wire is on my soil.' A machine came along and started shunting concrete wall blocks into a line, sandwiching metal posts in between and draping coils of razor wire between the posts. The noise of the machine scared the kids and they shouted at it.

I was not there to interview, though, but to demonstrate with them and I was handed a megaphone and asked to speak on their behalf to the soldiers. I told them how Saddam used to detain people without charge, arrest on the basis of false information and imprison people without trial, how families used to visit and bring food, how the name Abu Ghraib evoked fear. I told them people were saying nothing had changed, except that now you had no information and no right to visit.

On the far side of the wall a 14-year-old boy called Mohammed was herding sheep. Later, when the soldiers had gone back to the prison gates he came over to talk, stepping and wriggling his way through, throwing stones at the sheep when they came too close to the dirt road into the prison. 'All their relatives are in here,' he said. 'Many many people. Down Saddam, down Bush.'

On Friday's march they were chanting, '*Britanee, amreekan, Wayn al-haqooq al-insaan?*' [Britain, America, where are the human rights?] Women and children carried signs, photos, ID badges of their missing persons. The demonstrations gave them a chance to be seen and heard, the small hope of having the name of their disappeared one spoken around the world.

A young woman called Yasamin had three brothers in jail: Mohammed, Waleed and Younis. 'The Americans raided our house and arrested Younis and then came again and took all our money and jewelry and our ID. His brother was arrested from his workplace and my third brother was detained when he went to enquire about the others.'

Her dad added: 'So now we are not Iraqis because we don't have our IDs. In Iraq anyone who crosses the borders from Syria, from Iran, we are now like them, we are not Iraqis, and they stole about $11,000. That is our money. They stole everything, our jewelry. They are thieves.'

When the troops burst into the house, they came into the room where Yasamin and her sister Stobruk had been sleeping. They went to get their headscarves and the soldiers pointed guns at them. They said very firmly,

Yasamin at the demonstration.

'no, we're going to get our scarves,' and they did it.

None of the brothers was ever formally charged with anything though it was, for a while, alleged that Younis was plotting to kill Tony Blair. In fact he was a journalist working with British filmmakers. He didn't have tapes of the resistance, as accused, but still he and his two brothers were held for months.

A couple of months later the Americans promised to release a thousand of the people jailed without charge but by Eid, in early February, only a hundred had been let out. Their mother was in hospital for a hip operation having broken it in a fall. Depression at the absence of her sons was ageing her, day by day.

Instead in late January Esam, another independent Iraqi filmmaker who worked with Younis, was arrested too, his house raided at 3am on suspicion that he had footage of the resistance. Nothing was found but Esam was taken. The Iraqi translator, Mohammed Saddam, well known in Adamiya, told Noor that he'd make sure her husband was released in half an hour if he could hold her hand.

All day Noor, Uzma and some other foreign activists went to the CPA, the bases, the police stations. At the military-run police academy near Al-Shaab stadium the foreigners were allowed in to enquire while Noor was barred.

It was about eight months before Younis was released, less for Esam. The grounds of the prison were divided up into camps because there wasn't room inside for everyone. The prisoners were always given coded clues about when the place would be hit with mortars so they knew to keep out of the way. The US soldiers, not having the warning, would run for cover. Then one day the mortars hit without warning. The US soldiers didn't run for cover, just stood about as if they knew where the mortars were going to land.

Pictures of torture stun the world

It was almost half a year from those demonstrations until the news about Abu Ghraib finally reached the world: the pictures of torture, euphemized as 'abuse', blamed on a few bad apples, who were scapegoated. Even before their courts-martial General Ricardo Sanchez was shown to have signed off approval of a number of the common torture techniques but his command responsibility was never formally acknowledged.

Lawyers acting for the US soldiers charged claimed that it was a system-wide problem – which it certainly was and is – and that their clients were not responsible because they weren't given clear guidelines. Do you really need a guideline to know you're not meant to beat, kick and sexually abuse a prisoner? But their individual guilt shouldn't be used to absolve those higher up the system, right to the top of the military, right to the political leadership, the ministers, secretaries of state, prime ministers and presidents.

Several Iraqi human rights organizations had been taking statements and testimonies from released detainees and their relatives for months, as had the Christian Peacemaker Teams (CPT) and the awesome Italian human rights activist Paola Gasparoli, but The Photos made news in a way that countless Iraqi people's stories did not. The pictures that were published were the tip of the iceberg.

One prisoner told CPT about rumors of a mass grave under the prison.

He said that he and fellow prisoners investigated, digging under their tent, and found recently dead bodies a few feet down. There were stories, independently backed up by various former detainees, of demonstrations against conditions in the camp being brutally suppressed by soldiers: one man reported an incident where the prisoners were shouting 'Freedom' and soldiers opened fire, killing four men and injuring three.

There were reports in the cases known to me, CPT and the local organizations of extrajudicial executions during a raid on the wrong house, a man having his toenail pried off by guards, people being forced to swallow liquid, prisoners being left blindfolded in an open air passage, with a tank driving towards them so they thought they would be run over and killed. A minor reported having his buttocks held apart by soldiers who were kicking his anus.

Routinely, detainees and their families reported beating and kicking during raids and detention, guns being pointed at children or held to their heads, detention of minors, excessive chemicals being added to water so it was dangerous to drink, overcrowding. They also mentioned denial of water, food, medical attention, blankets, shade, washing and toilet facilities and space to lie down. They reported hands tied behind the back for prolonged periods, even when this prevented them drinking water, or tied so tightly that the arms swelled. They reported being forced to kneel, squat or remain in the sun all day in temperatures of up to 120°F (50°C), suffering severe sunburn as a result of being kept for their entire detention in only underwear or nightwear. They reported abuse from military 'doctors' and use of Kuwaiti military as translators and guards, who were apparently particularly aggressive in 'revenge' for the 1990 invasion of Kuwait. They reported severe verbal abuse, theft of money and jewelry by US soldiers during raids and failure to return documentation, IDs, passports and other personal property that was with the prisoner when detained.

There was no provision for access to legal advice or representation. From arrest, it could take weeks even to be processed. Detainees were often the family's only earner and driver, so that children couldn't get to school and the rent couldn't be paid. Depression was ubiquitous among the prisoners and some families reported severe behavioral changes following release.

Women were often detained because their husbands were wanted. There were many reports of them being kept naked. Other women were detained because they were prostitutes used by high-ranking officials of the old leadership. A female human rights worker from one of the major organizations working on detainee issues herself disappeared into a US prison.

Several bank clerks, mostly women, were detained and over a thousand threatened with arrest to force them to pay for the losses in the January currency changeover. They were told to pay out new money – Bremer's money – for all the old Saddam notes handed in, even suspect ones. This was because there was no way of verifying which were real – it was all just printed on ordinary paper without security marks of any kind. There was no suspicion that the bank clerks stole money or committed any fraud but there was a discrepancy between the amount of genuine money received and the amount of new money given in exchange. Some, in fear, signed papers agreeing to 'pay back' the money in instalments from their wages. The families, trying to fulfill the bail procedures, were delayed by a Baghdad traffic jam, then the judge was on holiday, and so it dragged on.

Lamia, a student I met at Baghdad University, said: 'The families send messages to the women inside the jails to tell them to kill themselves, or not to come home, because they are a disgrace to the family.' She was embarrassed to tell me why. 'They expect that the woman will have been raped in the prison and that is a disgrace to the family because they were unfaithful to the husband or they are not virgins any more. It's not her fault, but it will be her disgrace,' explained Mohammed. The other students looked away. This, more than anything, was too horrible to talk about.

Faleh Maktuf, the lawyer acting for the arrested clerks, said the procedures for bail were nearly done but it was a tortuous process. There was no legal basis whatsoever for the arrests but the still-flimsy framework allowed police, ministers and judges almost unconstrained power. Many, especially the judges, were part of the old regime.

The courts were in chaos, as I saw one morning when I attempted to get some British and American friends released. The court, it seemed, had no process. A statement was taken from one arrestee in the presence of another who was then asked whether his statement was the same as his friend's. There were no charges because no-one knew what they could be charged with. My friends were released but the Iraqi official in charge of liaison with the occupying authorities told us: 'You are lucky. If your friends were Iraqi they would be in prison at least one month before anyone even asked what they were arrested for.'

A couple of years later I would be embroiled in precisely that situation when Salam, my friend and companion during my first trip to Kurdistan, was kidnapped along with the British journalist he was working for. Even though he was gagged and bound, just like the journalist, when US troops found them by chance, even though we had the ears of the British security forces in Iraq, even though several of us vouched for his integrity, for over a month he remained in Abu Ghraib prison and for most of that time we were not even sure where he was.

Over a month incommunicado without charge, legal representation or access to a court – and he was one of the lucky ones. What kind of freedom was this?

8

START OF THE CIRCUS

January 2004

I'd begun to doubt my plan after I arrived in occupied Iraq in November. People needed everything, but did they really need clowns? Clowns wouldn't feed the children, supply the hospitals with medicine, build decent housing. Clowns wouldn't win them trade union rights, jobs, reasonable pay. Clowns certainly wouldn't establish security or public services.

I wondered if we could do something else with the money we'd spend, even on our minimal budget, but really the problems facing Iraq were not to do with lack of money or even aid agencies. I felt responsible for the safety of the clowns who were coming over, even though I'd told them the dangers as best I could and they were coming voluntarily. Workers from a couple of foreign organizations had been scornful, opining that a circus was not what Iraq needed, that people would be offended by such frivolity, and I started to fret that they were right.

As I wavered, I got an email from Peat. Peat went to Kosovo a couple of months after the war ended there. His group arrived in a village and all the kids ran and hid: strangers were people who hurt you, killed you. Eventually they coaxed the children out to play on the only space which wasn't littered with mines, a graveyard containing many of their friends and relations.

Peat described a scene of about 80 children around three play parachutes and, in the midst of it all, an old man, palms to the sky, wide smile, tears rolling down his cheeks, saying: 'Thank you, I never thought I'd see my grandchildren laugh again.' I remembered little Mohammed in the hospital, a few days into the invasion, and his reaction to the bubbles.

Fisheye emailed a story about Cirque du Soleil working with street children in Mongolia and how it boosted their self-esteem to receive, for the first time in their lives, some applause. Jenny emailed from Palestine, talking about picking up stones and teaching the children to juggle, the first time they had seen stones as something other than weapons. Between them they convinced me that this was something needed, something constructive, something potentially powerful.

Then I met Fadhil and I started to be excited about what we could do. A famous actor on stage and TV, he and some colleagues were being supported by the French NGO Première Urgence to perform two different plays around Baghdad for about a month. Fadhil talked about a school for autistic kids where they performed a play. He was a chef, trying to keep control over two mischievous cats who kept hiding the apples. The children, when they arrived, were introverted and isolated. He said he asked one of them if he knew where the cats had hidden the apples. 'And he looked at me and said "I c-can't tell you. The cats are my friends." He was relating to them. It was great.'

He took me out with them just before the other clowns arrived. The stage was created out of a leafy mat, tables making way for a tree and a fountain, branches concealing the hall's usual function as a hospital lecture room. Kids and families crept in uncertainly. A woman in an *abaya*, her husband in a wool hat, a toddler in dungarees between them, huddled in the very middle of the block of chairs, as weighed down as human beings could look. And, about halfway through, they started to laugh, and laughter rocked them and it shook them and it made the sun shine on them through the high window instead of just dazzling their eyes.

There are some men in the play who want to cut down a tree and a woman and two dwarves, comic wizards both, who protect it. One man gets turned into a cockerel and can only crow; another turns into a giant yellow monkey. At this point one of the smallest boys in the audience burst into tears, ran away and watched the rest of the show just peeping out from behind a chair with encouraging cuddles.

The director, Haider, once put on a play called something like Checkmate, about a dictatorial Chinese emperor from the olden days. He gave a poster to an ageing theater worker and asked him to put it up outside. Later the security services came to arrest him and investigate the whole production.

It turned out the old man's sight was fading badly and he'd inadvertently put the playbill over a portrait of Saddam. The other actors and the Ministry of Culture all tried to help Haider and he was released after a day, having convinced the authorities that neither the play nor the positioning of the poster was intended as a challenge to Saddam.

Plays had to be licensed. All drama had to be a celebration of the regime, Fadhil said. You could say you were against the war [with Iran] in your work but not that you were against the regime. There were no specific things that were symbols of opposition, no animals or figures that were widely understood as representing Saddam in theater or literature – you would be killed – but he said there would be things in the background that the lights would linger over.

Fadhil later showed us round the National Theater, the huge stage in the main auditorium, the echoing backstage, and talked about the plays and operas that used to be held there. The theater was looted after the war. Even props were stolen, never mind valuables like the lights. Fadhil excused himself to go and collect his Ministry of Culture salary from upstairs but came back empty handed.

The Ministry of Culture paid actors before the war as well, though Haider and some of the others were freelance or privately funded. Plays were still going on under occupation but Fadhil said there was little of any quality. A program of plays was starting soon about Al-Sadr senior, a Shi'a leader killed by Saddam, so the front of the National was covered with posters of him. There was a weeklong festival of children's theater and another of Iraqi theater but no new work of real coherence and power. People were still too bewildered, he said.

'We are waiting for the writers to start documenting and discussing the situation here now and the history of the last decades but they are still...' He put his hands across his mouth. 'They are afraid. They are afraid of all the different leaders, the different parties.'

Haider was translating a book and adapting it to fit the Iraqi situation. In it, a house is left standing alone after bombing destroys all the surrounding buildings. The generals want to know how this one withstood the demolition and the play is about their attempts to get in and to destroy the family inside. Haider hoped to be invited to perform it at a Moroccan theatre festival.

Things were uncertain for the theater, Fadhil said, because it wasn't clear whether the ministry would go on supporting actors and the economy certainly couldn't. 'We need the theater, we need drama, to preserve our ancient culture and also to move forward, to express and debate democracy and freedom and the future. It is important because the problem is with the Iraqi people. It is difficult for people to feel they have any control over the country and their lives so they don't take responsibility.

'Of course the problem is with the Americans as well – they came here and destroyed and they did not understand the culture or anything. They got rid of Saddam but they haven't done anything else.'

Stilts, kazoos and bubbles

Our first circus performance then, on 8 January, was just Amber and me after Fadhil's play in a hospital in Thawra, playing about on stilts, blowing bubbles and dancing, playing the kazoos and getting the kids to clap and dance along to the words 'Thawrat as-seerq'. 'Thawra' means revolution, hence 'thawrat as-seerq' is the circus revolution.

We arrived back at the apartment to find Peat on the living room floor, sleeping off the road journey from Jordan. He greeted us with a bad joke and assured us they'd only get worse. Like a bawdy old stand-up comic, Peat could never resist a pun or a double-entendre. He was also the first one up every morning, making sure we were all out in time, rock solid, often the peacemaker and really the heart of the circus. Luis had arrived as well but it would be another day before we tracked him down as he'd gone to a random hotel a few miles away where he knew someone. We were to get used to that kind of thing.

The mobile phone network had been delayed again, at least another couple of months, either to deny it to the resistance or because of incompetence and corruption, perhaps a bit of both. The communication towers being rubble, it meant organizing had to be done in person, not on the phone, negotiating treacly traffic jams clutching stamped papers from the relevant ministries saying we were permitted to perform in orphanages, hospitals and schools because no manager would dare let you in without those.

We eased ourselves in by working with existing organizations. In between a US military base and the Turkish embassy there was a building belonging to the city council, which an Iraqi organization called Childhood Voice had filled with kids, computers, musical instruments, art materials and teachers. There was a kitchen, a woodwork room, a sewing and knitting workshop, a ping pong hall, a theater and, outside, a volleyball and basketball court, a football pitch and a karate training space.

Odai pointed in one direction: 'This area is reasonably wealthy. They are not rich people but they are OK. Over here they are very poor. You can tell where the children come from by their clothes.' They all mixed together in the youth center.

Childhood Voice ran the Seasons Art School as well, a smaller facility which took more kids with learning difficulties and disabilities, running two shifts a day, morning and afternoon, because that was how the schools were running too. A lot of the kids wouldn't have had access to computers and musical instruments if it weren't for the center; there was also a psychologist available to help with trauma.

It was started by a group of Iraqi people in August 2003 with financial support from UNICEF and Norwegian Church Aid. The building that housed the youth center was owned by the interim city council. It was damaged in the war so it had to be rehabilitated for the project. Originally it was allowed to use the building on condition that it had a manager from the council, but in March 2004 the operation was fully handed over to Childhood Voice.

Odai said the location, between the base and the embassy, was a safety concern which was exacerbated by US soldiers coming into the center. They'd asked them not to, for the children's sake, because the soldiers were a target, but they kept doing it.

On the way we passed what sounded like a wedding: the drums, the bugle, the hooting, the shots in the air. Weddings didn't happen on Wednesday mornings. Funerals did. If the dead person – this time a translator working with the US military – was never married, they were dressed up and taken for burial with a procession as if for a wedding.

At the youth center I tied what felt like thousands of children to stilts, helped them up, walked them round, fended off the hordes of other kids dancing around my feet and their stilt bottoms and tried to remember in which order I promised the next few kids a go. Peat showed himself to be a fantastic entertainer and I began to believe this was going to work.

One of the boys joined me for some tumbling, taking a lengthy run up for a cartwheel that ended with a jump, landing in the splits, followed by a somersault, landing on his bottom. When we left the kids were begging us to come back tomorrow and, if not, then when?

It was interesting having new people around, because they saw all the things I'd stopped noticing, like bombed buildings. We passed the remnants of the Ministries of Industry and Higher Education – military targets, by some sort of logic – and the others asked what they were. Strange how soon you could forget that bombed buildings weren't always the backdrop to your life, which is why it was so important to bring childhood back to the lives of kids whose entire existence had been war.

Fadhil showed us the primary school near the Korean embassy, next door to his office. Now officially a target, the embassy is surrounded with concrete walls, sandbags and tanks. He acted out what he was saying, the way he always did. 'The children used to come along here skipping and singing. Now they creep along with their eyes on the tanks.'

Boomchucka begins

The queue went in a square round the entire block from each of the filling stations. Men waited outside their cars on the street parallel with the one where the actual pumps were and, every few minutes, opened the driver's door, put their shoulder to the frame and pushed the vehicle forward a few meters. To leave the engine running or restart it for every step forward would be unaffordable madness.

The filling station just past Wathiq Square said it had no fuel to sell, but still there was a motionless queue two cars wide and easily a hundred long, spiraling around the block. People waited all night in order to drive to work in the morning. Even the black market sellers had lines, managing to fill their cans despite the military guard. There wasn't even enough fuel to power the generators to work the pumps when the electricity was off. The queues blocked the road and the rage of waiting was amplified by the continued inertia of snarled traffic outside the station, burning the fuel so hard won. You never saw a humvee in a petrol queue: they, alone, were well supplied.

The Turkish drivers didn't want to drive to Baghdad any more and there wasn't enough fuel coming in from Kuwait and other neighbors to satisfy the demand for both cars and generators. Iraqi plants were generating too little because they needed repairs and the Iraqi engineers knew how to fix them but were not being allowed to.

In addition, the prices were going up, because Halliburton (the company that was paying US Vice President Dick Cheney a million dollars a year in 'pension') was charging, via the US administration, $2.65 per gallon (3.8 liters) to transport petrol in from Kuwait. Even the Pentagon used to do the job for $1.12 per gallon. Iraqi businesses were managing to bring it in for less than $1 a gallon.

As we drove away with a full tank after a half-hour wait for black-market fuel, driver Mohammed indicated another queue occupying two lanes of the highway we were passing over. The roadside sellers said an American tank had just crushed two cars in that queue and driven away. No-one was hurt, because they had been out of the cars, but they were very, very angry.

Fadhil and his colleagues invited us to join them in performing at the Haifa Club – once a sports club, now a Palestinian refugee camp. The kids

Circus2Iraq: Jo, Luis, Amber and Peat.

were waiting and the Iraqi group was stuck in traffic so we started without them, filling time with silly dances: the Birdy Dance, the Conga, Mexican waves with sound effects.

Paddy, a clown colleague of Peat's in Kosovo, once started shouting 'Boomchucka' and getting the kids to shout it back. Unfortunately the kids thought he was saying 'Oo-cha-ka', the acronym for the Kosovo Liberation Army (KLA) and began chanting that, which wasn't the idea, but here it was brilliant. We yelled 'Wo-oh' and the children yelled it back. We yelled 'Boomchucka' and they joyfully copied. It echoed off the walls and we decided to keep it, to make it the start of every show.

Then we started the show with the music box act. This involved a clown with a broom and a magic box that made music when opened, a mean, grumpy boss (first played by Amber, later by Luis) who kept taking the box and making the clown carry on sweeping, and lots of face pulling. The kids joined in with the shh-ing, nodded when the bullying boss was out of sight, but still cheered when s/he jumped up and down on the box and squashed it into the rubbish bin, then again when the bin lid was lifted and the music still played.

They loved Luis's didgeridoo, especially when he made it sound like an elephant, trumpeting through its trunk. Peat and Luis's juggling act was always popular, the two of them stealing the balls from each other out of the air. Luis had the perfect face for a clown, sort of gnome-like, with a pointy beard.

The kids had a football and almost nothing else to play with. The swimming pool was revolting, even for winter. We were required outside for clown football afterwards and stayed, talking to the mothers, playing with the children, juggling, spinning them round, turning them upside down, dancing to imaginary music. They renamed Amber and me 'Patata' and 'Tomata'. I think I was Tomata. Helicopters and tanks passed frequently and the kids stopped whatever they were doing to look at them.

They lived in tents with UNHCR stamped on the roof in the club grounds. How did she come here? Asmaa sighed. 'It is a very long story and I am tired and sick. I was born in Iraq and brought up here, married here and had my children here, but my father was Palestinian so I am Palestinian. I have no nationality, no identification, no right to own property.'

After the war the landlord had come to the house and threatened to douse it with fuel and burn it if they didn't leave. Her four sons lived at the camp with her but her two daughters had been squeezed into a relative's house. 'There are so many young men here. I am too afraid for the girls. But they had to stop going to school because of the situation. It is not safe.'

For a time they were supported by the UN and aid agencies, she said, but there had been no constant assistance for some months now. Half of the aid was taken anyway by the people inside. She and her friend gestured towards the buildings and offices of the club. 'They sell it outside the camp. But Dr Qusay owns the club and if he did not let us live here we would be on the streets, so what can we do?'

Fifteen families arrived back at the camp today, Eman said. They had been put in houses and the UN had promised to pay the rent but, after three months, without any rent being paid, they'd been evicted. They returned to greasy puddles between the tents, no electricity and little gas. Gas heaters inside the tents were dangerous in any case but there were no other options for warmth. The kids couldn't study when they came back from school because it was cold and dark.

Those who could, sent their children to other relatives during the winter, splitting families, rather than keep them in tents without even a hot water supply. 'We go to our relatives every two weeks or so to do washing,' Eman said, indicating the lines of clothes drying between tents. 'We cannot remember what it feels like to be clean.'

Dr Qusay said it was a myth that Palestinians were better treated than anyone else under Saddam's rule. 'We weren't allowed to own any property. It is not true that Iraqis hated Palestinians and that the Iraqi Government protected Palestinians from them. It was the other way round. Our Iraqi friends protected us from the Government. Iraqi friends used to help us by putting a car or a house or a business in their names so that we could buy them.'

Still the kids showed me tatty pictures of Saddam from the old banknotes. '*Saddam zain,*' some said. Saddam is good. I had to disagree. For me, I said, I don't like Saddam, I don't like Bush and I don't like Blair. One of the boys was angry with me. No, he insisted. *Saddam zain.* I supposed at least he had a home in Saddam's day.

Children with Post Traumatic Stress

To put things into perspective, doctors believed there was barely a child in Iraq who wasn't suffering some degree of post-traumatic stress, with a wide variety of symptoms. But Dr Ali, the child psychologist heading the Post Traumatic Stress Disorder (PTSD) Program, said there was virtually no awareness about the disorder and its symptoms, so bed wetting, for example, was a source of shame rather than a warning signal that the child needed help.

His colleague Dr Yousef explained that parents were in denial because of the stigma attached to any kind of mental illness. 'Parents think that people will believe there's something wrong with the child's mind and say maybe he inherited it from them.' Lack of a mental health network, using telecoms and the internet, denied doctors all over the country access to advice, leaving huge gaps in trauma treatment.

The doctors believed that play therapy would be the best, perhaps the only, way of diagnosing and rehabilitating kids with PTSD but there were no trainers. 'There are less than 100 psychiatrists in Iraq, but more than 300 Iraqi psychiatrists in the UK.'

Crisis Intervention Teams were urgently needed. 'Two or three months ago, when there were lots of bombings near schools, parents were scared to send their children to school and teachers were afraid to go to work. There were no psychologists working around the schools to get the kids back in and deal with everyone's fears. In other countries as soon as something happens near a school the support teams are there. We need crisis intervention centers as bases for multidisciplinary teams that can go where they're needed.'

The program was set up a little while after the war and Ali was the only doctor formally assigned to it by the Ministry of Health. Several colleagues who helped him were unpaid. Ali explained: 'We were doing workshops, an awareness program, we trained 120 teachers to look out for symptoms and talk to parents, funded by the Ministry of Health. We had everything ready for a huge campaign: Dr Yousef translated a lot of things from the internet and we made pamphlets and letters. We talked with the sheikhs and the imams and all the community places. We had the whole distribution infrastructure ready.

'After only a few weeks they were asking for my results. The senior advisor in the Ministry of Health is an American man called Jim Haveman. I wonder, what did he want? The details of how many centers I have built, in only a few weeks? How much office stationery I have bought? I explained that this is a project which will take years.

'Then I got an email from him to say the funding was suspended and I could not spend any more money from 2 November. You can imagine the magnitude of frustration. Everything was ready. We were writing a letter to go out with the ration cards, because every family would receive a new ration card within a few months. We would have given out one-and-a-half million letters. He was enthusiastic at the start. He said yes, let's do it, but in the end he wouldn't let us.'

Dr Ali was transferred away from the program and Dr Yousef assigned in his place but the two said they needed to work together. Still there was no funding. A psychology center for torture victims was opened with funding from the Ministry of Health, no doubt much needed but also politically expedient, prioritizing the victims of the last regime over those traumatized by sanctions and war inflicted by the present one.

The 'Safe to Play' and 'Back to Play' programs with UNICEF, for 6- to 12-year-olds, came to an end when the UN withdrew most of its international staff after the bombing of their HQ. There were manuals and kits for training play therapists and for carrying out the therapy, but they were all in Jordan.

Yousef said they'd prefer to work through an international NGO: 'It eases the headache if the money goes to someone else. Money is trouble. There is so much distrust.' He favoured a European or Australian organization rather than a US one: 'The American NGO people are nice and they mean well but now, even people who were happy when the Americans got Saddam out are frustrated. They don't want anything to do with Americans any more. They don't trust them. They were happy that Saddam was gone but the Americans treat people harshly.'

Dr Ali had his own example: 'My little boy, Haider, was playing in the street with his plastic toy walkie-talkie and the troops came and said what's that? Why are you playing with that? Where's your home? He pointed to our house and 24 soldiers pushed in and for two hours they searched my house.'

Running away with the circus

Amber had to return to Philadelphia after a month and Uzma, a British Muslim woman of Pakistani origin who was supposed to be working for another NGO, decided to run away with the circus. At the end of January a crowd of girls gathered to hold the make-up for us both as we got ready in front of a mirror in a corridor at Dar Al-Banaat, 'Girls' House'.

The girls' rooms either side had posters of boy bands and Shakira and pretty knick-knacks hanging on the walls. 'Workhouse for Orphans and Parentless Children' was scrawled in spray paint in English on the wall outside. One of Uzma's stilts had a screw loose so she was on the ground blowing bubbles while Afra, pig-tailed, seven years old, clowned for me, as I took photos from above. I was Tawila [tall lady] in multi-colored extra-long trousers and a silver dress.

The girls became part of the show, warning Uzma when the Boss clown was coming, nipping around the corner to check he was still out of the way, skipping over the rope. It could be hard to get girls to join in with stuff in a mixed crowd but here they were uninhibited, the only boys being a couple of workers' sons. None of them was wearing a headscarf. Uzma was melodramatically bawling her eyes out in a clowning act when Afra tiptoed past her in a charming act of solidarity, picked up the broom and finished off Uzma's sweeping.

Some 85 girls, from babies up to 18, lived there but that day there were only about 20 of them – some went to their families or other relatives on Fridays. Eid would start in a couple of days, so these were the ones who had absolutely nowhere else to go, which made it all the more important to bring them some laughter.

Some had lost their mothers, and their fathers couldn't cope with bringing them up. Some had lost their dads, and their mothers were too

Afra, seven-year-old volunteer clown.

poor to keep them. Some were rejected by the new step-parent when one remarried. We had heard of girls who were raped in the post-invasion chaos and were thrown out by their families as unmarriageable, a source of shame. We didn't ask these girls their stories but there was one, 12 years old, who whispered that she hated Iraqi men.

Parachute games with them were a joy. They worked as a team, they laughed a lot, they played parachute football with the passion of a World Cup tie, held the fabric with all their might for each other to run around on. When, at the end, one of the juggling balls was missing, they came and told Peat none of the girls was an *Ali Baba*. They wouldn't tell on the boy, the manager's son, who had it, but while we were out of the way getting changed, they got it back from him and passed it over.

Back in our normal clothes, Uzma and I sang with them. We didn't know any of the boy-band songs that were their favorites and could only manage the chorus of Queen's 'We Will Rock You', which they requested over and over. Heba started dancing, Arabic dancing with wild hips and swaying that I couldn't get at all, till Heba took my hips and moved them in a figure of eight motion.

There were others performing in Baghdad as well. We were taken to a concert at Al-Wazeria: immaculately dressed young men in the first half and a group of women in long, extravagantly embroidered dresses in the second, playing the *oud*, a stringed instrument not unlike a guitar except that the body is oval and there's a 90-degree angle at the other end.

Less traditionally, Waleed's metal band Acras Sicauda (Black Scorpion in Latin) played its first post-war gig in early January. The improbable backdrop to strobes and headbanging boys included colored streamers, a dangling strawberry and a bingo game board. A 4pm start was necessary because nobody went out at night.

The Government used to keep an eye on what they did. Waleed had to supply the Ministry of Information with approximate translations of the lyrics. The ostensibly pro-Saddam song was in fact, Waleed said, critical, while others had concealed attacks on the President. Younger people were sometimes less self-censoring than adults who had learned to be afraid. Now they sang about death, teenage angst and against the occupation.

Boris, a Hungarian journalist I met before the war, asked Peat to perform at a wedding reception. A young man from a powerful tribe but a poor family and a young woman from a lesser tribe but a wealthy family had fallen in love. His family didn't want him lowering the status of his tribe; hers opposed her marrying into 'poverty' and tried to marry her off to someone else.

She refused all suitors and was mistreated by her family for it. His relatives threatened to wipe out hers if they married. The couple talked about eloping to Yemen, even concocted a plan for him to kidnap her but it would be impossible for an unmarried couple to cross the border without her father's permission.

Eventually, faced with worse disgrace, her family agreed to the wedding but refused to attend while his family, if they knew it was happening, were in denial. Boris, who believed fiercely in people's right to choose whom they loved, arranged a wedding reception for them. When they visited their families, for the time being, they would each go alone and hope in time that the sides would accept their love.

A school in the Black Zone

The 'Green Zone' was the name given to the part of town fortified by the coalition forces for the accompanying civilian-military administration, the only place they felt safe and most commonly heard in the sentence: 'The resistance are attacking the Green Zone.' We were unable to find out whether there was or was not an Amber Zone but the Red Zone constituted most of the rest of Baghdad. Thawra, otherwise known as Sadr City, was designated the Black Zone, the wilderness.

It wasn't because we were fearless or had any illusions of invincibility that we were so flippant about it, but just because it was ridiculous. The people who made the decisions and policies did so from the far side of a dozen checkpoints from Thawra, or any other civilian district.

Constantly under attack and barely allowed out of their own Zone, a lot of those in there started to fear the Iraqi people outside. This was long before foreigners started being taken hostage.

At one of the Black Zone's schools, headteacher Mohammed looked out at the horde of kids outside the gate and mused that some might come back now they'd seen the circus. They wouldn't want to miss it if it came back again, he said. Loads of kids dropped out because of family poverty, the dangers and difficulties of getting to and fro or the poor conditions at the school itself. Kids from other schools had been kidnapped for money or attackers had come into the school. There was nothing to keep anyone out, Mohammed said, looking at the feeble gates.

Part of Mohammed's problem was the lack of textbooks. They were still working with the old ones, with Saddam's picture ripped out, and they hadn't nearly enough for all the kids, so the teachers could only lecture. UNICEF was close to giving contracts for the printing of new books to local Iraqi printers, who had started buying the inks and materials, but then the UN pulled out leaving nothing but ill-feeling between the different companies.

The school had no other teaching materials at all. There were a thousand boys in the morning shift and a thousand girls in the afternoon so there was no time or space for any sort of training for the 30 teachers. Each child was allocated 12 pencils per year, an average of one and a half per month of school. 'But the children do not keep a pencil for a month. They keep a pencil for a few days and then it is broken or lost or finished.' It went without saying that there were no art materials in the school.

Part of Mohammed's problem was that he was so starved of professional support that he had to ask a clown. He had a Masters degree in education and was studying for a PhD but the program had been stopped. To me, in pigtails, face paint and ridiculous trousers, he asked: 'What are the latest methods and systems of education in the UK?'

Then there was the lack of running water, so that even the single hole-in-the-ground toilet was unsanitary. Classroom furniture was scarce. But Mohammed's problems didn't end there. Teachers' salaries were not paid on time, leaving them broke for the weeks in between and at best they struggled to live on their wages. There had been thoughts of setting up a teachers' union but nothing was yet established.

We hadn't expected to do a second show, hadn't realized a second shift of children would be coming, but Adnan from the Italian NGO Un Ponte Per came in laughing, telling us the departing boys were all talking about the very tall woman and the men who made things disappear. We checked with Saba, Mohammed's counterpart for the girls' shift and began a second show.

The girls were incredibly loud. The noise of them shouting 'Boomchucka' was immense, a huge buzz, a thousand little girls happy and excited. In the end they got a bit too manic and we cut the show short. The ones at the back, standing, were pushing forward so the ones sitting at the front and squeezed in the middle looked likely to get hurt.

I thought the teachers would be furious with us for causing chaos but they weren't at all. 'They have never had anything like this, something happy, something fun in this yard. In this yard they used to have to sing songs praising Saddam. They are especially happy to see a woman in the show. They have never thought a woman can do this,' Saba said.

Bremer, she said, was not at all interested in women's rights: he hadn't done anything for women and nor had the Governing Council, overturning even the protections they only had on paper. Too many groups had focused solely on lobbying for 40 per cent representation of women on the Governing Council rather than taking on grassroots work with women. All urban schools had been segregated since 1999 when Saddam was trying to appease religious leaders. There was no sign of that law being dropped under the new leadership.

Saba also talked about attacks on the school straight after the fall of the old regime, armed men storming in, making threats, accusing her and other teachers of being Ba'athists. Like Mohammed, she'd seen a high drop-out rate among her pupils because of security problems, both on the journey to school and within the building. They would like armed guards who could escort the pupils to school and mind the place. With a thousand children coming from a wide area of narrow streets, a school bus would be impractical.

Ba'athist building reclaimed

Monday's school in Afdhalia, likewise, had no windows, nothing at all to work with. A tank was graffittied on the playground wall. Teachers said the 800 or so kids with their little blue UNICEF backpacks wouldn't listen to anyone except the headteacher. A woman in an abaya stood watching the show with one of the backpacks on her head. A dog barked in the school and small crowds of kids gathered at the ends of the upstairs corridors to look out over the crowd. As I took off my stilts a boy came down the steps carrying a colorful cockerel to show me.

As we arrived at the school in Diyala Bridge on Tuesday, a teenage boy wheeled a barrow past full of neon squeaking things. I took them to be fluffy toys that made noises when shaken till a younger boy picked out a handful, paid a little money and left with his dyed chicks. It must make good business sense to color them so as to attract the young customers who get sent out to fetch them.

Dozens of primary school age kids were out on the streets, not in school. Skinny dogs scavenged in the rubbish heaps, the pickings still not rich enough even amongst all this debris. The toilet here had running water: constantly running, so the toilet was overflowing. Several of the women teachers had tiny babies like six-month-old Zahra in Soulav's arms, her four-year-old brother Abdullah leaning on their mum's knee. The English teacher had no choice but to bring them to work.

The Bayaa kids get into the circus spirit.

Even by late March when the circus ended, a year after the invasion started, schools were still missing windows, sanitation and teaching facilities. Yet at Bayaa we saw what could be done. The kids had painted a mural on the wall outside what used to be a Ba'ath Party building – a harp, the tower in Samara, a lion – and now it was a youth center. Three different age groups used the center on different days: 6 to 10, 11 to 13 and 14 to 18. The Children's Council consisted of four boys and three girls elected by the other kids from all the age groups.

Marwan adopted me on arrival. A 13-year-old member of the Children's Council, he was enormously proud of the place. Khatar, the manager, gave him the bunch of keys: 'He's the only one who knows which one is which,' he shrugged.

Shiny, beautiful, multicolored fabric covers protected the six computers from dust. They were networked, with a printer, but there was no internet because viruses would destroy them. The covers were made next door in the sewing room where a dozen black sewing machines sat on workbenches along the walls. The workbenches were made in the carpentry room another door along, as were the display shelves for the pottery room. The kids all pointed out a horse's head, painted gold with wild green eyes and flared nostrils.

'Saddam made this,' they said, meaning the boy shown modeling the head on the center's leaflet.

'And this is me,' said Omar, a 13-year-old boy with strikingly blue eyes, indicating the photo of a couple of kids learning martial arts, and then they all took turns to identify themselves in the photo of the football team.

The yard served as volleyball court, football pitch, play space and anything else and the last room was the music room. Marwan and Omar picked up hand drums and fell into rhythm together, the other kids diving in to join them. Opposite the youth center was the theater where we did a show for them, where the kids did drama. The happiest set of kids I'd met yet, they joined us at the end to do acrobatics on the stage.

There, with a little foreign NGO support, the children and Iraqi staff had reclaimed a building from the Ba'athists, made something wonderful out of it, were learning how to run the place democratically and accountably and were healing themselves with creativity. The schools, the preserve of big US companies, went on crumbling, staggering, wallowing in sewage.

9

ASKING THE FAIRIES: THE CIRCUS IN THE SQUATTER CAMPS

January – March 2004

There are buildings in Baghdad – old government premises, secret police offices, properties formerly owned by members of the ruling clique and Saddam's family, officers' clubs, military barracks, half-completed apartment blocks – which are now squatted by thousands of homeless families, about 800,000 people in all.

Some were already without proper accommodation before the invasion because they were in hiding, for example. Others – a huge number – were evicted afterwards because they couldn't pay the rent and the Government wasn't paying for social housing any more, or their houses were destroyed by bombings, or they fled their hometowns for various reasons.

They weren't classed as refugees but as 'internally displaced persons' (IDPs) because they hadn't crossed a national border. It turned out it was a significant distinction: it meant nobody had to take responsibility for them.

In Rajdiya, about 400 families from the Maisan and Amara areas were living in an old army base. Dr Husni, now translating for us, said it felt like he was in a timewarp – he'd been based there for three years as an army conscript. Crushed buildings and barbed wire, reed houses, donkeys, cows and chickens had transformed the place.

Of course, there were almost as many stories as there were camp dwellers. Layla came north when her husband Muhammad, a sheikh or clan leader, started being abused by local government officials. The Mayor, a relative of Saddam, burned 65 houses which were alleged to belong to dissidents. Muhammad went to Saddam to complain. Investigators, headed by another relative of Saddam's, found it was true. The Mayor gave out a few irrigation pumps to influential individuals and the matter was hushed up but local government officials started persecuting Muhammad.

Informers accused him of supplying weapons to the resistance and he was arrested, jailed for two months, questioned, denied blankets, denied food except bread and beans, mistreated, his family not knowing where he was. A lot of his people were fighting Saddam, retreating into the marshes for cover, and Saddam ordered the marshes drained so there was nowhere to hide. The fish and birds died because of the drainage so there was nothing to eat.

Eman moved up from the south when her husband was sent to Baghdad with the army. Lack of work, electricity, facilities, drove others from the south to Baghdad but they weren't allowed to settle there. Unless you were registered as a resident of Baghdad in 1957, or were a descendant of someone who was, it wasn't legally possible to buy land or property.

Of the squatters at Rajdiya, some had stayed in Baghdad having managed to rent houses, but had been recently evicted; others returned to the south and came back after the war. Here they had next to nothing but still they said it was worse in Amara: worse than here where they had no hospital or secondary school, electricity was rare and they didn't know how long they would be allowed to stay before the new government demanded the land back.

Layla looked away when I asked about the women's health. To the floor, she said: 'For myself, I feel very tired. I do not feel that I am settled here because it is not our land. It is hard to find the energy to do things around the house when we might have to leave. Most of the women feel the same, depressed and without purpose. The children are sick, especially now that it is winter, with flu and diarrhea. I just want a place to settle, to know that we can stay on this piece of land and make our home here.'

'We have seen nothing so far,' her husband added. "We had hope before the war that things would improve but nothing is better. We are jobless, unemployment is high, there is so much crime and more religious division than we have ever known. Divisions existed before the war but they were limited. Now they are encouraged by the Americans. We need elections. We need to choose a government that reflects Iraqis. The Governing Council reflects different denominations, which is unjust, because we are all Iraqis.'

He and all the residents were Shi'a so this was emphatically not the bitterness of a group losing privilege. 'The Governing Council is weak and the US wants it this way. It's imposed. We want elections, for a real government that will stop the suffering, give us security, food, give our children a future after the sanctions they imposed on the people. Those never affected Saddam, only the people. We refuse the occupation. They cannot stay here.'

On the wall of Layla and Muhammad's house was an elaborate drawing of a tree, each leaf bearing the name of a male member of their clan, Al Bou Muhammad, the branches depicting the family tree, and a painting of a man called Faisal Ibn Khalifa firing a cannon. Faisal, Muhammad's grandfather, was known as Abu Tuwab – Father of Cannons. He built weapons for the fight against the Ottomans and after he died his son used them to fight the British occupiers.

Ali Kamel, a gray-haired retired schoolteacher, lived in a rented house in Hoseinia, a wave of his arm indicating an area nearby, again because he was not allowed to buy a home in Baghdad. Several of the squatters were evicted from houses in that area after the war when they couldn't pay the rent. He was headteacher of the site school for about 250-300 children, aged 6 to 11, with seven teachers, all of them squatters evicted from Hoseinia.

The show at the old barracks

Fadhil came with us to set up a visit to the camp at what used to be the air force officers' barracks. He kept shaking his head as we clambered in. 'All this money. All this money. Damn Saddam. He did not feed the people but he had money to build this. And all bombed by the Americans. Why?' Among the opulent rubble were two swimming pools, one indoors, one *al fresco*, likewise two theaters, their backstage doorways bricked up and a baby crying in the shack created behind one of them.

It would only take about an hour with some shovels to clear the outdoor one enough to fill it with people and perform. The indoor one was a ruin, stripped of everything by people desperate for a living. Around 400 families lived there. There was always someone acknowledged as the head of the camp: here it was a baker called Abbas. Fadhil teased the kids who were leading us to his house, a few rooms in the officers' quarters. 'Whose house is this?' 'Abbas's.' 'Where does Abbas live?' 'Here!' 'Where is he?' 'I don't know.' 'Oh. So whose house is this?' 'ABBAS'S!'

Abbas was busy in the camp bakery, but sent someone with us to pick a place. The garden was too uneven for stilt walking. Fadhil didn't fancy the stage dynamics of the hard standing where the boys were playing football. There was another open concrete space with people living in the remains of the buildings at one end, an enclosure built out of metal locker doors demarcating someone else's accommodation.

Rubbish heaps bordered the area, where barefoot children were playing. Women came out and complained about the habit people had of dumping rubbish there. Fadhil was excited about the dramatic effect of having us pop up on stilts from behind the locker-door contraption and, with his easy charm, gained permission from the woman who lived behind it.

I started doing cartwheels, inciting the kids to try. Some of them picked it up straight away, others just enjoyed flinging themselves about: this was something new and exciting. One of the boys wore a baseball cap to partly conceal burns to his face and a damaged eye from the bombing. His home was burned when a hospital nearby was hit. He didn't join in the cartwheeling, but repeatedly shook our hands and thanked us for each one.

Fadhil made a deal with them – the older kids would clean up the square and we'd come back and perform. Fadhil and his group would do the play about the tree and we'd do the circus show and play parachute games. The square would be clear of rubbish and broken glass, which made the women who lived beside it happy. Maybe more would be dumped later, but you never knew.

Maybe the act of clearing it themselves gives them some pride in their place, Fadhil thought aloud, such as it is, some feeling of control, responsibility, ownership, and maybe that would mean they'd keep the square as a community space. And maybe the kids would carry on practising whatever we taught them and maybe that would give them some hope, some fun, something. Maybe. He, at least, left with more hope than he had when he arrived.

So it was that on 16 January we got into our clown kit in Alia's place behind the locker-door barrier. There was a curtain across the gap in the barrier and another across the doorway into Alia's room. Inside were a couple of rugs on the floor, a gas cooker and a picture of Al-Sadr senior on the wall. The ceiling was a patchwork of pieces of wood, gappy, so the place was impossible to warm. The building housed an indoor swimming pool, no longer fully enclosed, and the family's space was concocted out of the bits of the walls and ceilings that were left standing and whatever junk they could seal it with.

The space we had picked last time looked better, more or less clear of rubbish, people leaning out of the windows in the accommodation overlooking the square as we started playing. There were 40 or 50 kids gripping the outside of the parachute. The first thing we did, as always, was get all the kids shaking the fabric, then lifting it and stepping in, underneath the red canopy. Next we turned it into a tent, by lifting it up, stepping in and sitting on the edges. Throughout all of this there were squealing, giggling children running under the color and billowing noise.

The circle was split into two semicircles – Baghdad City and Baghdad United – for parachute football. In this game a ball is thrown into the middle and the teams bounce it about by shaking the parachute. A goal is scored whenever the ball goes off over the head of a member of the other side. Usama became our helper, getting the other kids in order, explaining the game, a ginger-haired 17-year-old with natural charm and gentle authority. With his guidance the kids were the first group yet to manage the game of rolling the ball round the circumference of the 'chute – near enough anyway.

There was a near-catastrophe as Amber and I made our way over to the 'stage', on the rough tarmac, when one of her stilts snapped at a knot in the wood. Hayder, our driver, caught her as she fell, saving her head from hitting a metal stump sticking up, the two of them landing unhurt in a comedy heap of arms and legs. To distract the kids from leaping on top, I started the chants of 'Wo-oh' and 'Boomchucka' and added some 'Oompahs' that went down well.

Peat stepped in with his solo juggling act, fascinating the kids with the devilsticks (a stick that you keep in the air and do tricks with by knocking it with two other sticks) and balancing Joe the stuffed clown on a pole on his nose. He chatted away in a mixture of English and gibberish all the way through and the children laughed at the sound of it even if it didn't make any sense.

The kids jostled for the camera's attention, dancing the birdy dance with us, me on stilts, then swarmed for a go at skipping the rope, Amber on the ground this time after the stilt-snapping. Usama was the star skipper and the star organizer, keeping the other kids back safe from the rope and making them take turns. We finished with more parachute games: a few rounds of Cat and Mouse, where one of the kids crawls under the fabric and the others shake it to hide the mouse while the cat crawls on top, hunting.

The women watched, laughing, babies cradled inside their abayas, asking me to take their photos with their babies, tiny Abbas, a month old, with a woolly bobble-hat, beautiful Sabreen, six months pregnant, barely more than a child herself, with shining brown eyes and a dazzling smile.

Husni always wanted to protect us from the kids, ward them off from our stilt bottoms – 'they're wild, they're crazy, those are not kids' – but at last even he got carried away, started to clown himself. One of the women asked him to play with her kids while she went to make their tea. Two men, caught up in the atmosphere, hugged each other beside the locker-door wall.

The kids were still shouting 'Boomchucka' as we left, chasing the car, asking us to blow more bubbles, to come back tomorrow. Arriving at the camps the way we usually did, we were cushioned from the real grind of it all. People started to smile as soon as we got there, but once you looked at their surroundings, you couldn't forget that they were living in half-destroyed complexes of buildings without adequate walls and roofs, never mind amenities and stuff to play with.

The fairies and the blankets

The camp at Al-Shuala [the Flame] used to be a farm belonging to Uday, one of Saddam's sons, and became home to around 125 families after the invasion. People there pointed out the building which used to serve as a lab for research into animal growth enhancers.

I went first with Imad in November of 2003 because he'd been asked by a Swedish aid agency to find out what the children needed. Now and then amid the grime someone shines and for Imad and me it was Marwa: not a wide-eyed poster-child but an eloquent narrator.

Marwa was 11. She wanted to become a doctor but, as with many girls, after the invasion her parents became too afraid she'd be kidnapped to let her go to school. It wasn't an unrealistic fear – untold numbers of girls and young women had been kidnapped, even if their parents had no money, often for prostitution.

Her three older brothers were still going to school but because the schools were segregated and hers was nowhere near theirs she couldn't travel there with them and, even if she could, her parents didn't think she'd be safe within the school. A few of the girls still went, but most stayed at home helping their mothers. Ironically I had emails from people in the US listing good things that had come out of the invasion, including the statement that 'Girls are now going to school.' The implication was that they hadn't been before. Fewer and fewer girls were going to school because of ever-deteriorating security but some people still had Iraq mixed up in their minds with Afghanistan.

So Marwa's energetic brain tried to focus on the domestic instead. She said they fetched water three to five times a day. A family consumes a lot of water, she explained, for washing dishes and clothes. She wore a headscarf and had done for about a year because she had heard her parents saying that her hair would burn if it was seen by people she wasn't related to. Her favorite thing about school had been playing with her friends at morning break and she still hoped she could go back before she got left too far behind.

Asked what they needed, what they would like, most of the kids looked around for help before asking: 'What do you mean?' A lot of them had trouble expressing 'wanting' and 'needing'. Imad started talking instead about a fairy, a magician, who had come to offer each of them three wishes. What would they have the magician make for them?

The answer made me shiver. Blankets. Overall that was the commonest wish among the Shuala camp kids, because they were cold at night. They didn't even have enough blankets.

School and clothes were the next most frequent requests Toys were fourth, because none of them had anything to play with, followed by shoes. Some, prompted by their mothers, also mentioned cookers and fridges to keep food fresh and water cool during the day, when it's hot.

Despite the poverty of conditions at the camp, most wanted to stay in the compound, like the families in Rajdiya. It was better than being completely homeless. Umm Kadim told of losing her daughter to an unknown illness while on the run with her four children after her husband fled military service. They stayed in the desert because if they came close to the towns they were harassed by security forces and feared they would

Inside the Shuala squatter camp.

be caught. When the little girl got ill they couldn't afford transport to hospital. They set out to bring her but it was too late. They were one of the first two families in the camp, which was frightening because they felt exposed and vulnerable.

Aal'a dropped out of school at about 10 years old, when his dad died. He was now 17, an only child. He and his mum had been evicted from their house when they couldn't afford the $10 a month rent. Costs had risen since the invasion, wages had fallen and, amid the chaos, their ration card had also gone astray. There were no functioning services to issue a replacement so they could no longer even collect the monthly food handout.

Aal'a was working in a slaughterhouse. After the sheep were killed, slits were cut into their feet. His job was to blow into the slits to ease the skin from the carcass. His voice rasped and his throat always hurt from blowing constantly to earn a dollar or less a day. He said the only thing he wanted was a safe, stable place to live. He could support his mum in every other way. She nodded, her ancient face more tired than her 56 years. A safe place to live would be enough but we have nothing – no blankets, no cooker, not enough money for food.

Nobody's responsibility

There had been a decision some time before to clear some public buildings but to allow others to remain squatted. The Shuala inhabitants had received a letter from the Civil Military Administration saying their right to stay was recognized until such time as someone took responsibility for them. They kept the paper safe because it was the nearest thing they had to protection but ultimately it was nothing but a piece of paper and they were as precarious as ever.

Part of the problem was precisely that: nobody was responsible for them. Because they were internally displaced people and not refugees it was nobody's job to make sure they had adequate housing, water, food, medical care, education or even blankets. There was no international intervention, nothing to trigger assistance from the UN.

The position in international humanitarian law is that the occupying power takes over the main responsibilities of the deposed national government and is obliged to ensure an adequate supply of food, water and medical care[1] as well as clothing, bedding, shelter and other supplies[2] that are essential to the survival of the civilian population within the occupied territory. Relief operations from non-governmental organizations cannot be deemed to alleviate the occupying power's responsibilities.[3]

But that was that. There was a law that said they were to be looked after by the occupying powers; a law that was ignored and that didn't feed them or keep them warm.

Some of the smaller political parties were bringing supplies to people in the squats, clearly marked with the name of the party which delivered them, as a means of recruitment. Though far from ideal, it was all they were getting for the moment.

Coming back with the clowns, two months later, I did have a magician of sorts, if not the blankets and a school. Things were a little better than they had been. The clinic was receiving a visit from a doctor once a fortnight but it still took another five or six days to get the drugs that had been prescribed.

There was still no-one with overall responsibility for them. The German organization, HELP, had given them some blankets; the Workers' Communist Party had been supplying gas and other basics; but they had problems with 'the mafia', as Abu Ahmed called them, stealing some of what they were given.

Most of the 125 families in Shuala were from Maisan province in the south, like those at Rajdiya camp. Some said they would go back to Maisan if only there were jobs, houses and security, but there was more chance of finding work or getting help in Baghdad and now they, like many squatters, wanted the security of knowing they could stay where they were.

Maisan was one of the areas supposedly under British control but, as they explained to us, the British had 'Iraqified' their occupation: as throughout their colonial history, they had found a power broker on the ground that was amenable to them, in this case a local militia, legitimized them in that position and left them to exercise authority, denying responsibility for any atrocities committed by proxy and saving themselves the effort of actually running the place themselves. It meant those who had power and privilege before had it again, but now without the strong control from the center.

The mourning of Mariam

The only space to play at Shuala was a patch of cracked earth with spiky plants here and there. A few of the men got shovels and hacked out the thorny patches, scraping them out of the way. It was hard to get the girls to join in the games: some played at the edges of the parachute but wouldn't be a cat or mouse or run around. Dads encouraged their daughters to try jumping the skipping rope but most were still reluctant.

After playing for a while we went for a wander around, hands tugged by kids who wanted to show us their houses, their mums, the gardens among the rubble, between reed houses, tents and straw-roofed breezeblock shacks, living spaces cobbled together out of junk and the pre-existing farm buildings, like all the other camps, into the courtyard where Jamila was feeding Ali.

He was nine months old with no diapers and torn clothes. Everyone's clothes were torn, the kids' and the adults'. There were only three goats left in the yard, the others sold for essentials. None of the kids had toys to play with and some had parents who worked, so they were on their own in the day. Jamila pointed at a pile of fly-pecked, crusty shit in the corner.

'See that? That's what it's like living here.'

The rumble of yet another explosion seemed to echo in the sudden silence that followed it, cutting through the clamor and chatter of the kids.

Amal was making balls of dough, tossed and spun between her hands until they were broad and flat and round. She put them onto a round cushion-like thing and pressed them against the inside of the oven, with flames in the bottom. When they were done she reached in and retrieved them. She handed me one, warm, smoky, soft and gorgeous, and asked us to come back and perform again at Eid, in early February, because there was no money to give the children treats and it was important to them to have something special happen.

Abu Ahmed explained how they'd built themselves a small temporary bridge to make it easier to come and go, by collecting 1,500 dinars from each family and making it themselves. I don't know how much say women had in practice – although the Organization for Women's Freedom was active there at the time – but there was a meeting every other day in a reed house where everyone could participate in decision-making.

The kids were suffering from diarrhea and other illnesses because there was an open lake of sewage and wastewater in the camp. There were no toilets. They just dug pits and covered them over when they were full. They needed a drain to take the waste outside the camp. As with the bridge, they'd got a plan, but it would cost half a million dinars to dig it, cover it and pay some of the men to work on it.

Three days later we drove again through the street of listless sheep and squashed-up chickens, past the man blowtorching a cow's head, for leather, over the concrete bridge and down the dirt track into the farm compound.

There was a tent up in the entrance: long and semi-cylindrical, open both ends, with people inside drinking tea, eating together on the ground or sitting against the walls drinking *chai* (tea). It was a traditional Shi'a mourning tent for two-month-old Mariam.

'She died of the cold,' Abu Ahmed said simply.

Still no blankets. Still no blankets even though a blanket only costs the same as a hand grenade and there's never any shortage of those. The daily overpayment to Halliburton for the phantom meals they claimed to be supplying to US soldiers in Iraq could surely have wrapped up every Iraqi child a few times over by now and I'm sure I know which the US taxpayers would rather have had their money spent on, if they'd had any meaningful information or choice.

But they didn't and that's why Mariam died.

The dream of a drain

It had been raining the last two days and the place was a quagmire of mud and shit, sluiced through the camp from the lakes it normally festered in. Barefoot and barely shod children waded through it with us, following Abu Ahmed to the spot where the pipes were to go. They'd managed to buy three six-meter lengths of pipe, and needed another three which, at 30,000 dinars each, made 90,000 for the second 18-meter line.

The first would go from the puddle where the wastewater was collecting, the second from the shacks at the end of the camp, under the wall which marked the edge of the camp. It wouldn't be a full link up to the sewage system (which was still being repaired from the 1991 bombing, pipes and machinery having been embargoed under sanctions) but it was the best available. The main expense would be the machine to dig the ditches, at 250,000 dinars a day for two days, because the ground was concrete and they couldn't realistically dig it with shovels.

So the total cost for 125 families to build basic sanitation for themselves was $460 at that day's exchange rate. That was more than they could collect by asking every family to contribute so we thought we'd try and give them a real present for Eid as well as the show. It would mean a temporary wage for some of the men in the camp, improved health for all of them, but especially the kids, and it would be their project not something being done to or for them.

We told Abu Ahmed we couldn't promise anything but we'd do our best to get them the money. He said even the Government hadn't bothered asking after them. Peat and I sent out emails to our whole lists and posted it on the Circus website, asking people to help.

We weren't there to be a charity. Although there was a huge need for relief supplies, blankets and medical aid because the occupation forces weren't providing it, I felt strongly that Iraqi organizations like Ali's Malath Relief were best equipped to do that kind of thing; that this was a country of sophisticated people able to look after themselves with a little support.

Play, laughter, a sense of community with the outside world and a bit of psychological healing, on the other hand, were things Iraqis were barely able to give one another so that was what we tried to bring.

Charity is about doing things to the 'deserving poor', a paternalistic ideal which is all too often disempowering for the ones to whom it is done. Mutual aid, on the other hand, is about supporting people, empowering them, acting in solidarity with them, letting them lead and being accountable to them for the things you do, not to some alien donor. This was a reconstruction project devised and planned by the camp residents, without Bechtel and Halliburton. This was funded by ordinary people, in solidarity with Iraqis who wanted health and education for their children and themselves.

It was impossible to stand in that place, among the animal sheds they called home, and not help in any way possible, knowing that a drain would save some of their lives; knowing it, because there could be no doubt about it on a day like that when the sewage was flowing freely past the funeral tent for the tiny girl.

The kids came running out to meet us, arms out, when we arrived to do the Eid show. The girls joined in with the parachute games this time, asked to be picked as cat or mouse, lying on the fabric to be lifted up and to run around on it. The women watched through the reed fence of the house next to the concrete square where we performed. We gave them the money for the drain at the end of the show and explained it was from ordinary people, in solidarity. The place was full of smiles: they would start preparations straight away and then get the digger in. It would be built within a week.

We went a few days later to take some pictures for them, to give them a record of how they built their drain. Already the reed hut that used to stand at the edge of the water, its wendy-house shape reflected in the sludgy edges of the pool, was landlocked. There was but a puddle, several meters away. The drain wasn't completely finished yet but there was an enormous improvement.

Within a couple of weeks they'd been able to take in the entire compound so there were no toxic ponds left at all. Still most families were quite a walk from a water source. There was one tap in the roofless farm building where some had made homes and one beside the bit of empty ground where we played with the kids, where they hoped to build a school.

But for every glimmer of hope there was another piece of unremitting grimness. A man took me aside from the others and asked me to come and see his son. He took me to a tiny part-breezeblock, part-canvas and raffia-mat square building, open to the elements in dozens of places, stinking of infected, rotting flesh like a warning before my eyes could adjust.

Abbas was four, his legs a bloody, pus-oozing mess. He'd burned them three weeks ago on the paraffin flame from the stove that was their only heat source and he hadn't been seen by a doctor or a hospital yet. He lay under a blanket, naked from the waist down, eyes huge and glazed, unresponsive except when they creased and spilled silent tears.

The doctor hadn't been for over a month by the end of February. There used to be one every two weeks, through the Organization for Women's Freedom in Iraq, but once Layla wasn't there the doctor stopped coming. It only cost 500 dinars to be seen by a doctor in the hospital, but most of these hadn't got even that and the cost of a taxi there and back made it impossible to go. In any case, they couldn't pay for the medicine even if it was available to buy, so what would be the point?

We went the next day taking medicine, antiseptic and antibiotic creams, but it was worse. We tried, but failed, to get a doctor to come to the camp in the morning. I had to go out to Jordan for a few days so Peat and Raed returned to take him to the hospital. They were turned away because the hospital was full with more casualties than it could handle from a bombing nearby.

Eventually they found a doctor who could get out to the camp. He said Abbas was only days from losing his leg to the infections if they hadn't been treated. A week and he'd have died of blood poisoning. Within a few days, though, he was walking about, sleeping at night, smiling and laughing, wearing trousers, still whole, the look of exhausted agony and despair gone from his eyes although I doubt Peat or I will ever forget it. Alaa went with them to translate when Peat brought Abbas to the hospital and she couldn't sleep until she knew he was all right.

Eight-and-a-half months and billions of dollars after the war had ostensibly ended, lives and limbs were still so precarious that they could still depend on a bunch of clowns arriving at the right moment.

Blaming the Americans

Tanks came by blasting out some message over a loudspeaker and throwing brightly colored leaflets behind them. A couple of the boys ran to pick them up. They showed a cartoon man planting a bomb in a newly built school, while the cartoon kids were happily dancing about. An Iraqi sees him, finds a police officer and reports it. The bomb gets safely removed, the school is saved, the criminal is arrested and everyone but him is very happy.

'We think probably half of the bombs are planted by Americans,' Abu Bassim said. The recent party office bombings in the north, they were convinced, were the work of American provocateurs trying to create divisions; likewise the bombing in Najaf of Al-Hakim a few months ago. 'There is no division between us and Sunnis. We are all Muslims, but the Americans are trying to create divisions. They have done it all over the world, everywhere they go.'

Abu Ahmed brought us to the home of one of the sheikhs and we went together to the reed meeting house to drink sweet *chai* and discuss things. The place filled with people but still these two did most of the talking. Iraqis seem to have an incredible capacity for creating hierarchies and authority and then deferring to them. Elections, they said, were a priority. Bremer was wrong to talk about delaying them. They would support Sistani. Whatever his policies were, they would follow him, but they didn't mind who won, even if he was not a Muslim, as long as he was elected by the Iraqi people, not chosen by the Americans.

If Sistani called for jihad, they said, they would fight. Over lunch in Abu Bassim's compartment, made out of a corner of a roofless farm building, they said they weren't backing the current resistance because it was killing innocent people and, Abu Bassim repeated, they were convinced that a lot of the attacks were American-perpetrated.

Jihad, they said, would include attacking the Americans, with bombs aimed at their bases, not at convoys in the street, where innocent Iraqis got hurt, but the main focus, Abu Bassim said, would be unarmed jihad: refusal to work with the Americans, total non-cooperation and so on, something in which all Iraqis could participate.

'The Americans are the same as Saddam,' Abu Ahmed declared, 'They are from the same line. We can criticize the Americans, that's true. We went on a big demonstration a few weeks ago and chanted against the Americans and the British and the Governing Council and we were not stopped. We can complain, but that is all.' They weren't represented by anyone at the time but there were four sections to the camp, each with its own sheikh so, with Abu Ahmed, there was a committee of five.

We were meant to be meeting a sheikh who represented 4,500 families or about 25,000 people, living in 35 squatted former government buildings. They were expecting that the new government, when elected, would want those buildings back and would evict them. There was no housing for them to go into, so they'd be on the streets.

There were some rights for squatters, which was what we were going to talk to the sheikh about – the rights they had and what support they wanted, but for various reasons the meeting was to be in the Convention Center and was cancelled because of 'an important ceremony' there – apparently more important than people's right to have somewhere to live. Ceremony trumped substance any day in occupied Iraq.

Less than 200 of the camp's 800 child residents were registered in school. 'Child' referred to those under maybe 13, 14 years old. None of them went to school when it was raining because the mud was impassable. They'd talked to the Ministry of Education, which had said it would provide teachers but only for a purpose-built school made of bricks. We talked through some other possibilities: what about a reed house, like this one? What about just a big tent to start with, so you can get moving.

Peat talked about a community in Albania, where he'd clowned before, which had no school and lived, likewise, on state-owned farm premises. He got them a tent, someone else got them a couple of teachers and, when another organization came along a few months later, they were so impressed with what the community had already achieved that they built them a proper school.

But the squatters here said – and they had a point – that there was no way the kids could deal with the extremes of weather in a tent or reed house, the freezing winter and long, scorching summer, and they didn't think the Ministry would give them teachers for such a structure. There are issues over the desirability of building a permanent structure in a squatted place which is without proper services. It starts to create a permanence which has positives and negatives.

They didn't know whether they'd be allowed to stay or whether the new government when elected would demand they vacated the complex. They didn't much care whether they stayed all together in that place or split up and moved into housing elsewhere in the city, just as long as they were housed. But they felt that something like a school building would help their claim to stay.

But if they remained where they were then, like the Palestinian refugee camps, the slums might remain for decades without anyone taking full responsibility for their welfare. Jamila pointed out the tap that supplies them with water, cold only, and the electricity cables, amenities brought in for the farm animals which used to be bred here. 'We don't have any facilities for the humans. We are living like the animals.'

Unlike the homelessness problem in Britain, there actually isn't enough housing in Baghdad for everyone, so there genuinely is a need to build houses to accommodate the displaced people. Provided there are amenities, the new communities don't have to be slums and shantytowns. On that basis a drainage system and a school, especially ones designed, built and controlled by their users, would be a good start.

Marwa's world

Marwa came to kiss me with her eyes shining. It was hard to imagine how she might manage to become a doctor because she hadn't been to school in months and she was from a very poor family, without even a real home, but I couldn't bear the thought of her becoming a housewife like the other women there, hidden under a headscarf, producing child after child and trying to keep them all alive, looking out through a reed fence and hoping her daughters would have better chances than she did.

Marwa pointed to a young man, his arm in a sling, a striped towel wrapped around a plaster cast. 'My brother,' she said. A pile of bullets on the ground, Sattar explained that you could melt them and sell the brass for 500-1,000 dinars per kilo. You could scavenge them anywhere. A few days earlier, while he was working on one, it blew up and took his finger with it. A finger was cheap enough though, when 500 dinars a kilo was your only income.

The kids ran out shouting 'boomchucka'. There was a tiny boy called Abdullah whose head had been bandaged back in November. He was shy, scared of me, scared of noise, scared of crowds, hiding behind his mum. When we first brought the parachute he wouldn't come near it. Gradually, over the weeks, he'd crept closer, his face brightening. Finally, that day, he came running and hugged me, grabbed the parachute and shook it, bouncing, shouted and begged to be the mouse.

Beyda grumbled about her husband's preference for his other wife. 'He only comes to me to say hello and then he goes to her. I've only got one daughter.' But her sister Fadma, who had got married in January, was pregnant now, so Beyda had given her the only mat to sleep on and lay on the bare floor herself. Fadma had been engaged for five years before she and Ali could afford to get married.

Ali was called up to the army when he was 18, as usual. He and his friends turned up for training but weren't given proper uniforms, food or wages. The money wasn't enough to support the two young nieces and other family members he was responsible for, so after his first month he paid off an officer to give him false papers and cover for him and didn't return from leave.

'I carried on working, using the false papers, until I was caught at a checkpoint and I was put in prison for a year in Kirkuk, where my unit was based. When I was released I was returned to my unit but I did the same thing again and after that whenever I was caught I paid a bribe to the police who caught me, so I didn't go back to jail again. When the war happened all that was over, but Bush has betrayed us again.'

The women eventually confided, when there were no men around, that they were desperate for underwear and sanitary towels. With their families hungry, needing medicine and without work, there was no money to spend on other basics. 'Normally they would use rags, since the sanctions, if they couldn't afford sanitary towels,' Alaa explained, 'but it's so hard for them to wash things now.'

Marwa.

By the spring several of the squatter camps were under threat of eviction. Abu Ahmed at first said there was no threat at all but then admitted that a contractor came: they didn't let him near the camp, threatened to kill him or his colleagues if they came back. He said they would fight for the place, wouldn't leave just because they were told to.

He said the man was from the animal welfare department of the Agriculture Ministry. The land, having belonged to Saddam's son Uday, had reverted to the Iraqi Government. There was no specific move to evict the camp but all the squats depended on the whim of the Ministry in question. Squatters in Thawra, for example, were given till 10am on 16 March to leave a building on Mudhafa Square which used to belong to Saddam's Fedayeen. Hamed Selman Majid, a 33-year-old father of ten, went out looking for alternative accommodation for his family but couldn't find any, came back, collapsed and died of a heart attack.

During April there was no aid at all at the Shuala camp. Most of the international organizations had pulled out for security reasons. There were no jobs for the same reasons – the security problems and the fighting. Even we are afraid to go out, they said, even the Iraqis. Wasn't I afraid to go out?

The women scolded me, when I went in early May, for staying away so long. 'The children miss you. They're always shouting 'Boomchucka' and asking when you're coming.' I apologized, from under a heap of children. Alaa explained, unprompted, that I'd been in Falluja, as the kids played with the drawing things I brought, Abdullah covered in felt tip ink, and I was forgiven. The old Iraqi flag featured a lot in kids' pictures, Shi'a and Sunni alike, since the extremely unpopular attempt to introduce a new one.

Between them they'd raised the money to run some more electricity cables from the nearby pylons into the camp. Abu Ahmed had been ousted as representative of the camp and Abu Bassim elected to replace him. Beyda rolled her eyes as Abu Ahmed explained that there had been a conspiracy behind his removal and, when he was gone, everyone else explained the conspiracy for which he was removed.

Mistrust was virulent. Both the conspiracies and the conspiracy theories were products partly of a love of intrigue and a lack of other entertainment but largely of the sores from years of living with surveillance and corruption.

Over the months after I left, we carried on fundraising for the school, still hoping we'd be going back to Iraq in a few months. As things got worse, not only did it become apparent that it would be a long time before the clowns could go back, it also became more and more difficult to get news about the people at Shuala. The Iraqis I knew whom I could keep in touch with and who could have found a local contractor and got the money to the camp left the country, one by one, because of the everyday danger to their lives. Shuala itself became, by whatever accounts we could get, effectively a no-go area.

As for Marwa, I don't know. She didn't come out when I last went to the camp. I just saw her looking through the window of their house, without a smile, her world shrinking week by week.

1 4th Geneva Convention, Articles 55 and 56.
2 Article 69, Protocol I Additional to the Conventions.
3 Information from Programme on Humanitarian Policy and Conflict Research, Harvard University: http://www.ihlresearch.org/iraq

10

ANOTHER DAY

31 January 2004

It's the last thing I hear before I sleep, unfolding the spare mattress for Ahmed to sleep off the alcohol he drowned his sorrows in, and the first thing I hear in the morning, when Hamsa opens the door and sits on the end of my bed.

He is dead. He is dead. Four bullets destroyed his skull on the road from Hilla back to Baghdad.

His name was Durayd. His four-year-old son is called Ibrahim and his wife is known as Umm Ibrahim.

She's too young, Hamsa says. She can't deal with it. They ask her does she want to see the body. She doesn't know. How could she know? If she waits until the body is cleaned then she can't hold him. If she holds his body it will have to be cleaned again before burial. But if she sees his body before it's cleaned... Four bullets destroyed his skull on the road from Hilla back to Baghdad.

Durayd was a presenter on Shebab FM, the Voice of Youth radio station, before the war. That's how Ahmed got to know him, calling in to win prizes all the time. Hamsa knew him from the College of Languages first and then they worked together at CNN, as translators and producers. A lot of the young people with good English got jobs with the Western media after the war, supporting their whole families – English being one of the few skills that could get you employment in occupied Baghdad. She said he looked after her, helped her get her packages finished.

Who killed him? Whose were the fingers that fired the bullets? Who determined that CNN should be the voice of the White House? Who decided that young Iraqi fathers who worked for them should be targeted? Who decreed that there should be this chaos and destruction where you could just be shot at random (because it wasn't certain that he was specifically targeted), and that it would be just another day?

Husni says Hamsa hasn't eaten for two days, hasn't slept, just cries and cries and cries. We drop her at Durayd's home and go to Première Urgence to meet Fadhil and the others and go to the camp at Rajdiya. Fadhil was down, crushed under the weight of his everyday sadness, even before he knew.

'You know, we are tired,' he said. 'We don't go out and meet people. We lock our door. We don't even see our friends. I am depressed.'

Then comes the knowledge that Durayd is dead, his skull destroyed by four bullets on the road from Hilla back to Baghdad. Durayd, who always tried to help everyone, had time for everyone, loved his son like there was no tomorrow and then there wasn't.

Today the funeral process begins, delayed from the traditional and important almost-immediate burial by various requirements and rigmarole.

As you come home along the road from Hilla back to Baghdad, burnt tanks mark the kilometers, some tucked in among the palm trees, some stark at the roadside, for some reason not thrown into the tank cemetery at Ad-Dora, a huge expanse of wasteground where burned-out tanks and vehicles are piled.

One more is dead, after four bullets destroyed his skull on the road from Hilla back to Baghdad and it's just another day.

11

PLAYING WITH THE LOST BOYS

January–March 2004

After the invasion, Baghdad's children's homes stopped operating, and in those first months the street children constituted an appalling crisis – sick, injured, high on drugs, malnourished and abused on corners, in basements, on dusty patches of grass, no-one to protect them from the violence of the street and each other, no-one to feed them, no shelter from the searing heat of summer.

Gradually Iraqi groups and international NGOs started setting up orphanages and taking in kids. Some fell through the gaps though, turned away because of persistent glue habits or antisocial behavior, or just couldn't readapt to walls and rules.

Ahmed, Laith and Saif used to live on Abu Nawas Street, outside the Palestine Hotel, sleeping in the closed road all huddled underneath a blanket. Imad and I taught them a counting game which they loved. The staff of the hotels gave them leftover food sometimes. Journalists and some soldiers would give them money. Within the fortress surrounding the big hotels was a relatively safe place to sleep. Often they would be moving in slow motion, inane grins plastered over their faces, as they floated over for a hug.

Even as you told them that sniffing glue was no good for them, you wondered whether, in their position, you wouldn't do exactly the same – fill your head with a solvent that made the ground feel less hard. Yet inevitably they couldn't make the sudden transition from the complete freedom and independence of the street, the solvents they were addicted to and the dirt and the grime, straight into a pristine, sanitized orphanage with strict rules and controls, where they couldn't smoke and swear and fight.

'Our Home Iraq' was set up by a few activists from around the world and started taking in some of the kids the orphanages wouldn't or couldn't. Their crisis center was something in between, in Bab a-Sherji, close to the basement where several were already sleeping. The rules included prohibitions on violence and drugs, enforced breath tests to detect solvents, but the boys could come and go as they pleased. Sometimes they kicked one of the kids out for a night for serious transgressions. Most came back the next day and asked to be forgiven.

They took in 20 boys and within about six weeks, 4 had moved on to long-term accommodation and care. Some were barefoot because they'd sold the new shoes they were given. 'Then they'd have tantrums because they had no shoes and they'd ask for more,' said one of the founders of the home, Donna. 'We'd tell them if you sell your shoes then you won't have any, and we'd leave them a few days without any. Then when they get some more they don't sell them.'

As we drove up Donna explained that they'd had trouble the night before with a local gang, threatening them and the boys with knives. The gang said they'd be back at six. In fact they were already there when we arrived but the kids came racing out anyway to hug us and carry our stuff in, even the stuff we didn't want carried in and had to bring back out again. Ahmed was there, his eyes clear and bright, free from the glue glaze: now he was one of the 'vigilantes', breath-testing the other boys to check none of them were high.

The cold, ramshackle building had a mezzanine level and a high ceiling perfect for stilt walking. We started with parachute games, shaking it, looking underneath it, creating a tent, playing cat and mouse. The gang members joined in for a while, some of them, but they were mostly high and aggressive, and instead Peat silenced them by contact-juggling a single ball so it seemed magnetized to his hand.

The gang left and we got the boys up on stilts. At first only a couple of them were keen, but then everyone wanted to try, tying them onto bare feet. The cords have to be tight but the children were all too tough to make any fuss about the severing of their circulation. The queue of kids wanting a go kept getting longer, but the gang was back making threats: 'We'll be back later and if we see any of these boys on the street we're going to kill them.' The shelter was taking away their young clients and servants.

I promised Mortada and Ahmed with solemn handshakes that we'd be back and they could learn to stilt-walk then. We emptied the circus car of all the gear, packed in all the boys and drove them to the house that they were meant to be moving into for long-term accommodation, an orphanage run by the Kurdish Children's Fund. The managers there had been saying for weeks that the place wasn't quite ready but the gang's threats had forced the issue.

A new home

At the Kurdish House the boys were glad to see us in their new home, grabbing our hands to tow us on a tour of the building. This is my bed, this is the office, this is the garden. They were in clean clothes, their hair cut and their faces clean. They were starting to realize that there were stricter rules in the new place – they couldn't just come and go like they had before. Smoking had been abruptly banned. Ali, a tiny 11-year-old, hung about outside, reluctant to detach himself completely from either the new home where his old mates were or the solvent-soaked cloth that he was still addicted to.

Peat taught them some juggling. The older of the two Ahmeds picked it up like he was born to do it. In the crisis shelter he hadn't spoken. He

Little Ahmed and Laith.

hadn't responded, hugged, laughed, fought, anything. He'd just been there. When we arrived now, though, he was painting a sign. He hugged Donna and chatted happily.

Saif came with us, one of the boys who had a home of sorts but used to hang out on Abu Nawas Street with Ahmed and Laith, both of whom were now in the new house. They hugged each other and ran off to play, none of them smelling of glue. We played rowdy parachute games, then Peat and Luis did their juggling act again. We had the children skipping in the street between stilt walkers, along with the boys and girls from the other houses on the road, and little Ali, still a bit high, joined in.

Perhaps it wouldn't influence Ali's decision on which of the two worlds to commit to – the home or the drugs and the street and the gang that controlled them. There were no guarantees that any of them would stay but if we could boost their self-esteem, help them enjoy themselves for a while and ease the transition a bit then at least that was something.

Adapting wasn't easy. Glamor attaches to the violence and drugs of the gang members, the appearance of power that comes with their weapons compared with the rules and adult authority of the orphanage. The next time we arrived, walking between cracked houses and marble-playing kids among the roadside rubbish heaps, five had left the night before and gone back to the basement where they used to sleep. Peat and Donna left us to play and went to Bab a-Sherji to look for them. One refused to return to the house at all. Four decided to go back but one of those, Aakan, was frightened out of it when one of the gang showed him a big knife and gestured, pulling it across his throat as a threat.

The three who came back were told they weren't welcome by the child psychologist there because they said 'nasty things' to him before they left. He was persuaded though. It was, of course, difficult for the staff too, taking on a group of very troubled and needy boys when they had no experience of working with kids in a practical setting. They had university degrees in things like psychology and social sciences. The science of childcare had always been more important to them and suddenly they were faced with the practicalities of dealing with 20 difficult boys.

Good things were happening too though. Playing the familiar parachute games with the boys, there was still some scrapping, not much concentration or listening, but for the first time we gave them a try at lifting each other up on the parachute to run around on top of it and it worked. It gave me goosebumps, seeing them able to do that, able to communicate and co-operate, remembering them the first time in the crisis shelter.

They had to work together to lift each other off the ground; they had to trust each other and look after each other, because all the kids round the outside, holding the parachute, had to keep it taut or the one running on it would fall. It was hard to keep them there, holding the edge for another boy after they'd had their own turn but Baghdad wasn't built in a day.

The older Ahmed – Gypsy Ahmed, they called him, because of his dark skin and long curly hair – was learning karate at the Magreb youth center nearby. He showed us, a bit shyly at first but glowing with the attention and praise and his own achievement. Little Laith from Abu Nawas Street had a new haircut, really short all over and a big tuft at the front like a very small punk. He still remembered the counting and clapping game Imad and I used to play with them.

From there to the main road we bounced and kicked the ball with the kids we passed. On every street, every verge and every piece of wasteground there were boys playing football. There was something sad about the dirt pitches with metal goalposts and yet more rubbish piles stacked all around them. We picked up a grown-up too, a man in his forties, or thereabouts, his amble home with shopping brightened and delayed by the meeting, absorbing a second man in a *dishdasha* whose eyes twinkled as he abandoned his reserve and joined in the bouncing.

Aakan came back from Baba Sherji, from the gang who'd terrified him so much that hadn't dared leave them. Aakan and I became friends. He sat on my knee in the bus to the park and we set the world to rights.

Ali went back to his family and Laith left to live with his grandma. It would be a long process, and the members of the extended families would need economic, psychological and other support helping to accept one another and settle into living together but maybe it would work.

Enormous problems remained though, worsening as poverty spread and security declined. IRIN (the UN Integrated Regional Information Networks) reported on boys being forced into commercial sex work by threats and violence from street gangs[1] and on abuse faced by street children, for instance being hit or knifed when selling items in traffic queues. As a result, the report said, drug abuse was increasing among the children.[2] Al Jazeera reported that 'more than 1,000 homeless, most of them children' in the Battawin neighborhood alone were affected by drug addiction, alcohol abuse and glue-sniffing.[3] This was the crisis left by sanctions and occupation.

But these boys showed what was possible: when I went to say goodbye to them Aakan was back with his mum and had been for a little while. Some of the older ones had got jobs for a few hours a week and seven were going to school, including Laith and the younger Ahmed.

Six months earlier they were filthy, glue-addicted, violent, with no self-esteem at all, living on the streets around Abu Nawas and Baba Sherji. Now, thanks to a few individuals operating on a small amount of money and a lot of determination, and to a few Iraqi people who struggled to overcome their lack of practical experience with children, a few boys had another chance.

1 IRIN 8 August 2005.
2 IRIN 26 December 2005.
3 4 December 2005.

12

HAPPY FAMILY

January-March 2004

On one of our regular afternoons with the ex-street boys at the Kurdish House we met Safaa, an old university friend of the manager, Asmaa. He was part of a group called Aila Saida (pronouced Eye-la Sy-eeda), or Happy Family, who were doing theater projects with kids and wanted us to work with them. We started by doing a show with them at the Al-Talia Theater.

The boys from the Kurdish House and some of the kids from Childhood Voice's Maghreb youth center were among the audience so we were already popular and got huge cheers from the kids. Happy Family did a couple of plays in which Laith appeared – a long way from his days sleeping on the road outside the Palestine Hotel. The karate group from the Maghreb youth center did a display; a single small pony-tailed girl among the boys.

Safaa's family home doubled as the group's base, their logo in English and Arabic on the wall, a concrete patio with a canopy serving as a stage in a garden with chickens pottering between tall straight palm trees. A busy main road just visible beyond the house was the only sign that we weren't in the middle of nowhere. A screen hid the part of the garden that was all puddles and bits of dead cars and a curtain marked the border between the group's office and storeroom and the rest of the family house.

Small hands held out four, five, six colored glass balls, picked a prize piece each for the contest, lined up the rest of the marbles, flicked one from an open palm at the row on the road by the stone wall. Crouching between puddles on the crumbled street, Fatima directed play, a feisty, dark-skinned 12-year-old girl.

Hanging over the wall they watched Fuad and Mustafa from Happy Family teaching Uzma and me a dance. Fuad had been jailed for a year for refusing to join the army, then conscripted anyway. When the invasion started he escaped, hiding out in Safaa's house till it was all over.

Happy Family started a few years ago. 'We were the first group to perform in the burned-out remnants of the Al-Rasheed Theater in the days after the war. It was a kids' play with the fox and the rabbits, no lighting, heating, décor or anything. Safaa was the fox.' Raed translated, as the only member who spoke a significant amount of English. Raed had been a member of the Iraqi national basketball squad and now ran a music and sound recording shop and did all the music for the performances. To differentiate him from my old housemate Raed, who ran Emaar, this was Music-Raed. Music was his passion, his obsession.

Of course, like most grassroots groups, those not registered with or of interest to the occupying authorities, they had no funding other than what they earned themselves and, apart from Raed, most were students or employees at the fine arts college. They had a Tweety Pie costume and one of Sylvester the cat which they referred to as 'muppets' – by which they meant any big cartoon costume. With little more than this they tried to do good work both for themselves and for the country.

Safaa's big idea was this: that we would create a show, Happy Family and Circus2Iraq together, book a slot at the National Theater in Baghdad and invite a thousand children to watch it for free. We would join in their ghost play and dances and they would be included in our clown routines. I was slightly concerned about the dancing part: I wanted to do it in clown costume so if I were to spin in the wrong direction it would look like I was just being daft, instead of incompetent.

Aila Saida, or Happy Family, with Luis (second from left), me and Sam (second from right).

The children crowded into the garden to watch every time we went for a rehearsal, singing and dancing along. We told Raed about the 'boomchucka' part of our show because we wanted to include it at the National Theater. The thought of a thousand laughing children yelling 'Boomchucka' back at us gave me goosebumps.

He was sceptical. 'I don't think the children will join in.'

'Oh, yeah. They always do.'

He wasn't convinced. 'Come on then,' we said. We took him outside to the patio stage where a couple of dozen children were waiting for something to happen. Peat started: 'Hello.'

'Hello,' came the echo.

A few more hellos, then all four of us shouted, 'Wo-oh.'

'Wo-oh,' all the kids yelled back.

'Boomchucka.'

'Boomchucka,' the kids repeated, loud and gleeful, louder each time. Raed was so excited he came with us to the next show to see if it would work again. It always did. He had a joyous afternoon.

There were times when we were all so tired, felt so burned-out, so fed up with explosions splintering our sleep, that it was hard to crawl out of bed, hard to bear another traffic jam, hard to get into costume and up onto stilts, for all that we knew things had been much harder, for much longer, for the people around us. But from the moment that first 'boomchucka' of the morning bounced back at us, we revived, we felt ten feet tall, we felt like we really had all that joy to share.

Lack of electricity delayed the start of the Eid show on 1 February at the Happy Family base so I climbed up on my stilts and we started clowning and boomchucking. The kids and the Happy Family lads all shouted it at us whenever we arrived after that first time. I stole Luis's hat from above and started posing and strutting about with it. He tried jumping for it, demanding it, then found a child to put on his shoulders to try and reach it.

Waving the hat like a matador, I whisked it out of reach. Finding another, taller child for his shoulders, Luis tried again and failed. Sam, nicknamed 'Abu Lahamm' [Daddy Meat] for his size by Happy Family, made as if to climb onto Luis's shoulders next and he ran off in terror. In despair, Luis began to wail. Looking sheepish and guilty about upsetting him, I rolled it down my arm and back onto his head. Pretending not to notice, he continued to howl till the children persuaded him the hat was on his head and we were friends again. Just then the power came back on, the music burst out and the kids jumped up and danced with us. Hat stealing was simple but fun so we kept it in the show.

The boys from the Kurdish house started break dancing and took turns wearing the Sylvester and Tweety Pie costumes, performing for the

Safaa's mother, 'Ummi'.

smaller kids. It was fantastic seeing them using their creativity, playing, doing something to make other children happy. Applause must be life-changing when you've been a drug-addicted street beggar refused by the whole world.

The Eid fun and games were cut short by rain and Raed showed us the drawing of Happy Family's plans for the garden. They wanted to turn the wasteground part at the end into a play space, plus library and dressing room and to extend and cover the stage because your fingers hit the wall when you spun with your arms out during the dance. In the summer it was too hot for the kids to watch without shade, so they planned a cover for the garden as well. They were also desperate for a generator – not surprisingly, given the frequent disruptions.

I had to teach Mustafa a new word: 'poser'. He was always checking himself out in the mirror, wetting his curls, making sure they were in the right place, making sure he was still tall, dark, handsome and elegant. He was a professional singer and dancer, so we got him to show us some folk dances.

Uzma and I were adopted by Safaa's sisters and mother, who instructed us to call her Ummi, 'Mum'. Ummi cooked us breakfast when we got there and Damia and Maryam whisked us off for beauty treatments, clearly the most important preparation for the show.

For those who are interested in such things, for facial hair Iraqi women use a length of cotton, one end held between the teeth, the other end in one hand, with a loop in between, that's pulled tight around the offending hair to wrench it out of the skin. For non-facial areas they use an abrasive sugar solution. I'm all for mutual grooming and gossip, but had to escape having my eyebrows ripped out of my head by pleading the need to practise the dance.

Damia was a dressmaker, working from home. She wanted to find a husband but was so shy, and her family so traditional, that she wouldn't even go out and talk to the Happy Family boys when they came to the house. She only knew their names. Maryam was married to one of Safaa's brothers, with baby Abdullah, her first, a wide-eyed sweetheart of six months. She parked him on the windowsill, legs out in the sunshine, one either side of the window bar, fixed in place with her headscarf so he could wriggle but not fall. I taught Ummi to juggle chiffon scarves, neon yellow, pink and blue, the only thing I could juggle: Peat had taught me how that morning.

The women bustled in and out of the kitchen where immense pots bubbled, full of beans and rice. I, Uzma, Ummi, the men and boys of the family and a very small girl passed freely between the worlds but the women of the family and the circus and Happy Family men kept to their own sides, except sometimes Fuad, who was more or less assimilated. When we all ate there, it was on the floor, from shared bowls, shoes left at the door of the neat room. The family sitting room was the realm of the women, girls and small children, sewing, reading, playing, rocking babies, watching TV and questioning Uzma and me about our lives and loves.

Raed took the dubious decision to idolize Peat and wanted to be just like him. He adopted him as a brother and tried to learn Peat's accent. The music shop was full of bootleg CDs – the only kind you could get in Iraq – of film soundtracks, Arabic singers, Western boy bands, Britney clones and Eighties classics. As time went on and things got worse, Raed was forced to shut the shop because of threats from a politico-religious group that deemed it decadent and inappropriate.

Raed's boundless enthusiasm for life was infectious; when the other clowns left and Jenny and I wanted to start the Boomchucka Bus, a mobile play centre, Raed set himself the tasks of finding a bus, designing a mascot for it, decorating it, equipping it with a sound system and doing the music when we went places. He became an integral part of the circus. In fact the abrupt deterioration that followed the first attack on Falluja made it impracticable to run the bus – unsafe for the children who played with us, never mind anyone working with us.

The news from the National Theater, meanwhile, was that repairs were finished. The date for the show was set to avoid Ashura, a Shi'a festival commemorating the death of the Imam Ali, grandson of Muhammad, during which time a performance like ours wouldn't be acceptable.

The night before, though, someone threw a grenade into Safaa's garden. No-one was hurt although the cat got a bit singed. Safaa insisted he knew who it was, that it was a personal vendetta, nothing to do with working with foreigners but the same person threatened a couple of schools and orphanages not to bring their kids to the National Theater, saying it would be bombed if they did.

When Ashura did come, on 2 March, the world knew about it: they saw the bodies on TV. Four of Waleed's old school friends, now at college, were killed in the Kadhmiya explosions. The worst of the carnage was in Kerbala, the most important of the shrines. The BBC World Service reported that some people blamed the Americans for 'letting' the bombings happen. It was more than that though: people blamed the Americans for *making* the bombings happen.

The taxi driver asked had we heard. Everyone asked had we heard. And all of them said, 'This is the Americans. They are trying to make us fight each other.' That belief led to defiant unity: Ahmed was in Adamiya, the Sunni district next to Kadhmiya, and said lots of Adamiya people went immediately to give blood for the Shi'a victims at the hospital.

Hands and eyes: Damia.

At Safaa's house there were portraits of the Imam Hussein on the stage. They were having a quiet Ashura, except that a brick had been thrown into their garden with a message threatening them to stop working with us. This time he couldn't tell us it was a personal vendetta. It was written in English, Safaa said, which he thought was odd, but he'd already destroyed it in disgust.

Damia said we were to ignore it and not dare to stop coming to hang out with her. Safaa said the same: he wouldn't let threats destroy everything we were working on. But how do you arrive, smiling, at someone's gate wondering who's watching; wondering which of the men in the street outside, watching his children hugging us, shouting our names, asking for this or that trick, is going to say what to whom; wondering what might happen to our friends in the night after we've gone.

Abu Safaa [Safaa's dad] came in, breaking into a big grin when he saw us, greeting me with the nickname he'd given me, Hassan. It was better than being told never to darken his family's door again, better by far, but I still felt like the worst friend in the world. It's not pleasant to know that you are putting someone in danger by spending time with them; still less pleasant, I'm sure, to be the one put in danger. They said they refused to let fear get in the way but you could see it mingling with their anger nonetheless. We still went, still played with the kids outside, still slipped behind the curtain to Damia and Ummi, but it was never quite the same. It was poisoned somehow.

Postscript

In April 2006 Fuad was murdered. Happy Family had gone from strength to strength since we left, appearing on TV, and giving drama lessons and shows to kids of all sects. A note was left on their van threatening to kill them unless they stopped. Just before they were due to take part in a children's festival, Fuad, Haider Jawad and a woman friend of theirs were traveling in the van when they were fired on. Haider and their friend were killed instantly.

Fuad was dragged out and beaten to death. Punched and kicked and clubbed until his body was so damaged it couldn't live. For making children laugh, for helping them think about something other than violence.

It's not clear whether the murders were ideological – more than 80 artists have been killed and theater, music and dance are considered 'un-Islamic' by some factions – or sectarian (because the group worked with all children). Their small government grant may have made them 'the enemy' or there may have been some other perceived offense. Many artists have simply stopped performing. The others in Happy Family, though, all agreed to go ahead with the festival and have sworn to carry on, knowing the importance both of their work for the kids and of not giving in to violence.

No doubt some would say that Fuad and Haider's murders are proof that this is a war of good against evil, life against death, light against darkness. That's nonsense. Fuad and Haider were – and the kids they worked with are – caught between multiple violent groups including states, paramilitaries, criminal gangs and ideological extremists.

Fuad was murdered because he lived in a country where, having invaded, the occupying powers did nothing to establish law and order, only to prevent attacks on themselves. There's no protection, no investigation and no security.

Fuad Radi, you were a brave, gentle, good man and the world is sadder without you.

Fuad Radi.

13

THE MOST FAMOUS CIRCUS IN IRAQ

January-February 2004

As if taking their job titles too much to heart, the Environment Minister was off sick and the Foreign Minister was abroad, so their meeting with the National Association for the Protection of the Environment and Children (NAPEC) was cancelled.

Undeterred, Kerim Hassan, a famous Iraqi writer and one of NAPEC's founders, announced to the dozens of journalists that his group was about to bring one of the most famous circuses in the world to perform in Babylon and Diyalla.

He'd seen us perform at the Al-Talia theater. He knew we were only four people making a lot of brightly colored noise. It was pure propaganda. But an Iraqi journalist who was also at Al-Talia was inflating our reputation as well: he'd interviewed Luis, who was French, in Spanish.

The reporter had asked Luis how many countries he'd been to. He'd used the singular word for you and Luis had taken it to mean how many countries had he personally visited? The way the journalist interpreted the reply transformed us into an internationally renowned troupe of performers with a tour of 26 countries behind us.

The fact that we were called 'Circus2Iraq' was no obstacle: he'd filled the logical gap by writing that we'd changed our name in honor of the Iraqi people. Now he wanted to know what our name had been before. Husni declined to translate the truth. He said he didn't want to upset the man by telling him that he had his story completely arse-backwards.

That was how we became the most famous circus in Iraq.

So it was that we went to Hilla, the modern town beside Babylon, to perform for about a dozen kids and 60 or so adults. In a hangover from the old Iraq, the front rows were full of dignitaries, officials, the mayor of this town, the mayors of the neighboring towns, with the kids an afterthought. Eventually the grown-ups did get into the spirit of it but it wasn't the most exciting show ever. We made the NAPEC group promise to invite children instead next time and let the dignitaries sit at the back if they wanted to come. Even the dissidents against the former regime

THE MOST FAMOUS CIRCUS IN IRAQ

couldn't help follow some of its habits.

Babylon, the ancient site itself, had been occupied since April 2003 by Polish and US troops – visitors were not allowed, except by prior arrangement and prior arrangement was usually impossible to make: 'They will shoot you.' Two-and-a-half years earlier, on my first visit to Iraq, I had gone to Babylon for a couple of hours' respite. Overlooked by one of Saddam's latest palaces and in the eyeball-boiling August heat, I'd nonetheless found it extraordinary.

Bricks bore the stamp: 'Nebuchadnezzar, King of Babylon, who provides for Esagila and Ezadila, the eldest son of Nabopolassar, King of Babylon, am I.' Processional streets where Hammurabi would have walked – Hammurabi who created the first written code of laws – were still there between reliefs of dragons and lions on the walls. There were those parts of the Ishtar Gate that hadn't already been looted and taken to Berlin; there was the magnificent Lion of Babylon.

As with our all-too-brief trip to the Iraqi Museum, it was like walking backwards through history into the dawn of civilization, law, philosophy, writing: Sumerians, Akkadians, Babylonians, Assyrians, Chaldeans, Persians, Greeks, Romans, Parthians, Sassanids and Muslims in turn battled and studied and debated here.

John Curtis, Keeper of the British Museum's Ancient Near East collection writes that: *'Babylon is unquestionably one of the most important archaeological sites in the world, and was the capital city of two of the most famous kings of antiquity, Hammurabi (1792-1750 BCE) who introduced the world's first law code and Nebuchadnezzar (604-562 BCE) who built the Hanging Gardens of Babylon, one of the Seven Wonders of the World. Excavations at Babylon during the last 150 years have uncovered some parts of the city but much remains buried beneath the earth and there is still a great deal to discover about the ancient city.'*[1]

He goes on to say that, *'Infrastructure works to support the military camp were the responsibility of Kellogg, Brown and Root [a subsidiary of Halliburton]. The camp (150 hectares) was established in the middle of the archaeological site (900 hectares) and surrounded the central enclosed part of the ancient city.'*

Before describing extensive and irreparable damage to the site, Dr Curtis cautioned that his report was based on only two-and-a-half days' work and could not cover all the destruction and interference, not least because some parts were fenced off and mined. Broken bricks with Nebuchadnezzar's stamp, he writes, lie in spoil heaps and many tonnes of archaeologically valuable material, including bones and pottery, have been used to fill sandbags. The dragons around the Ishtar Gate have been damaged, apparently by someone trying to remove a decorated brick.

Military vehicles have crushed the bricks of the processional streets which had survived since the sixth century BCE; huge tracts of the site have been leveled with gravel; trenches have been dug into the Ziggurat, a pyramid thought to be the original Tower of Babel. The gravel, other imported material, chemicals and leaked fuel are damaging as-yet undiscovered layers, while buried bricks are likely to have been destroyed by the heavy vehicles, meaning that what is unexcavated may never be properly explored. We will likely never know where the Hanging Gardens were.

But even Babylon, which was initially protected from looting by the troops' presence (though later looted by troops), and the National Museum, National Library and Library of Korans, which were unprotected, were not the sum of the destruction and pillage. Chalmers Johnson writes: *'At the 6,000-year-old Sumerian city of Ur with its massive ziggurat, or stepped temple-tower (built in the period 2112-2095 BCE and restored by Nebuchadnezzar II in the sixth century BCE), the Marines spray-painted their motto, "Semper Fi" (semper fidelis, always faithful) onto its walls.*[2] *The military then made the monument "off limits" to everyone in order to disguise the desecration that had occurred there, including the looting by US soldiers of clay bricks used in the construction of the ancient buildings.'*[3]

Ur, near Nasariya, now sits beside a massive air base, Tallil, with four camps, two runways, two Burger Kings and a Pizza Hut.

Iraqis, with or without formal education, have a strong sense of historical pride and many saw the desecrations as a deliberate insult, both by individual soldiers who stole and vandalized and by the authorities who chose the sites as bases and prioritized protection of the oil ministry above the museum and libraries.

US military lawyers would no doubt point out that the US never signed up to the Hague Convention for the Protection of Cultural Property in the Event of Armed Conflict and US collectors had carefully prepared the ground pre-invasion by persuading their government to relax laws against sale of Iraqi antiquities.[4]

Laughing from their insides

We went to Mahaweel, a small town in Babylon governorate, to put on a show that was filmed by an Iraqi TV crew. I didn't notice how dirty the stage was till I started sweeping, between dancing about with my magical music box, and the audience disappeared, spluttering in a cloud of red dust. The kids seemed to come to life as the show began, like the cartoon cat Bagpuss waking up and bursting into color. In the middle of the first act, the lights went out. No-one noticed, nor when they came back on, part-way through Peat and Luis's juggling extravaganza. The downside was that the TV crew's very bright light suddenly dazzled the jugglers.

The youth center hosted about 750 kids a day, mostly boys, for sports and games and drama. It reopened in June and the youth workers said the children were visibly scarred by the war. Explosions still shook them and their play was more violent, their concentration disrupted. 'They are fearful,' Ali said with a shrug.

At the end, as we were leaving, one of the men came to Peat and me. 'I want to thank you for coming. This is the first time since the war that I have seen the children laugh this way, from their insides.'

The sheep were making some kind of effort at grazing on mounds of sand and heaps of discarded plastic while people crouched weeding out carrier bags in plots of green. A woman in black with a stick in one hand and a donkey on a string in the other hurried slowly into Baquba town center, in Diyala province, north of Baghdad. The letters outside the Iraqi Grain Board premises were peeled so as to look like Chinese-style decorative writing, in front of a building devoid of windows.

Mud and mud and mud. Three wedding dresses sparkled in front of a roadside shop, hovering above the bog like the spangles were holding them up. The writers who were guiding us asked the way to the children's hospital, calling it by its new name. 'You mean the Saddam Hospital,' was the firm reply, before directions were given. Resembling a building site more than a hospital, the place was bare.

The two ladies' toilet cubicles were without water. One, a sit-down arrangement, had a tin can wedged in the bowl. The other, a hole-in-the-ground, was overflowing. We occupied the police office as a dressing room, the desk too low, really, for getting on to the stilts, doing our make up in the mirror on the back of a pink hairbrush borrowed from a police officer. We were besieged by women asking to borrow Peat's juggling ball case for carrying presents for the kids, by a man in an army uniform requesting the loan of some make-up (he was part of the show) and by assorted security officers bringing large automatic rifles in and out of the room.

Lots of sick kids had a good time, which was what mattered, and it was good for an over-tired and somewhat burned-out clown to be cuddled and kissed by a crowd of smiling children at the end. Farah, the nine-year-old daughter of one of the writers, adopted me as her friend, which was great because it meant when we were taken for lunch afterwards I could run off to the playground instead of smiling nicely and trying to make polite conversation. A small donkey by the playground fence made her nearly fall off the slide by shouting loudly right behind her.

Baquba, to the north of Baghdad, was another of the hotspots: less so than Falluja, Ramadi, Tikrit and their surrounding small towns but still tense. Uzma and I went out to listen to people and found that no-one wanted to talk. No, there was no resistance here. Yes, everything was fine in Baquba. The trouble was only outside Baquba city. But the same people who were telling us Baquba was calm and peaceful were also telling us the center was too dangerous and we should go back.

There was a fear in people's eyes I used to see when anyone asked them about Saddam in the old days. It was the look when they knew there was an official line and that was what they had to tell you. The eyes glazed over and they repeated exactly what the person before told you, the tone flat. Things are fine. No, no resistance here. Deny the visibly obvious. Finally Khalid, one of the writers hosting us, explained: 'They think you must be American soldiers.'

The campaigning writers' group.

'There are many house raids and they destroy everything and take everything and then they come and say it was a mistake,' Khalid said afterwards. He was the leader of the Diyala Young Pens Association, an arts and cultural group set up in 1998 to encourage upcoming writers and artists and to make contacts with those in other provinces and countries. Since the war they'd helped establish the Iraqi Woman Rising organization based in Baghdad as well as the new popular poets' and writers' unions in Diyala.

'Everyone in Baquba is opposed to the occupation, both Shi'a and Sunni,' Khalid told us. Consultation brought forth a guess of about 60 per cent Sunni, 40 per cent Shia in the local population. 'The resistance so far is Sunni. The Shi'a are opposed to the invasion as well, but they were so badly brutalized by the past regime that it has taken them time to recover. People feel shame because it was not the Iraqi men but foreign invaders who deposed Saddam. They are against both Saddam and the occupation.'

Writers in resistance

The National Association for Protection of Children and the Environment, which took us to Hilla and Baquba, was created on 1 May 2003 with around 1,000 members, many of them writers, artists, musicians, journalists, religious figures and teachers who were opposed to the former government. They first campaigned for a ban on the import of militaristic toys, like replica guns and tanks, then met with the Minister for Health trying to persuade him to extend the milk ration for babies from one year to two and to make all hospital treatment for children free.

They made a film about damage to the environment before and after the war and met with the Minister of Justice to ask him to indict the former Ministers of Education and Health. The previous week they'd asked the Minister of Trade to test imported food for fitness for human consumption. There was also a problem with imported toys being already used and unsafe.

They had been meeting with the Environment Minister, asking for environmental legislation, for families of newborns to plant a tree, for the new government to sign the Kyoto Protocol on carbon emissions. They had asked the Minister of Agriculture to ban the use of pesticides in summer and to license pesticides for use only after testing the levels of poisons in them. Disastrously, for the soil and water, there had never been any limits before.

'We asked for a law preventing anyone from cutting down any trees at all, even the Americans,' said Kerim Hassan. 'My philosophy is to ask for everything and get what we can.'

The group met among the sculptures in the garden of an art gallery where Kerim introduced Mr Sami, a musician, Mr Wisam, a sign writer, Mr Ziyad, a clothing designer, and Dr Hanaan, who used to teach childhood education. Several of them met in the political prisoners' wing of Abu Ghraib jail.

'There were many high religious people there, as well as writers and politicians,' explained Kerim. 'We taught each other, to avoid being cut off from society. We were 25 or 30 men to a room but we were able to meet with prisoners from other rooms as well in the daytime.

'I wrote many stories in prison and five plays and gave them to my family to smuggle out when they visited me. Two of the plays have been performed and Iraqi newspapers and magazines have been publishing the stories. We secretly had paper and pens and books about politics. We got them sneaked in and hid them under the beds and we cut the water barrels to make secret compartments.'

Kerim was arrested in 1996 for membership of the Wafaq Watani party, in opposition to Saddam, was sentenced to death after a year in Al-Haqmeeya, a Mukhabarat prison, and then transferred to the political prisoners' wing of Abu Ghraib, where his sentence was commuted to life imprisonment. He held out his arms to show the uneven bones where his wrists had been broken.

'I was surprised that the place where I was most abused was a place where we used to publish magazines about children. When I was first taken there, on 8 November 1996, I remembered working there with my friends, but the regime changed it from a place for education to a place for torture. I was kept in solitary confinement for the whole year there. I did not see sunlight.'

Kerim's party, its leaders having apparently been promised roles in the new government, believed Saddam could only be removed by force: 'I agreed with the invasion because there was no other choice. The US let Saddam stay in power in 1991 because their main aim was to prevent a Shi'a government like in Iran. The sanctions helped Saddam because they made people weak. They were just on the people, not on the Government and Saddam's policy was also to keep the people thinking about food and not about political change.

'They kept him in power because they needed him to stay, but the policy to remove him began long before 11 September 2001. The CIA and White House did not need him any more, like Anwar Sadat: they kicked him out after he fulfilled his purpose of making peace between Egypt and Israel.

'But the US did not do anything except remove Saddam. Why did they destroy ministries and everything, allow looting, and stop the army? This was the main mistake they made and the other was to disrespect the Iraqi people and our beliefs and rights. What we need now is an independent government, not one named by Bremer. I am against Bremer's view that Iraqis are not ready to lead the country. He wants to delay elections.'

Of resistance, Kerim said, 'Non-cooperation through peaceful means is the best way, because the US is strong and it is impossible for us to kick them out by force. Personally I think they did not come to stay as a military force but as an economic one. I don't believe there would be a civil war if the US troops left. For 6,000 years we lived together without civil war. We were the first people to have words for peace and freedom – salam and hurriya. We are part of history.

'We are not writing now, just talking, talking. The US does not want the writers to work now. The budget for the Ministry of Culture is only

$1 million for the year. It's not enough for a month and the money is only for maintenance of Ministry buildings damaged during the war. It's a disaster for Iraqi culture.'

Bashir Al-Majid, a poet, was a member of an Islamic organization, which opposed the former government. He was tortured for nine months in the Mukhabarat [security police] prison then transferred to Abu Ghraib. 'I am sorry. I still cannot talk about that time.' Instead he took out a laminated card bearing his name, year of birth, 1962, the length of his sentence and the insignia of the Independent Political Prisoners' Association, based near the National Theater in Karrada.

'I used to smuggle my poetry outside the country, to friends in Canada who would publish it for me. I was caught by the security police. I was in hiding and they arrested my relatives then my wife and my two-year-old son, so I was forced to go to them. Even then they did not release my family straight away. They were not tortured but while I was questioned they kept them in jail for about a month, as a form of pressure on me to answer all their questions.

'It is too difficult to explain life in jail. The time that I suffered most was when my little son came to visit. He could not understand that his father was in jail so he asked me always a lot of questions, which I could not answer so I was forced to lie to my own son. It was impossible to write

Bashir Al-Majid, poet.

during the nine months in the security jail. There was not even a pencil.

'But even in Abu Ghraib, where there was some sort of comfort after the security prison, I could not write. Even in the prison there were spies and there could be searches at any time. I was not in the same section as most of the political prisoners. I was in a special section. I tried to write in my mind instead and to repeat the poems in my head to remember them. I would like to publish them now but there is no money.'

He disagreed with Kerim on the need for invasion, despite having been liberated after just a quarter of his allocated 12 years in jail when Baghdad fell. 'To remove Saddam is good but to invade the country is a violation of our beliefs and thinking. It is nice to feel free and not invaded, but unfortunately this is invasion. Freedom has no meaning here. There was no freedom with the invasion.

'The gamble of removing Saddam wasn't dependent on an external power but on us, because Saddam always ran away from things. He always backed down under pressure. The Iraqi people could have removed Saddam, even if it took a long time. Yes, I would have been in jail for longer, but there are other people. I knew Saddam was a dictator and a criminal. I was subjected to his crimes and dictatorship, but it was up to us. The French freed themselves with the French Revolution, not by US invasion. The Bastille fell by revolution, but this is a new way to colonize a country.'

I asked him nothing, just let him talk, his eyes burning with the same sadness I saw in those of the political prisoners in Suleimania. 'I was tortured by the past regime but when I saw Saddam on television, captured by the Americans, I was sad because this wasn't the way it should happen. I can't agree with showing him that way. As a human being I can't agree. As an Iraqi I felt suffering when I saw him, even though I know he was a criminal, but he was my president and we had to remove him by ourselves, not by US invasion.'

Did he ever regret writing the poems that got him into trouble? *'Ani, akeed la*. For sure, no. As a human being I had to do it and even if I paid with my life, I have to stand by my beliefs. Voltaire said: "If I stand in the dock for a moment, I shall forget a thousand books I have read about the meaning of freedom." I say, if I stand for one second in the dock knowing that I am innocent, I shall write a thousand books about the meaning of freedom.'

1 JE Curtis, 'Report on Meeting' at Babylon 11-13 December 2004, www.thebritishmuseum.ac.uk/iraqcrisis/reports/Babylon%20Report04.pdf
2 Ed Vulliamy, 'Troops Vandalise Ancient City of Ur', *Observer*, 18 May 2003.
3 Chalmers Johnson, *Nemesis: The Crisis of the American Republic*, Metropolitan Books 2006.
4 Oliver Burkeman, 'Ancient Archive Lost in Baghdad Blaze', *Guardian*, 15 April 2003.

14

'COLLATERAL DAMAGE'

March 2004

'**W**e are farmers. We are farmers.' Fatima had kept screaming it, over and over, cradling one child after another, the fourth dead in the rubble of the farmhouse they had fled to for sanctuary from Baghdad. Three people had been killed: little Zahra, Fatima's sister Hana and her brother Khalid's new wife Nahda, who was 18. Almost a year later the circus was in Diyala Bridge, near to the farm, and Julia was back in Iraq so we decided to go and look for them, to find out what had happened.

Surviving family members and neighbors said at the time that they saw the plane circling overhead for some minutes before it fired three rockets, one of which hit the house, destroying the entire upper storey. Everyone said there was nothing military in the area, nor anything that they could imagine was the intended target. We always wondered though, even after we drove around the district and couldn't find anything, whether they were told by the security services what to say to us.

Taalib, who had driven us there last time, gave us approximate directions and said to ask for the house that was bombed in the war. We drove down the track past a few houses, none of them familiar. We stopped and asked and were directed back to the first house we'd passed. We didn't recognize the woman outside, whose name was Layla, nor the children who peered out through the windows. They talked about most of the family being killed, at midnight, on 29 March – six days after the attack that we knew about. It was a different house.

Layla pointed out the remains of the house, which hadn't been rebuilt. Altogether 16 or 17 people died. She was the second wife of the owner's brother; the first wife was killed in the attack. Her husband was now staying with family members in Britain, receiving treatment after losing his arms in the bombing.

Mustafa Taha, a 16-year-old boy, listed eight of his family who were killed. Kamila Abid Kadem, his 50-year-old mother, his sisters Muna and Abir Taha, 24 and 20, his 13-year-old brother Mohammed Taha, 50-year-old Ismail Abbas, 11-year-old Abbas Smail and Mustafa's cousins Ezhar and Sabiha, both 27-year-old women. Mustafa had shrapnel wounds in his shoulder but had physically recovered.

'We heard the plane above us for about 15 minutes and suddenly we were underground.' He pointed to a smaller boy, 14 years old, sitting on the edge of a step from the house. 'He lost all of his family.'

Nabil Sabah stood up very straight. 'I was at the house of my uncle and I came back at noon and the house was destroyed. My mother and father and all my five brothers and sisters were dead. The rocket hit the house directly.' Speechless, I looked around at the family, their faces still devastated, their bodies still weighed down with grief.

Taha Abbas, Nabil's uncle, with the rubble of their house behind.

'*Asafa*' I said to Nabil – I'm sorry – although it was a pointless thing to say.

He nodded, dignified, and he didn't cry but his little body slumped somehow as if something was crumbling inside him, consumed by the pain which was undiminished, still raw and unaddressed.

Taha Abbas, the uncle whom Nabil lived with now, said: 'We came back to the house and there were many people missing. We searched in the rubble and there were pieces of them everywhere. Some of them we found with their heads off. We are farmers. We have lived here since 1958.'

He'd rebuilt his own home and his brother's. There were eight in the house now, with water and occasional electricity. He supposed the military base three kilometers away might have been the intended target. In truth, though, either you accept that the bombing is so imprecise that, after 15 minutes of circling, the pilot could miss by 3,000 meters and massacre civilians by accident or you have to call this a deliberate attack on non-combatants.

'The tanks and troops come through here all the time,' Taha said. 'It is hard for us to like them after what they have done to us. We have nothing. We are just hanging around trying to live. The Iraqi Government has never asked about us, nor the Americans. No-one has come and asked about us until you.'

They knew nothing of another bombed house in the area so we crossed the river and asked more people. 'Do you mean the house where two women and a child were killed?' someone asked. That was the one.

Though the house was in pieces last time, we knew it when we saw it. There was a drop from the dirt track down to the house. I knew the man who came out. When I'd first seen him I'd thought he was smiling. He'd been on the far side of the emergency room, covered with blood and grime. An older man, his father, had been brought through in a wheelchair and he'd come to him, held the arm of the wheelchair, asked him a question I couldn't understand. It had been a grimace, not a smile, his face desperate.

Ajama had shaken his head and Khalid had collapsed, gasping to catch his breath as if it were trapped in his wife's chest: Nahda was still under the wreckage of the house. The next day he'd been hunched in the corridor, still bloody, head on his knees, tears falling silently, endlessly.

They welcomed us in, Khalid, his brother Omar and their mum, Umm Khalid. The rubble was now swept away, the second storey replaced and the walls repainted, the windows whole and cushions laid around the outside of the room.

Among the photos was one of Hana, Khalid's sister. 'She was in the last year of her studies,' Umm Khalid said. 'She was studying to be a teacher of Arabic. She would have finished in the summer.' Khalid hadn't got any photos of Nahda. They were all destroyed in the bombing. The only one was a passport photo in her ID papers, that of a very young woman. 'She was only 18 years old and they murdered her,' Umm Khalid said and had to wipe her eyes.

'Can you imagine how we felt?' she asked. 'It was the seventh day after the wedding. We brought the bride to the house at four o'clock and at four o'clock we were bombed.'

Umm Khalid talked about Nada, Fatima's eldest daughter, with a

Khalid: bitter memories.

gesture, a long sweep of the hand along the thigh: the gouge in Nada's leg was unforgettable and still causing her problems. How was Rana, I asked. Rana had been eight when the bombing happened, suffering badly with concussion and struggling to breathe when we met her.

'Rana is alright. For us, we are all alright,' Umm Khalid said. 'You can see we are alright. But for them, they are broken. Their family is broken.' Fatima had gone back to Baghdad with her three surviving children: Nada, now 15, Rana, 9, and Mohammed, 5. 'They came from Baghdad because their home was close to the Air Force Center and the National Theater and they thought the Air Force Center would be bombed. Of course it was bombed, but how could they have expected that we would be bombed as well?'

We asked them again what they had thought was the intended target. Still they said there was nothing military in the area, nothing even related to communications or electricity generation. We'd driven all over the area looking for the house and again had found nothing that explained the attack in terms of a mistake, an attempt to hit a legitimate target. We passed the Tuwaitha nuclear power station quite a distance away, drove around its heavily wired perimeter wall but, even had that been close to the farmhouse, it didn't explain the attack. It's unlikely that anyone would aim to blow up a nuclear power station close to a city they plan to occupy.

Ajama, the father, came back from a funeral. One of his relatives was killed in the crossfire of an ambush, some Iraqi militia, some US troops; he happened to be traveling along the road. Ajama was friendly, polite, thanked us for coming. No one has been to ask about us since you last came, he said, not the new Iraqi Government, not the Americans, nobody has offered any help.

'But we are afraid. We welcome you but I am afraid that if we are seen with foreigners in our home people will tell the Americans we are working for the resistance or tell the militias we are working for the Americans. They will ask: who are these people, how did you have communication with them, how did they know where to find you to come and visit your house? I don't know anyone who this has happened to but we hear stories. We hear of it happening and we are afraid.'

He ran a small company with a few employees. Khalid worked as an engineer in the electrical plant in Karrada, which took him on after he'd graduated a couple of years before. They were somewhere between the traditional and the modern, still farmers but also going to university and working in the city as professionals.

Before we left, we had to ask whether they had been told by Mukhabarat, the security police, what to say to us. 'They did not tell us anything,' said Ajama. 'They did not come to us.' There was no reason, now, to disbelieve him. Yet he was more afraid a year later, more afraid to talk to foreigners, more afraid to draw attention to himself. All the same, Ajama thanked us repeatedly, kept apologizing for his fear.

We'd gone looking for the bereaved of three dead and had found the still-devastated remnants of the families of 17 more.

Akael and Ibrahim

I searched as well for Akael, the man I'd met in the hospital during the invasion, after the bombing outside the mosque on Palestine Street. Shrapnel had been embedded in his forehead, the doctors unsure whether it had pierced his brain. I still had their address: Street 9, House 12, which in theory had to be close to the mosque.

'The streets are all in a mess,' a lad explained, referring not to the heaps of festering rubbish nor even to the craterous holes in the road but to their random order. 'This one is Street 3 and that one is Street 43.' He gave us an apologetic look. What could you do when the world around you made no sense?

Nobody we asked knew where Street 9 was. They could tell us what this one was and the one next to it. This is 14 and that one is 26, they would say, with an apologetic gesture. Someone suggested we ask the Responsible for the district, the Mukhtar. There's one in each area, the senior gentleman of the district, a source of information and social authority. He came out from his siesta, pulled up the metal shutter of what looked like a garage next to his house to reveal a tiny shop but he too was unable to tell us where Street 9 was and didn't know the family.

We went to the mosque that was closest to the bombing and our driver Dhafur went in to ask. Yes, they knew the attack we meant and the street where the houses had been damaged. A man who was leaving offered to lead us there in is car, but tanks and armored personnel carriers blocked the way. The soldiers waved guns menacingly and Dhafur remarked that there was only one God but also only one death; with that he reversed up the street and we decided to find Akael's family another day.

Emaar-Raed co-ordinated a survey of deaths and injuries, organizing teams of volunteers who went door-to-door asking about casualties of the war. The teams recorded 2,000 dead and 4,000 injured in parts of Baghdad, nine southern cities and Kirkuk, so the numbers recorded do not refer to the entire country. They collated data from hospitals as well, ensuring their records didn't duplicate individuals but a doctor in Nasariya estimated that perhaps a quarter to a third of the dead actually came to the hospital; the rest were simply buried.

Yet with the end of the invasion the carnage was far from finished. A local police officer came with us from the outskirts of Ramadi to show us the way. He gave us his full name but asked to be identified only as 'Hussein'. He told us the story of Ibrahim Odai, whom he'd met as a police cadet – an uncommonly honest man who refused to accept bribes.

'He was very ambitious to be a lawyer, so he studied and got his degree and when he became a lawyer he started coming back to his friends who were still in the police, asking us to send him our cases in which the people in prison were illegally or dishonestly accused, in Saddam's time.

'He graduated two years ago and started to work with those people accused by others. He wouldn't work for anyone who was trying to harm anyone else – it was the first time I'd ever seen a lawyer who wouldn't accept bad things being done. Beside Ibrahim's house there was an office of the Ba'athist party. When any soldier left his unit and went absent without leave the Ba'athis used to come and take him from his house and send him back to his unit.

'This was near Ibrahim's house and he told all the police that when people escaped from the army they shouldn't tell the Ba'athists, he told them do not take anyone from his house, just talk to them and try to persuade them to go back. Don't take them to the prison. This was a good thing for Ibrahim to say, because they weren't punished if they went back on their own, only if the Ba'athis took them back.'

On 20 November, two days before the end of Ramadan, just as they were about to break their fast, Ibrahim's family was interrupted by two groups of US troops from the 82nd Airborne Division. A man called

Khalid explained that he was outside the house with Ibrahim, his brother Sabah and their cousin Mohammed, waiting for *futtoor*, the meal.

'American vehicles came on the road. Ibrahim's mother asked what was going on. He said it was only traffic control. We stayed outside the house, not thinking the troops were coming for us. The first vehicle stopped beside the bush there and the others were standing on the road.

'The soldiers came from the road towards the house and they were running. They surrounded the house. We were outside the front of the house. The soldiers came and put ties on us and put us on the ground. The Americans entered the house through two doors – this is one and the other one is at the back – and started shooting each other.

'The soldiers were terrified and reacted thinking each other were the enemy. They were firing as well from outside the house, through the windows. Three or four Americans were killed inside the house, killed by Americans. As revenge they came outside and shot us on the ground. We were forced face down in the mud. They killed Ibrahim, Sabah and Mohammed and I was shot in the arm.'

Khalid carefully removed the coat from around his shoulders and undid enough buttons to show us the wounds on his arm, dark scabs surrounded by yellowed bruising, a smallish entry wound and a larger exit wound. He'd no idea why they let him live. The house was devastated by continued attacks: Khalid said a tank opened fire on the house. Shell casings littered the ground outside. The US troops threw a grenade into a front room with no-one inside. The soldiers took the papers for all of Ibrahim's legal cases from his car.

His brother Ismail said: 'The Americans came the next day and smashed the car. On the second day after, they came and said we are sorry, you are not the people we want, it's a mistake. They were from the 8th Brigade – the commander was Isle.' (No one had any idea how the commander's name was spelt, so that's my guess).

The women and children had mostly been in and around the outdoor kitchen building when the Americans arrived. Ibrahim's nine-year-old son Ibed stood outside among the adults in silence, the devastated, lonely, powerless rage in his eyes answering any question you might think of asking him. I wasn't clear exactly where he had been standing during the attack but his uncle said he'd seen his father shot.

The house was more or less destroyed, the white car a strainer of bullet holes. There were marks on the ground where the three had been executed, covered by stones which the men lifted to show us. The survivors were now living in the medical aid building. Ibrahim's wife was indoors, in mourning for three months along with his daughters.

Ismail Odai had gone to get the bodies of his brothers. The doctors wrote and signed death certificates saying the men had died from 'fractures and body wounds' from shrapnel. Ismail was enraged. 'The Americans were on the head of the doctor when he wrote the death certificate. It was not wounds and fractures, it was assassination – they shot them on the ground, but the doctor refused to write that. There are bullets in the ground where they shot him. The doctor was sitting writing and the Americans were there standing over him.

'It was Dr Khattan Abed Hanish at Ramadi Hospital who signed the death certificate for Sabah. It was obvious that the doctor was under pressure from them. A different doctor, Dr Hamdi, signed the certificate for Ibrahim but he gave the same cause of death.'

We failed to find either doctor but an Iraqi friend who worked with foreign journalists said he'd encountered Dr Hamdi before. He'd signed the death certificate for a Hungarian civilian worker killed recently. Three different causes of death were given in public statements by the US authorities, none of them mentioning shooting, though witnesses insisted that the man was shot by American troops. Reporters who went inside the hospital were told nothing. Away from the cameras the guards told my friend that the man had been bleeding from bullet wounds when he arrived.

We went to the army base to ask the commander for an explanation about the raid which killed Ibrahim, Sabah and Mohammed but found ourselves surrounded by guns and an incoming convoy of humvees. The base was already 'on lock down' when an attack on the other side of the palace rocked the ground.

When the soldiers returned to Ibrahim's house they brought forms for claiming compensation. That process did exist but only superficially. To attempt to enter it was to step into a void. You went to the administration centers and you went again and you went again and each time you were told to come back another time. You tried to submit proof of fault, photographs of damage, medical reports, death certificates, details of the amount of money claimed, and so on. But at the end of it all the US military would say it was a combat situation – someone had fired on the soldiers, so compensation wasn't payable – or they would falsify the cause of death, saying it was not their fault.

Baqer's story

Saif, who used to work in the hotel I stayed in during the invasion, asked me to come and meet his neighbors in Thawra (formerly Saddam or Sadr City). The neighbors' son Baqer had been shot by US soldiers and survived – but with a 9mm bullet lodged in his head.

Baqer was four-and-a-half. On 26 May 2003 the family was going to visit relatives, and were waiting for a taxi when there was an explosion. US troops opened fire; Baqer fell. His left cerebrum and cranial nerves were damaged, impairing his sight, hearing, speech and walking. One eye unfocused and unmoving, he listed and staggered and fell over whenever he tried to get off someone's lap. His dad Ali said he couldn't sleep properly, so he cried with tiredness.

Baqer screamed, wriggled and squirmed out of his dad's arms and flung himself out of the room in panic because he was sure my friend Michael and I must be more doctors, come to poke and stare. The doctors only prescribed medicines that the family couldn't afford to buy. They'd sold the furniture, the TV, almost everything, to buy medicines. The house was bare but for rugs on the floor, a single light bulb and a lamp which took over when the electricity was out.

The Coalition Provisional Authority had promised to help with his treatment and medicines but had given the family nothing: no money, medicines or treatment nor any assistance with traveling out of Iraq to hospital in Jordan or beyond. A lawyer from the Civilian-Military Operations Centre (CMOC) had promised money for Baqer's treatment but they'd been unable to find the lawyer again on subsequent visits. Each time the authorities told Ali they were busy and to come back another time. The family was more fortunate than many in having support from various groups including Care International and Human Rights Watch.

There was no dispute that US soldiers were responsible for Baqer's shooting, that it was a US army bullet in his head. There was no knowing how many more desperately poor families and individuals were going through the same struggle, trying to find the money for medical care or to survive after the main earner was killed, trying to get the forces responsible to give the financial help they promised.

Even if you could get a lawyer to help, getting any kind of recompense was unlikely. Thabat, the lawyer from one of the Iraqi human rights groups, checked down a list of the dead: 'This is cluster bombs, this is cluster bombs, this is cluster bombs, but you know, there are no cluster bombs. They say there are none and they will not come and clean them up.

'A doctor was standing outside his home waiting for a taxi when he was shot dead by American troops. There were thieves nearby and they ran away. The soldiers chased them in the vehicle and they were firing, firing, everywhere, and they killed the doctor. And they pay nothing. They say he was in the wrong place. If they shot him in his house they would say he was in the wrong place.'

On 8 November a man was waiting in the bus station when US soldiers came and began searching people. He reported to Thabat's group that they stole 160,000 dinars from him – about $80. He didn't see the face or rank of the soldiers responsible because they'd covered his head with a bag. They didn't give him any paper stating that the confiscation had been made, nor the value, nor the reason. This happened a lot, according to Thabat's list of cases, in people's homes as well as on the street.

Thabat said that in only one of all the cases reported to the group had the victim been given a paper stating what had happened but even in that instance the paper was worthless. It didn't bring anything from the CPA or CMOC. In not a single case that had been reported to him had any compensation been paid or any action been taken against the perpetrators.

I told Baqer's story on my blog as an account of how an innocent person could be injured by US troops in Baghdad and their family then struggle to get treatment, compensation, even an honest answer from the occupation authorities.

I told the story of Ibrahim and his brothers on my blog as an example of house raids by US troops – showing that houses were raided by mistake, that extrajudicial executions were carried out, that doctors were compelled to lie on death certificates, that even in the most clear-cut cases, compensation could be refused on the basis that it was deemed a 'combat situation', backed up by the falsified cause of death.

I told the stories of people whose homes and families were destroyed during the invasion as illustrations of the apparently deliberate attacks carried out against civilians and of the complete lack of reparation by the occupying powers or assistance from the new Iraqi leadership.

None of these were one-off aberrations. They were part of a pattern, military training being designed to dehumanize the enemy, subjugate conscience, make killing reflexive, overcome the natural reluctance to shoot another human being that afflicted two-thirds of US soldiers sent to the frontlines in World War Two. US soldiers who have left Iraq have since talked about being told to fire on all taxis or about deliberately killing unarmed people, including children.[1]

These stories were repeated, with variations, thousands of times over – thousands of bereaved and crippled people knocking at the high palace gates of the new authorities and being turned away.

I explained at the time that the compensation process was deliberately vague, the occupation authorities deliberately obstructive and the soldiers and commanding officers deliberately unaccountable for their actions and orders. What was needed was not an appeal for Baqer but sustained and vigorous protest against impunity and for a fair and open system of investigation and compensation. Reparations are due not only to individuals but also to the country as a whole, just as Iraq has been forced to pay for its invasion of Kuwait.

Baqer was not necessarily the most needy but he was – with no disrespect to him – perfect poster-child material and money raised as a result of people reading about him meant in the end that the bullet was removed from his head in Greece. The damage had been done though and he would need long-term care, requiring long-term funding. Others, who might have benefited more, but with lower propaganda value, were not taken for treatment. Of course solidarity with individuals is important, but it has to be based on need and accompanied with a wider perspective.

The corporate media, though, never makes visible the wider perspective. It's all about 'human interest' on their terms and pictures of starving children are not accompanied by a commentary which comes close to telling us who is truly responsible. By focusing on an individual and neglecting to relate that single experience to the wider context, it is possible to divert energy from resisting a bad policy into fixing a bad consequence of an otherwise-ignored policy. The time for marching is over. There is no need to get out on the streets and loudly and fiercely demand justice. There is no bigger picture. Cry and donate. Cry and donate. And then shut up.

It's the Media of Small Things. Like Arundhati Roy's God of Small Things, who deals only with individual suffering, leaving the large-scale national suffering to the God of Big Things, the corporate press shows only the personal disasters, the dead child, the day's biggest car bomb, the kidnapped Westerner. Meanwhile the mundane, everyday carnage, the hundreds of bullet wounds, the homelessness, the human trafficking, the deeper pattern of occupation authorities actively fomenting sectarian conflict, are bypassed. Let cause and consequence never be seen together.

So far the US Government has given a paltry $20 million to the US Agency for International Development to 'aid' civilian victims – the US authorities do not use the term 'compensation', much less 'reparation'. Raed from Emaar explained that mostly the money is used for 'aid projects' that indirectly benefit bereaved dependants or injured people. Some have been given sheep or bricks to build houses, rather than cash to use to satisfy their most urgent needs.

As Raed put it: 'Yes, a sheep, as in *baa, baa*. I wonder if they send a note saying "Sorry we killed your son, here's a sheep instead".'

1 See, for example, Iraq Veterans Against War www.ivaw.net ; Christian Parenti, *The Freedom: Shadows and Hallucinations in Occupied Iraq* The New Press, 2004; various accounts by Dahr Jamail, www.dahrjamailiraq.com

15

THE BOMB

18 March 2004

I set off for the internet center. I'm wearing The Face. I've learned this from the Iraqi women as a way of deflecting harassment: staring straight ahead, slightly fiercely, not responding to any shouts or remarks, even greetings, because as soon as one man sees you say hello to another, you're fair game.

The air seems impossibly full for a second and then bursts with a roar, sending a tremor through the ground that shoots up the leg my weight is on, unbalancing me slightly, but The Face doesn't flinch. Young men start running past me in the direction of the explosion. That's when the shock hits me: I've learned to ignore things blowing up behind me. Bombs have become normal.

A burst of gunfire sends a crowd of children and young men running back the other way. '*Wayn? Wayn?*' people are asking. Where? '*Kahromana,*' someone says, referring to the sculpture of Ali Baba's wife pouring hot oil into the barrels where the 40 thieves were hiding, which stands at the junction between Karrada Dakhil, Karrada Kharitj and Saadoon.

The shopkeepers scoop up the boxes of electrical goods, fruit and toys from the array on the pavement and haul down the metal shutters in front of the windows, if they've still got any. The less fortunate sweep and shovel the splintered glass. Towards Kahromana most of the windows even on Karrada Dakhil are destroyed; on Karrada Kharitj there's barely one intact.

'*Wayn infijar?*' someone asks me. Where's the explosion?

I don't know but you can see smoke from the road towards Simona and Paola's house. A raw clatter of gunfire, very close and very loud, drives another crowd of young men running. They're saying it was a car bomb, saying it's a hotel.

As I carry on towards the internet, the old men ask me the same question. '*Wayn infijar?*'

I tell them the *shebab*, the young men, say it was a hotel.

'*Al-Sadeer?*'

I don't know, but they say it was a car bomb.

No, they insist straight away. It wasn't a car bomb. It was a missile. One of them points to the sky and traces the arc of the thing just to make sure I understand.

It's weirdly dislocating to find the next street live on TV. Al-Jazeera bring on the scene almost instantaneously because the hotel where they live and work is behind the one blown up. The men in the internet center say it was the *Funduq Burj Lubnaan* – the Lebanon Tower, an apartment hotel used mainly by families from other Arab countries. No-one can think of a reason why it was targeted. People speculate that the bomb was being taken somewhere else and blew up there by mistake.

Fisheye comes back in shock. He's never seen the flames, the panic, the craters, the impossibly copious smoke before. The mobile phone network is jammed so I can't ring anyone to see if they're OK and say we're all OK. In the morning we walk over because Fisheye needs to see it in daylight, to know that the flames are out.

There's no front on the hotel and the street is a mire of bricks, puddles, foul stinking mud and craters filled with water. Smoke still limps out of windows and doors inside houses, their front rooms exposed to the world like dolls' houses, men with shirts wrapped around their faces sweeping out the debris from a first-floor room, the side wall split like a rotten trunk.

Wrecked houses opposite the Lebanon Tower Hotel.

When they discover I understand a bit of Arabic, everyone wants to talk. I can't find anyone who accepts that it was a car bomb. The US soldiers on the scene say it was a thousand pounds of plastic explosive wrapped in some kind of artillery. It's impossible to see what's in the crater, whether there's any part of the skeleton of a car, because it's full of water from the fire hoses.

Local people unanimously insist it was a missile. It came from the air. I ask everyone, did you see it yourself? No, no, they all say, but as we're leaving there's one who says he did. He points to his right, my left, opposite the demolished hotel, but behind the row of buildings which faced it. He says he was standing close to where he is now and he saw it. He thinks it was the Americans, as do all the men around him, all the people who come to talk.

Of course, it could be denial, scapegoating, wanting to blame someone and something else, something foreign for all the problems, to avoid having to address them from within. It could be. Like the Ashura bombing, like dozens of smaller explosions, a lot of people think it's a tactic by the US troops to foment troubles between Shi'a and Sunni as a justification for prolonging the occupation.

Either way it's impossible to investigate properly because a US military bulldozer rolls past us scooping up whatever forensic evidence there might have been. A CNN reporter swoops on a small child carrying a plastic doll, bereft of several limbs, and rearranges them for the camera. Where is the truth?

On 18 March, a year after the war, where is the truth? Bulldozed and rearranged for the camera, dead and buried under the rubble.

The spiral of violence

Car bombings, roadside bombings, suicide bombings, bombings of all sorts were on the increase, from sporadic to daily to several times daily and, alongside that, the rise of sectarian paramilitaries, assassinating, torturing, imprisoning. In late 2005, more than 170 Sunni prisoners were found in an Interior Ministry bunker having been detained by Shi'a paramilitaries and tortured. It was clear that these paramilitaries were either part of or working alongside the police, by then dominated by Iranian-backed Shi'a groups, death squads carrying out disappearances and killings of Sunnis.

John Negroponte, the US ambassador to Iraq after the 'handover of power' in June 2004, made covert paramilitary operations, disappearances and death squads his stock-in-trade in Latin America in the 1980s. Negroponte's successor, Zalmay Khalilzad, had a background in marshaling politico-religious forces in covert operations in Afghanistan, the Soviet Union and Bosnia.

The suspicion that bombs were being planted by the occupying powers could only have been strengthened when, in 2005, two British Special Forces operatives were arrested by Iraqi police in a car containing explosives and then released by British troops smashing through a compound wall before investigations could be carried out. In fact much of the suicide bombing is thought to be the work of Ansar al-Islam, a Kurdish group which has more followers than Zarqawi but rates fewer mentions in War-On-Terror speeches.

Increasing identification by sect or ethnicity was deliberately driven. First, the occupying powers organized elections along ethnic rather than regional or even political lines and created a particularly divisive mode of federalism. Second, conflict was actively fomented by, for example, bringing Kurdish Peshmerga forces and Shi'a militias into Sunni areas of resistance and by support, explicit and tacit, for those groups' operation within the police.

Economic measures also played a part. Enforced 'structural adjustment', driven by Iraq's debt, meant that fuel prices were increased seven-fold in December 2005 as subsidies were cut under pressure from the World Bank and its President, former US Deputy Secretary of Defense Paul Wolfowitz.[1] Fuel price rises inflated the cost of all commodities while unemployment was high and wages were low. Poverty and deprivation, the inevitable consequence of privatization for the benefit of outsiders, cause increased rivalry and an emphasis on division.

A 'Council of Notables of Nineveh Province' warned of sectarian escalation caused by Peshmerga militias of the Kurdish parties, the Badr Brigade – a Shi'a militia under the command of Abdel Aziz al-Hakim, leader of the Supreme Council of the Islamic Revolution in Iraq (SCIRI) party, part of the transitional government – and the Wolf and Thunder brigades which were acting as regular forces of the National Guard. They said Sunni Arab residents were being forced out of Tel Afar, the left bank of Mosul and surrounding villages. As well as checkpoints, arbitrary road closures and arming of young men, they said Kurdish gangs were controlling towns and villages in Nineveh province, appointing party functionaries to run them and replacing Iraqi flags with Kurdish ones.

Mosul was not part of the area designated Kurdish with the creation of 'safe havens' in 1991, and nor was Kirkuk: oil-rich areas which would be central to any territorial battle between an Arab center and a Kurdish north. Were Kurdish forces to succeed in seizing those oilfields, some suggest the mainly Shi'a south would also seek to separate from the oil-poor, ethnically mixed but Sunni-dominated center.

The situation is more complex, though, than just Sunni, Shi'a and Kurd. Even leaving aside the many other groups living in Iraq – Christians,

Turkmen, Yazidis – those main groups are by no means united. Kurds are split by party and class. Civil war in the 1990s between the Patriotic Union of Kurdistan and the Kurdish Democratic Party – both more clan-centered than ideological – left the region with two of every major institution, ministry and service. The Kurdish Islamic Union blamed the two main parties for a campaign of arson, intimidation and destruction of its election materials.

What is more, land and political power in Kurdistan still belong to a large degree to the Agas landlord class, many of whom sided with Saddam against the Peshmerga and whose privilege, like the Ba'athists, enabled

The bombed-out street outside the Lebanon Tower Hotel.

them to reinstate themselves into powerful positions post-invasion.[2]

The south, perhaps less divided, is still torn between supporters of Abdel Aziz al-Hakim and those of Moqtada al-Sadr, a leading young Shia cleric known for his extreme conservative and anti-occupation views. It is by no means certain that the lines would be drawn simply either side of the center. Of course there is the conspiracy theory which says the occupiers always wanted a civil war and the cock-up theory which says they never had that degree of control. The truth, no doubt, is in between. Nevertheless, blatant provocation of sectarian fighting was evident with the impunity of militias and the deliberate placing of Shi'a and Kurdish dominated forces in Sunni areas.

It can be no surprise that the Kurds, assaulted by state governments and successive occupiers, should want to seize significant areas when they have the chance. In districts where Kurds' property was given to Arabs who then lived there a long time and had nowhere else to go, mediation is urgently needed, backed by funding for proper compensation to those who lose out.

A combination of oil revenues and contributions from those in the international community who were responsible for arming Saddam against the Kurds ought to fund the process. Mediation between all communities in Iraq would be beneficial, with neutral facilitators, provided that all-comers were equal and that nobody was able to be obstructive on the basis of partisan support from foreign militaries. It's a powerful tool which has been successful in conflicts all over the world. Otherwise there can only be a few winners and many losers – and there cannot be a peaceful future based on justice for everyone.

The bomb at the Lebanon Tower Hotel was not particularly significant in the scheme of things – not particularly provocative in the sectarian context, just another fragment of violence in the spiral, just one story, my story, of another scene of devastation where the truth was bulldozed by a military machine, rearranged for the cameras, killed and buried in the rubble.

1 Dahr Jamail and Arkan Hamed, 'Iraqis Reject Increased Fuel Costs', Inter Press Service, 21 December 2005.
2 Christian Parenti, 'The Question of Kurdistan', *The Nation*, 14 November 2005.

16

CIRCUS TO KURDISTAN

March 2004

We were acting up in Kishmisha, the juice shop at the end of our street in Baghdad, taking bright red lights out of each other's ears and pockets, making hankies disappear, Peat apparently taking 30 or so ping-pong balls out of his mouth and so on, as we seemed to do most days. People expected it of us.

A man we didn't know came in. 'Are you some kind of magicians?'

That's how we met Shakhawan, a journalist from the Kurdish newspaper *Al-Ta'akhi*. The staff lived in the offices in Baghdad from Saturday to Wednesday, returning to Erbil and their families in between. The walls of their common room carried pictures of Salah Yousifi, the former editor in chief, killed by Saddam in the 1970s, and another journalist from the paper who disappeared.

Shakawan was arrested, questioned and released under instructions to give information about fellow journalists and students in his university. He fled and the newspaper retreated from Baghdad, returning after the invasion. They interviewed us for the newspaper and invited us up to Erbil.

We had to stop at every single checkpoint except one on the way north and there were lots. Raza, from the newspaper, and Firas, the driver, seemed quite pleased to tell everyone we were a circus. Two US soldiers thanked us, said they were trying to do the same thing as we were: 'We give the kids candy to try to win their trust.' So, not quite the same thing then...

Erbil is a small city which has grown around an ancient walled medina on top of a green hill in the center, a winding bazaar to one side of the newer part, an enormous statue of a man sitting halfway up the slope to the old part. A photographer was working beside the statue, and schoolboys and young men climbed onto it, for fun or to pose. His other backdrop was a canvas, hung from the wall, of distant mountains which could have been Kurdish but for the Alpine cottage in the foreground.

Police and Peshmerga soldiers walked around singly, still armed but

Sky juggling: Peat in the Kurdish mountains.

nothing like the four-to-a-car pack movements of the Baghdad police force. Things were infinitely more relaxed here, although we were still told to be careful at night, that it was better to be home before dark. In any case most things were closed by night, unlike Karrada, where we lived in Baghdad, whose food stalls only started to open up at dusk.

The shop mannequins had beards, either painted on like the rest of the facial features or with ginger bristles actually attached. Ginger hair and green or blue eyes are common among Kurds. The roar of generators was mostly absent: electricity went off for the same couple of hours every day, twice a day, so people were able to work around it, whereas elsewhere in Iraq it came and went erratically.

The first task was to go to the police station and get travel and residence permits for Kurdistan. We dropped our passports off when we arrived, in exchange for a yellow piece of paper, and went back for them, equipped with passport photos, in the morning. We completed interminable forms, English to Arabic to Kurdish, and eventually we were asked for $60, apparently either an admin fee or some sort of refundable deposit for good behavior.

Either way we didn't have that much money to spare. We'd been filling time with the guards outside and they followed us into the office asking us to perform. All right, we said, but this one will cost $60. It was a deal. If we could impress them with some circus tricks they'd let us off the money.

Fisheye commissioned a volunteer and had him take off his jacket, a big leather thing he was evidently proud of. Borrowing the man's cigarette, he pressed it into the fabric. The owner let out a small whimper, swallowed hard and managed to say 'OK' while the others' mouths hung open. I knew how it worked, but still I had to bite my lip and hope there was no way it could go wrong.

The wisps of smoke died out and Fisheye put his hand into his pocket to fetch some invisible magic dust to sprinkle over the wounded jacket, which he then held out, unscathed.

'*Wallah!*' [My God], in chorus.

OK. We were going to get out alive; maybe even uncharged, given the wide eyes. Clutching his coat, our man looked everywhere for the burn, for the cigarette, for the secret. Where was the cigarette, everyone wanted to know. '*Rahid*' [gone]. We all gestured dissolution into thin air, shrugged: '*Huwa sahar,*' he is a magician.

Peat was, for once, without ping-pong balls so he scoured his pockets for small things to juggle: a bottle of shower gel, a stray beanbag and a roll of tape. The soldiers gaped. I plundered the desk-tidy and threw him some correction fluid for an attempt at four balls. I had no stilts with me, so contributed a couple of cartwheels. It had to be time for the grand finale.

'Can I borrow your Kalashnikov?'

Emptied of ammunition, the automatic rifle went on Peat's chin, point downwards because it's easier to balance things that are top heavy. He moved about a bit to make it look harder, like he was having to make some effort to keep it there. You could see them all thinking this would really impress the wife and wondering how long it was going to take them to master it.

The outcome of it all was four official papers bearing our photos and entitled 'Kurdistan Region Ministre of Interior. Trevleng and Stayng' and no fee. 'But where did the cigarette go?' they were still begging as they followed us to the taxi, the jacket's owner still sneaking surreptitious looks into his coat pockets and under the collar.

The streets of Erbil

Boys sold chocolate and toys on the streets of Erbil, standing at stalls, wheeling wooden carts over broken pavements or winding their way between cars at traffic intersections. A young lad with horrific scars pulling his face and body out of shape adopted and followed us. As in Baghdad, any car was a potential taxi. The US and UK had carried out bombing raids in the northern and southern no-fly zones throughout their existence and had turned an unsubtle blind eye to frequent Turkish military incursions along its border.

In Baghdad, when we announced that we were going north, people asked us why. 'The children there are all right. They don't have problems.' Though avoiding the obvious post-war chaos of the center and south, the north too had suffered 12-and-a-half years of sanctions.

Certainly the Kurdish region suffered less under the sanctions than the rest of the country. There was more money per head in the north, for a start. The Oil For Food money was divided on a percentage basis but the north got its share from the gross revenues. From the remaining funds the deductions were made: a percentage for administration costs and almost a quarter of the gross revenue for the compensation account, to pay reparations and so on. What was left – much less per head of population – had to cover all food, water, health, electricity, education and other infrastructure for the entire center and south of the country.

The north also received a cash component. While the rest of the country could only issue credit notes for goods, the north had some hard cash to pay workers, to buy local components and so on, both boosting the local economy and enabling regeneration work to be done much more cheaply. Increasing clean water output by a cubic liter costs many times more when a foreign company is importing everything than when local businesses supply parts and labor. Negotiations over a cash component for the rest of the country were not held in good faith by either Saddam or the sanctions committee.

In addition, because of the restrictions on international NGOs in the south and center, they had much greater presence in the north. Peat and I arrived at an orphanage for boys, whose address Raza gave us. Signs outside displayed the names of organizations from around the world like humanitarian graffiti tags but we were distracted from a closer look by a small boy arriving at the gate from outside and beckoning us in, around a crumbling guard's cabin to a patch of grass and weeds.

There was a young man on a chair, a couple of kids playing around his head. There were apparently no toys at all. Fifteen or so boys screamed and giggled and ran after bubbles. The windows in the boys' rooms were patches of jagged glass, the rest lying on the ground outside. Karovan explained that an American organization was doing some refurbishment, had mended the boys' beds and given them blankets, but still there was thick dust all over the floor in the rest of the building. One corner was filled with broken cupboards, another with bits of furniture, either part-built or part-collapsed.

A generator in the yard was a gift from Peace Winds of Japan, a sign announcing that they'd run summer camps in 1997 and 1998 and given the generator a year later. There was no update. All the NGO signs were chipped, peeling, several years old. The home was built by

Saddam, Karovan said, because he wanted to help all the children whose parents were dead or remarried. After 1991 it was not run by the Iraqi Government any more. Some Kurdish organizations helped them as well as the international groups.

Karovan was a student in the College of Law and Political Science. He lived at the orphanage because he couldn't afford the student hostel. He had a room, a thin mattress on the floor, a desk piled with books. He introduced others who arrived while we were there: a fellow student, a telephone engineer who worked nearby, all helping to look after the boys in exchange for a room. The boys were clean enough and seemed healthy despite living in a building site.

The place looked better by Saturday morning when we turned up to perform: there was still broken glass and heaps of half-furniture but a woman with a mop was making *jihad* against the dust. The dust was still winning but the grime from the floor had gone and there were more workers about, the morning shift already gone to school and the afternoon shift milling about hoping Peat was going to regurgitate more ping-pong balls.

We were still without a translator into Kurdish and I somehow got the job of miming instructions, which worked surprisingly well. When there were lots of kids, it was sometimes hard for them all to hear the instructions but they could all see the clown in the middle of the parachute. We even managed to co-ordinate rolling the football a few laps around the fabric.

I was teaching a few of the boys to do cartwheels after the games were over when I realized that one of them only had one-and-a-half arms, so we all switched to one-handed cartwheels.

As Omran, one of the workers, was driving us home we met a school bus full of kids. We couldn't help ourselves. It happened every time. One or other of us would start, blowing bubbles, pulling faces, making things appear or disappear. All the kids piled against the windows. The boys selling stuff in the traffic queue were drawn in as well. Omran couldn't stop laughing. We couldn't hear the laughter of the kids in the bus, but we could see it and it made us completely high.

The laughter relaxed Omran and he opened up, telling us about his only other experience of the British. '*Uhuwye,*' he said, my brother. '*Tiyara Biritanee*', a British aeroplane. '*Papapapapa.*' He gestured firing. '*Mat*' – dead. He was in his home. He wasn't with the army, wasn't with Saddam, just waiting it out at home. Somehow, seeing us making the children laugh was important.

His foot had entry and exit scars from two bullets, courtesy of Saddam, in whose prisons he spent two years, 1988 to 1990. There were other torture wounds as well, because he was a member of a political party that opposed Saddam. His brother had fled to Canada, married a Canadian woman, and now had a child. Jail seemed such a common experience in Kurdistan: the man at the front desk in the hotel had been a political prisoner for 17 years.

We found a fellow clown in the Ministry of Culture, Anwar, brought in from his own department to help translate. Offered a sweet, he took the entire bag and stashed it in his jacket, chuckling. Many years a refugee in Iran, formerly a Peshmerga fighter against Saddam – 'Our revolution started in 1961' – he walked with a stiff, short step, claimed to be 93 but young at heart, claimed to be 19 but mature for his years, laughed often.

All over the Ministries of Culture and Education were pictures of Mustafa Barzani, killed by the Ba'athists, father and predecessor of the current Kurdish Democratic Party (KDP) leader and Governing Council member Masoud. This, the western side of Iraqi Kurdistan, was run by the KDP. The east was controlled by Jalal Talabani's Patriotic Union of Kurdistan (PUK).

The Culture Ministry's 2004 calendar featured Mustafa on the front cover and, youngish, smiling, in January, as well as seated, in military uniform, in June, next to a picture of members voting in the Iraqi Kurdistan National Assembly building, the outside of which was on May's page. Other photos of Kurdish beauty spots and musicians were interspersed with, in March, the bodies on the ground in the aftermath of the chemical attack on Halabja and, for December, a Kurdish man hanged by the neck. Though the picture told an important story, it was hard to imagine you would voluntarily look at it for an entire month.

Anwar said he was grateful to the US for finally getting rid of Saddam but angry as well, for all they did to keep him in power. 'We had weapons from the First World War, old British rifles, and the Ba'athists had all the technology that America gave them.'

He took us to meet the Minister of Education, who seemed to like us well enough because he not only permitted us to go into any schools we liked within the Erbil governorate but also gave us a guide, translator and tour bus from the Ministry.

Chnur, our translator, told us how her family had been forced out of Kirkuk in 1989. They'd been driven from their home into another quarter of the city and later 'dismissed' from the entire area. They were settled in Erbil now, working or in school and, with Kirkuk still dangerous, there were no plans to go home. Relations between Arabs and Kurds were no problem in Kirkuk, she said, but there were still disputes over property that had been seized. We were told it was too dangerous to go and do shows there.

We'd passed through oil-rich Kirkuk on our way to Erbil, the surrounding hills sprinkled with tall thin chimneys spouting bright

Chnur (bottom middle) and her family, with Luis (right rear).

Chnur, me and Khadij.

orange flames, columns of smoke behind the horizon signifying more oil flares farther away. It was not part of the Kurdish autonomous zone demarcated in 1991 and unprotected Kurds in Kirkuk were forced out by Saddam, their former homes given to people from elsewhere in Iraq. Those people, of course, now had nowhere else to go.

It took almost an hour to get to Bistana, a village of about 35 houses and 300 people, with 40 children attending the sand-colored primary school next to the sand-colored mosque. The village had been burned down six times by government forces between 1963 and 1991. Ahmed, the headteacher, and Mr Daoud, our guide from the Directorate of Education, hugged each other as old Peshmerga comrades. All the village men and some of the women had been Peshmerga.

'The kids were shy at the beginning,' Chnur commented afterwards. 'If you go back I think they will eat you.' It was only 40 minutes before the end of their shift when we arrived so we launched straight in, finishing on the dot of 12 as the secondary pupils from all the surrounding villages arrived. Both shifts followed us on foot up to the cemetery for parachute games.

It was the best grassy space in the village, free of mud, with plenty of space. Lots of the graves belong to Peshmerga fighters. 'One woman was burned here,' Chnur told us, 'for helping the Peshmerga.'

You can make the parachute into a dome by all lifting it up, pulling it down behind you and sitting on the edge. Jwan, next to me, in school blouse and skirt, gave me a huge grin, put out her hand to squeeze my arm in excitement.

We filled the hillside with laughter, the men joining in as well, joyfully bouncing the football around the fabric, some unable to work because of wounds from their time in the resistance. They really needed to play like children.

Habitat – the UN agency, not the furniture chain – funded the rebuilding of the houses and they'd been planting trees but still there wasn't enough electricity and the water wasn't clean. What was it like in Baghdad, they wanted to know, compared with up here? I told them about people struggling to get on with things amid traffic jams, explosions, pollution and erratic electricity. There were some explosions here too, they said, in the city, at the political party's buildings. People were frightened in Erbil too, but not here in the villages. They thought Ansar al-Islam were responsible for the 1 February bombings.

We went the slow way home, through the mountains, diving into landscapes of green slopes and clear streams. There were red flowers, still just buds, somewhere between a rose and a poppy, and Chnur said when they open, it's spring. And there was air you could really breathe, cool and soothing.

The federal state of Iraqi Kurdistan

Drums announced the coming of a parade, men and boys, the red, white and green of the Kurdish flag, with a many-pointed gold star in the middle, the placard featuring the murdered Mustafa Barzani. The Kurds had been stateless people in the empires of others more or less for ever – ruled by the Ottomans, the British, the puppets of the British and, until 1991, the Ba'athists. Winston Churchill authorized the use of poison gas to crush their demands for an independent state in the 1920s.

On 8 March 2004, with the signing of the interim constitution, a federal state of Iraqi Kurdistan was created. At last. At long, long last.

Sinan and Selim, English students at Salahudin University in Erbil, stopped me to chat. We talked about the war, why it happened. Kurdistan wasn't the target of much bombing and there were no troops on the streets, no house raids, no detentions without charge, no random shootings. People here knew as little about what was going on in Baghdad and the rest of Iraq as people in Jordan did. It was another country.

'You know Kirkuk?' Selim asked. 'Kirkuk is Kurdish. It is part of Kurdistan, but it was not included in the area that was given to us. Why do you think they did that? Is it because of the oil?'

Sinan shushed him nervously. 'No, Kirkuk is not really Kurdish.'

Selim looked shocked. 'How can you say that Kirkuk is not Kurdish? Well, we are different there.' And although the war ended the sanctions for the Kurdish people, Selim tentatively wondered whether the reason for invasion might have been oil, more than concern for human welfare. They knew nothing about the vast sums of money going to US companies in reconstruction contracts.

Peat muttered to Luis, 'She's talking politics,' and they sneaked around the corner for a cup of tea. A crowd, though, had gathered to watch the novelty of two local men talking to a foreign woman. When the crowd spread to block the teashop entrance its proprietor came out. We shifted to the edge of the pavement and the crowd went on growing. Eventually the police came and dispersed us as a security risk.

Inside the teashop we smoked a narghila and watched the signing of the constitution on TV. The men made no noticeable response to Barzani but laughed at some joke when Talabani walked up to sign. The signing was followed by patriotic songs and footage, a military rhythm accompanied by shots of dramatic scenery, old film of Peshmerga on the march and images of the persecution by the old Iraqi Government. It happened every day, several times a day. Television up here was still government-controlled.

Two shots were fired as we walked home, I suppose in celebration of the new federal state. A whole street of heads turned: all but ours. In Baghdad, no-one looked around at the sound of gunfire. In Baghdad, everyone laughed at you if you did. It was another country.

In the first school we went to on the 9 March, Chnur came out saying there was no place in the school for the show, but not to worry, we could go somewhere else. We were already standing in a big open space that stretched a few hundred meters to the farms and mud brick houses one way, to the horizon the other.

'Here would do.'

The kids gambolled out of tiny classrooms, hardly believing their luck, and the rest of the village crept around desperate to see what was happening but reluctant, for the first little while, to be seen childishly enjoying a kids' show. The girls were fiery: one of them stood up facing Luis in his role as the bullying boss.

'*Bash nia*,' he was insisting. No good. Clowns ought not to be dancing with music boxes instead of sweeping the floor.

'*Bash*,' she replied firmly, not about to be intimidated by any dictator.

When, for the third time, I was in trouble for capering instead of cleaning and Luis was about to explode with fury, another girl stood in front of me, spreading her coat to protect me. We arrived at the second school still in costume, again doing the show outside the school with the whole community gathered round. The teachers had to leave for their afternoon lessons but the kids played with us for ages.

This school opened in 1993 after people came back to the village of Girdesory in 1991. Saddam's army never took the area until they were given helicopters by their foreign backers but the village was then destroyed and the people chased away. Despite the no-fly zone which supposedly protected the Kurds, attacks carried on after 1991 because the village was so near the border with the government-controlled area that it could be bombed from tanks.

Headteacher Muhammad had two wives and 12 children. Mr Daoud from the Ministry, who traveled with us, had two wives and 13 children. At their mother's direction, Rawa, Ahmed and Selim chased the sheep around their pen with much arm waving to position them appropriately for a photo, alternately fussing and persecuting the lamb, yanking his floppy ears in a kind of 'good shepherd, nasty shepherd' routine.

The drive home was bordered on both sides by minefields, marked with red-and-white tape, red triangle flags, small rock piles and white stones. Peat started telling us about landmines, just in case. 'If you ever find yourself in a minefield, never, never retrace your steps. Some are designed to blow up when you step on them, some when you step off and some when the fourth person steps on or off them.'

'So you might have been the third on your way in?'

'Exactly. And some fly up in the air and explode. Then there are the new "intelligent" mines, which give off a radar signal when they're disturbed, like when the minefield is being cleared, which triggers all the other mines in the area to explode or to fly into the air and explode. They're supposed to have a metal ring on them so they can be detected but all the manufacturers make them detachable so they can be taken off before they're planted.'

What kind of twisted mind sits in an office or a boardroom to invent those things, planning that kind of murder, while someone else works out ways around the flimsy export controls? Why aren't those people forced to come out and repair some of the damage, to crawl on their bellies through the mountains and let one child or one mine-clearance worker live instead of them?

The girls and women of Jejnikan

In the village of Jejnikan, four teenage girls sat on rugs by a heater under shimmering chandeliers, minding the children. The oldest granddaughter of the village chief was 14. Silver glitter around her eyes sparkled like the tear she wiped away, explaining that she had never been to school. Her mum and dad had wanted her to go, at least for a few years, but her grandfather hadn't allowed it. Zainab and Ashti had been to school for three and four years respectively.

These days they got up at six, with the rest of the women in the household, to bake bread, then to cook breakfast. Then they would begin cooking lunch and when that was ready and served and cleaned up it was time to start preparing dinner. In between and after there was washing to be done, cleaning, looking after the children.

They weren't allowed to go out and meet with the other women in the village, which was about 70 families strong. They weren't allowed to go to the market. They weren't allowed to watch the television their grandfather had bought the year before so as to watch the war coverage. They weren't allowed beyond the edge of the courtyard to the broad patio where the men sat in the sun. They couldn't read because they weren't allowed to go to school. Liberation never came here. Their dictator didn't flee, wasn't arrested.

They stared at me as if I were a space alien for the first half-hour. They'd never met a foreigner in their lives, much less a female one. Finally one of them found the courage to whisper to Chnur: 'How is she allowed out of her *country*?' They knew, of course, that other women were allowed to leave their houses, even their villages – but their countries?

Everywhere else I'd been in Iraq, I'd been able to mix with the men but allowed to go into the women's places as well, to move between the separate worlds. Not here. Here Chnur, her sister Jwana and I were segregated from the men at the door of the bus and taken out of sight.

We went to Jejnikan to do a show, the second of the day, but the primary school shift was over, the building now populated with teenagers. We were invited for lunch and agreed we'd do a show for the younger kids on a bit of open space afterwards. Chnur asked the exhausted-looking wife of one of the chief's sons whether they'd come out and watch the show.

'No. We would not be allowed.' In the event the men started singing religious songs after lunch, beating a drum, and Mr Daoud decided it was time to go.

Being watched as a clown is fine but being stared at so intently as myself was too uncomfortable so I hid behind faces and bubbles, making the kids laugh. The women, weary, just watched. Zainab and Ashti smiled, laughed a bit with the smaller kids. I started chasing the little ones, going 'Grrr' and pouncing on them, tickling their bellies and bare feet so they squealed and at last the women laughed. They laughed at Kala's face and her yelps as she jumped out of the way, laughed at her pushing her little brothers into my clutches, laughed at the helpless squeaks. I carried on for them not the children. It was the only entertainment they had.

At 14, Arjin was already thinking of marriage. It would come within two years, to a close cousin of her grandfather's choosing. It would be no escape. Grandfather controlled the whole village and the husband would be under direct family control. Her grandmother, one of the two wives, came in bent 90 degrees at the waist, held up with a stick.

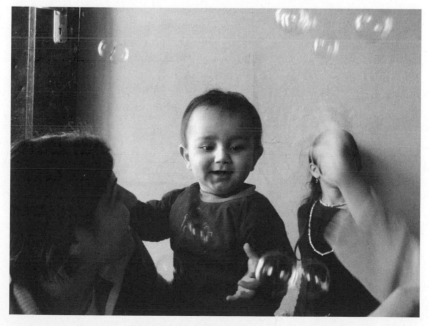

Bubble bliss: Chnur's nephew Roj.

At a message from Mr Daoud, we left them, the young ones following us out as far as they dared, halted at the edge of their world, waving with a longing that almost suffocated me too, trying to smile for us. We left them in the prison of religious and class conservatism where they were losing their minds, the older ones as bent, inside, as the old wife of the chief.

The weight of misery, of boredom in that room weighed on me long after we left, and on Chnur and Jwana too. Their mum, the next day, argued that perhaps the Jejnikan women were happy, fulfilled and satisfied that way but it wasn't true. Life dragged for them; they longed to go to school or even the market. All we could hope was that Grandfather would die before he could marry Arjin off and force the smaller girls out of education; hope that the next patriarch would be better: not liberation, just a more benign dictatorship.

The next day we went to Perpidan where, as ever, Mr Daoud seated himself at the headteacher's desk. Again we were invited for lunch with the chief's family, segregated like the day before. The women teachers, Senur, Banas and Ishtima, came with us. They lived in Erbil and traveled in by bus each day, bringing their children to the village school. One of them asked what I thought about the situation of the women here, in this village. I talked about the women imprisoned in their home in Jejnikan.

'We are related to them. Our aunt is one of the wives of the chief, but it is not so bad here as it is with them,' Kamar said. 'We are allowed to go out and the girls can go to school.' They mentioned that 13-year-old Chanas had been in school and had chosen to leave. 'It is because she is lazy,' her mum and the teachers agreed. Chanas was wearing a long skirt and a blazer, non-traditional clothes that the Jejnikan women were not allowed to own.

There was a television in the room. They asked whether we were going to do the show again, so they could come and see it. At 18, Kamar's daughter was not yet married. It was visibly different from the situation the Jejnikan women were trapped in. Even the air in the room was less oppressive. They laughed. Of course there were still restrictions on their freedom, but it was about a century away from Jejnikan.

The refugee camps

We carried on through the mountains to another school. It, too, was closed in the afternoon. Mr Daoud wanted to keep going, village to village, till we did find an afternoon primary school but we spotted boys sliding down the hillside on metal trays and asked to stay.

'But there are not enough children,' Mr Daoud fretted.

'They will come,' we assured him.

By the time we'd got the tray-sliding boys to help us pull the parachute out of its bag and opened it out, the village telegraph had done its work and a stream was beginning to flow towards us, a crowd of little girls running, kids carrying smaller brothers and sisters, to see the clowns.

Mohammed, too small to join in, stood on the outskirts, clutching a bunch of red flowers, overcome with amazement. A little girl in a gold tinsel dress jumped up and down with the shaking of the parachute, spangling in the spring sunshine; another in a long pink velvet frock, another in a shiny green and black ballgown, three princesses on the hill.

Dara laughed and laughed, his one foot tucked underneath him at a right angle, his missing leg no disability when it came to cat and mouse. Parachute football was harder, trying to grip the fabric when it was being shaken by standing kids around him and he was sitting, or to hold that and his crutches in order to stand up. He gave up and just sat on the fringe of the game until I sat on the ground beside him, playing at his height, and he made the save of the game with his head.

Thursday was a holiday, a celebration of 13 years since the creation of the Kurdish autonomous zone. We went to Chnur's house for lunch with her dozens of sisters. Dilana graduated in geology last year and now worked in the Directorate of Education in the geography department. Jwana was studying law and Dilhosh economics. Senar was in high school and would go to college next year.

You submitted an application stating your course preferences but the Government made the decision, based on your grades and the numbers applying for a given course. You could turn down that offer but it meant going to a lesser college. The brothers, Ari and Ala, at 16 and 13, were the youngest of the family but there were Jwan and Jila too, daughters of one of the married sisters, and baby Roj, 14 months old, petted and cuddled constantly.

Baba, the father of the family, had a piece missing from the top of one ear, indicating that he had been tortured at some point. Luis had brought photos for Chnur to give to Mr Daoud to pass on to some of the teachers and kids we met in the villages. The photo envelope was made out of re-used paper and when someone looked inside it turned out to have a picture of Saddam. The envelope was passed round and everyone looked in. Mama started crying. Just the thought of Saddam, just his picture, was enough.

On the Friday, with all the schools closed, we went to refugee camps. The Iranian refugee camp had been there seven years, since 1997, though some of the residents had fled to Iraq back in 1979. A sign on the wall said 'PDK Iran' – the persecuted Kurdish Democratic Party. UNICEF had given some assistance with the school but mostly they were independent or helped by the Party. The houses were built of stone or breezeblocks, basic but safe and people said there were no problems.

In 1996 an Iranian plane was able to bomb the camp despite the no-fly

zone in force and, in the chaos of the struggle between the KDP and the
PUK a few years ago for control in Iraqi Kurdistan, they were attacked by
Iranian ground forces as well. But now the kids were healthy, there was
water and electricity, it was just like living in any other village. The only
problem was that they couldn't go home.

Almost 10,000 people lived in the Turkish Kurds' refugee camp at
Maxmur. The camp had existed, in different places, since 1979, moved on,
from time to time, by Turkish troops, the Iraqi Government or the UN
High Commission for Refugees (UNHCR). Medya, a German woman
who had lived and moved with the camp since 1994, explained that the
UNHCR forced them to move saying the camp had grown too big for
the organization to provide for them. 'But really the UNHCR is just
controlled by the US military, the same as everything else.'

The last move, to land outside the village of Maxmur, was in 1998
because of attacks by Turkish troops, destroying the camp despite
the 'protection' of the No-Fly Zone, set up to prevent the Iraqi army
attacking the Kurds. There were countless reports of incursions by Turkish
troops into the areas along the border with Iraq's Kurdish zone, in the
conspicuous absence of the usual Allied air patrols.

Speaking Kurdish, like the use of Kurdish names, was not allowed
in Turkey, an ally of Britain and the US, and a favored client for arms
and torture equipment. More recently, after the enactment of dozens
of reform laws aimed at securing European Union membership, the
language had been legalized but still, Medya said, if it was used in public
speeches or approaching elections, anything important, the police were
likely to interrupt and prevent it.

Many thousands of people were still missing, still being imprisoned
for political opinions or party membership. They said they wouldn't go
back because they were scared of the Turkish Government. The reforms
existed on paper only. There was no practical improvement. Lots of them
had nowhere to go back to anyway because their homes and villages had
been destroyed or the grazing lands that used to be their livelihoods were
minefields.

Around the camp, too, there were walls with 'MAG' painted on
them: the Mine Action Group. They'd cleared lots of places but still the
residents said they still heard explosions. Inge, the German doctor who'd
lived at the camp for the last three months, said four children had been
killed recently by unexploded cluster bombs blowing up at the Al-Tash
camp of Iranian Kurdish refugees in Ramadi, in central Iraq.

The biggest health problem, though, was malnutrition, the food ration
being devoid of vitamins and fresh food. The kids didn't eat enough either
because they hated eating the same things every day, the same rice, beans
and flour. Although it rained, the land wasn't fertile. There were no trees

at all when they arrived there and there weren't many still. 'Look,' one of the women pointed at the bare slopes of the mountains behind the camp. 'It is desert.'

There was a water supply for one hour a day and erratic, infrequent electricity. The nearby village had a bit more electricity but there was still only one hour a day when water came out of the taps. That wasn't so bad in winter when it rained as well, but in summer it was a nightmare. It was hot and there was no other source of water. A tank on the hillside supplied water from the river, heavily chlorinated and cloudy.

Infectious diseases, especially typhoid and brucellosis, were rife and malformation of broken bones was common. In addition, Inge said, there were huge psychological problems because of the living conditions, the depression and, for many, many women, the trauma that followed being raped with impunity by Turkish troops.

The women's center had been founded about a year-and-a-half earlier as a venue for education and empowerment of the women. Men were allowed to use the facilities and visit but it belonged to the women. Medya said the women there were very strong. They didn't take any problems from men objecting to their center. 'It took a long time though. They used to ask: "why would you bother sending girls to school, when they are only going to get married and have babies?"'

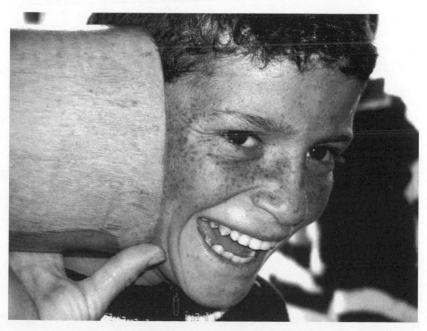

Nuredi, hearing music for the first time ever.

A young woman walked through in tight jeans, another one in the balloon-like trousers worn by Kurdish men and a slim-fitting long-sleeved top. I hadn't seen women in those clothes anywhere else and Medya said you didn't see it anywhere else in the camp. 'Here is a sanctuary.'

The center held classes in music, English, writing, women's health and so on. A group called Mothers For Peace met there, a row of women with deeply lined faces who had lost sons or brothers and were sick of war and repression. They shook hands with the circus lads and kissed me on both cheeks, four, five, six kisses: the circus was welcome. Within the camp they visited the lonely ones, took part in the general organization of the place, but they were part of a wider Mothers For Peace network as well.

Within the center a boy's eyes sparkled with joy and tears. For the first time in the 11 years of his life, a refugee for all of them, Nuredi was hearing music, holding Luis's didgeridoo to his ear. He was profoundly deaf but the vibrations from the instrument were detectable to him and a huge smile of disbelief and delight lit up his bright brown eyes, amid the freckles and sunburned nose, and didn't leave him the rest of the day.

We'd arrived unannounced because it was hard to contact the camp, so a loudspeaker announced that at two o'clock there would be a show for the kids on the stage. The steps filled immediately with children, waiting an hour to see what was going to happen.

We started out on a huge stage at the front of a concrete amphitheater, a thousand or so children yelling 'Boomchucka' back at us. Bit by bit the stage got smaller as the disbelieving kids pushed closer, till we were performing in a broom cupboard-sized gap, one of the doorways onto the stage completely closed off by the crowd.

There was no translator to do the usual pie-in-the-face act so we improvised, Fisheye and I plotting conspicuously, getting Luis, the bullying clown, to hold Peat as he juggled, believing that Peat was the target of the pie. Just as the pie began its arc, Peat dropped a ball and the pie got Luis. The kids howled with laughter, Luis howled with rage, we all ran away, the pie foam went everywhere and we had to sit in the Cultural Center behind the stage for ten minutes while they persuaded the kids that it was the end.

The Cultural Center's walls were hung with banners quoting Ocalan, the imprisoned leader of the Turkish Kurds. 'Without victory, there is no life for the Kurdish people.' His words were on the walls of the women's center and the youth center as well. They spoke the Kurmanji dialect of Turkish Kurds rather than the Sorani spoken by the local population. They also ran on Turkish time, an hour behind the surrounding villages.

The refugee camp looked permanent enough, like any other village. The houses were made of bricks and stones. A couple even had satellite dishes on poles, for when the electricity was on. There were a couple of shops, one selling clothes, one with fruit and vegetables, a cigarette stall. Women gathered between the houses, one standing knitting beside a younger one baking bread in the fire barrel. About 3,000 pupils were enrolled in the schools, one primary, one secondary. Some families had moved to Mosul, but even if they could afford to move out, a lot of people preferred to stay, to be in a place which was more like home.

There weren't many jobs in the camp. A few people had found jobs in Mosul lately, about an hour-and-a-half away, depending on checkpoints. There were dozens of checkpoints so it could take longer, could be impossible, but it was easier than it used to be when the KDP and PUK were fighting each other.

An eight-year-old girl stood watching us in the women's center after the show, too shy to come to us but too spellbound to leave. Woodbine the racoon charmed her and she wanted to learn how to make him wriggle and jump, shyness forgotten as she posed in Peat's sunglasses and his baseball cap with its peak sideways. Her name was Tekoshin – Resistance. Over the last few days we'd met several little girls called Kurdistan as well.

After our last show in Kurdistan the river sparkled as boys waded across with their schoolbooks and bags. Birds were building nests in the pits in the side of a building. Mela drove the bus into the mountains. He knew a place where you could stand on the crest of the hill, wildflowers tumbling

Tekoshin.

down purple and red and white between the white painted stones marking the graves, down to the rectangular plot of land the farmer was plowing with a tractor while the cows chewed idly.

The kids and women came out to see us, Khadij in a long purple dress and black headscarf playing Luis's didgeridoo, a woman with hair gray before its time from raising too many children and losing her husband, her face alight as she remembered what it felt like to play. And here and there, in the soil, empty shells lay half buried like a reminder of the battles between the rival parties, 1994 to 1999. 'It was shameful,' Chnur said.

It was spring. No place, no moment, had ever seemed so charmed and I felt like the luckiest, free-est woman alive. The refugees at Maxmur and the imprisoned women in Jejnikan couldn't see this: despite 'liberation', despite the fledgling federal state, despite Kurdish autonomy, freedom hadn't come to them. Autonomy hadn't come to them. Spring hadn't come to them.

17

CIRCUS IN THE SOUTH

March 2004

A sign on the wall opposite said 'Idle Association Thi Qar'. Thi Qar is the southern governorate which includes the city of Nasariya. The road in front of the Idle Association was closed off every morning by a couple of vehicles of Italian troops, dark blue *carabinieri* in tight trousers and sunglasses, smoking cigarettes out of the roof hatches, a few more on foot and some Iraqi police, while hundreds of unemployed – or idle – men gathered outside looking for work.

Next door on the other side of the hotel was the police station. Within a minute of walking out the front door we were accosted by an Iraqi police officer whose superior then told us we couldn't walk down that road. Why not? Because it's dangerous. Go back to your hotel and stay there. Don't walk anywhere.

Less than an hour in Nasariya and I was already being sent to my room. Disobediently we carried on past the hotel door and into town. The hotel manager said it was safe to walk anywhere in Nasariya. As ever, people were curious, friendly, protective, asking were we Italian, what were we doing here and did we want chai. In the streets of Baghdad you didn't see a lot of unarmed foreigners but in the south we were a rarity.

Another time police came over to the bench we were sitting on outside a teashop and asked what we were doing. I held up my glass of tea and stated the obvious. They demanded our passports. 'It's in the hotel,' I lied, because otherwise they'd wander off with it, pass it around, find things to ask pointless questions about. 'Is there a problem?' No, the first one conceded, eventually, there was no problem, except that by now his colleague was eyeballing the men on the bench and had to be coaxed away.

In the playground between the hotel and the shops there was a hand-turned big wheel with all its pods hanging off at awkward angles, a peeling eagle standing guard in the entrance. The streets were filled with heaps of rubbish, festering in the heat, emitting clouds of black flies when a child or a flock of sheep trampled through. A toddler stood in one, picking at the bits and pieces, raising a piece of pipe to his open mouth as he gawped at our passing. As everywhere, there were children selling things between the cars.

A child called Mustafa claimed us and became very particular about whom he would share us with. We were his friends, he said, but he really meant we were his territory: there was a point in the road where he always started asking us for money. He waved at the troops as their vehicles passed but then told us all the things he didn't like about them. He just waved because then sometimes they gave him sweets.

The big roundabout in town was surrounded with teashops where the men sat smoking and playing dominoes. You didn't see the women at all unless they were hurrying from shop to shop, fully covered. People stared as if they'd never seen a woman smoking a narghila before and in all probability they hadn't, at least in public. After long hot days of work I didn't care though. Let people stare – I wanted narghila.

Passing the water pipe between us, we met a man called Yousef who said things were better now Saddam was gone but he didn't trust Blair and Bush either and didn't like the Italian troops. He thought they were arrogant, rude and treated people harshly. Worried about offending me, he added that he was sure the British soldiers in Basra were better.

Nobody was fighting the soldiers down here though, Raheem* said, even if no-one actually had a good word to say about them. People just wanted to get on with things, to live in peace. Raheem was a water engineer by profession, who taught English to subsist in the meantime. War Child, who'd organized things for us in the south, had introduced us to Raheem and we'd employed him as a translator.

Raheem said about a million people lived in Nasariya, but he called it a small town where everyone knew each other. Certainly everyone knew Faisal, a man with Down's Syndrome. Delighted to meet strangers, he stopped to say hello while the young man with him tugged at his hand, a bit embarrassed. Another time we were smoking a narghila on the roundabout and he stopped, in kaffiyeh and dishdasha, no-one to chivvy him along this time, and sang us a song. People teased him a bit but I didn't see anyone being cruel to him as so often happened in Baghdad.

Everyone would soon know us too: the first couple of shows were in schools in the center of town and also on that evening's local television. Plenty of the kids were not in school any more, like Duha and Wafaa, two wild-haired little girls in sparkly frocks who accompanied us to the internet center, but they'd heard the stories from the other children.

---

* This is a pseudonym, as are most other names in this chapter: many people in the south are afraid to have their real names used.

The first school was all girls, really excited girls. Most of the teachers were women and also really excited. I was bombarded with questions, trapped in the toilet while they all asked at once about the circus, England, me, everything. Though only March, in the south it was already getting too hot for shows and games in the school playgrounds. A couple of the older girls crept away from the audience to peep around the door where I was getting ready for my next bit and sneaked me away to their classroom upstairs, where you could sit in the shade and see over the crowd.

The second school was all boys. It was looted after the war and though

The music box routine always went down a storm.

things were better there was still a void where the chairs and tables and books ought to have been. We had to cut the show short because the parents were outside waiting to collect the kids. They came even if it was only a short walk home because of security worries and equally the women were scared to be standing waiting. The third school was very poor, a few kilometers out of town, the playground guarded by armed police, no pictures on the wall except the Ayatollah Sistani.

It was strange: some people would tell you there were no problems even as they stood among a load of armed guards thought to be necessary as protection. Raheem was one of those. His wife, Safiya, taught at the fourth school we worked in, where his eight-year-old daughter Azhar was a pupil. While I was off stage, Ana, the PE teacher, came in to talk to me. There were bits I couldn't understand so I asked Raheem to translate for me the problems she was talking about.

'No, no,' he said smiling. 'There are no problems in this school.'

Ana contradicted him with a litany of difficulties much the same as every school faced. There were not enough books, the few textbooks were out of date; there were no teaching materials, no art materials, no pictures on the bare walls; there was not enough furniture; there was no running water at school so the children brought water in bottles from home while the teachers brought flasks because the children couldn't carry as much as they needed for a hot day.

Ana did the security patrols around the school. 'In front here, always I get bad words shouted at me, even here.' A lot of teachers had been attacked, threatened and killed throughout the country. 'Because they are free now they can do anything. If the school says we do not have room for your child, or if the child fails the exams and has to stay another year in the class, sometimes the family come with the gun and make the teacher change it.'

Raheem said it was safe to walk on the streets. Ana said no, women don't go out on the streets unless we have to, and Safiya agreed. Raheem declared that there were no health problems. Ana told me she got typhoid from unclean water. A lot of the children were depressed, she said, and the women were very, very tired. Again Safiya agreed. Raheem wanted to focus on the positive, to show other people the positive. Saddam was gone and that, for him, was enough to outweigh any other problems.

People started off by only telling you the good things, giving you the positive. Alex, from War Child, explained it was because they didn't want you to leave. It only lasted until they were sure you were going to stay. After that they started telling you about the problems, both those which had carried over from the old days and the new set. Nasariya was badly bullied and badly neglected by the old government. Sattar, our driver, spent two years and four months in jail for being part of the 1991 uprising against Saddam before being released as part of a general amnesty.

Ana said she didn't expect or want the rights of women in other countries, just security, just a government. 'We are religious,' she said. Safiya, though, said when there were no men around, she liked to take off her hijab and abaya and do cartwheels.

The only international NGOs working in Nasariya at that time were War Child and the International Medical Corps. There were a couple of others in Amara and a few in Basra but over the next couple of months almost all would pull out their non-Iraqi staff. War Child ran a bakery, employing several people to bake bread each day for thousands of people through a couple of hospitals, some orphanages and other avenues for reaching poor people. They were planning to open a street kids' drop-in center, among other projects.

Nasariya was tangibly more conservative than Baghdad, Alex said. All the alcohol shops in Nasariya were targeted and closed down. She also told us to watch out for the landmines in the garden. Even the young boys there, from about nine or ten years old, started out by shouting sexual insults and suggestions before they found out I could actually understand them and then they came and chatted.

Laughter in the old Ba'ath Party building

There was a youth center in every town in Thi Qar province, run by the Ministry of Youth and Sport, every one exactly the same, from the basketball hoops in the yards to the layout of the rooms and backstage area. The only difference between the stages in each of the identical theaters was the precise location of the holes in the floor underneath the standard burgundy carpet. Qala Al-Suka had one sewing machine, two computers, a sparse library and, alongside the basketball hoop, a lone football goal frame, denuded of its net. In each of the first two, Al-Nasur and Al-Rifa'ie, about 130 kids, mostly boys, used the center each day after school.

'This was a Ba'ath Party building. The girls have never been in this hall before,' Nafi'a said by way of explanation for the ones who burst into tears and went and hid. 'Only three girls use the youth center and they only come for sewing lessons.' For the last couple of weeks she'd been visiting the girls' schools and talking to their parents, reassuring and negotiating for them to be able to come and see the show. Still she was surprised at how many were allowed to come.

'Some of these girls, I have not seen them smile since the war and today they were laughing. It makes me think there is still hope.' Nafi'a was the computer teacher for the center, which had two machines. She was well respected in the community for her honesty which was why she'd managed to persuade the parents to let their daughters come to the show. The center manager, less popular with the staff and community, was known as 'Little Saddam' and was reluctant to let the girls use the facilities at all.

The girls, as always, were excited to see a woman in the show, like the women who worked there, mostly as cleaners and cooks, clustered at the back of the room. Nafi'a was hoping the show would be a precursor to more of the girls coming regularly. There was nothing else for them apart from school. There was some kind of plague that claimed them around 11 or 12 years old. They disappeared.

A lot of them had very poor co-ordination and spatial awareness because the physical side of their development was neglected. They didn't get to run around and become aware of their bodies and the space around them and consequently they had trouble even with things like writing, arranging things in a room, stacking stuff against a wall, convinced that it wouldn't fit in the space available. The kids in the kindergartens, even,

Preparing for play: Fisheye Sam, Jo and Luis.

were developmentally delayed by the lack of activities and materials. They just sat in rows with their hats on while the teacher talked.

War Child had just received a grant to raise the standards in all eight youth centers in Thi Qar. Nafi'a said she'd been thinking of leaving because of Little Saddam but now that new resources were coming she'd stay, otherwise the stuff would just disappear. Besides, the girls might not be allowed to come back if she left. It wasn't just about giving the kids something better to imagine than guns and bombs, it was also about bringing hope to the adults who lived and worked with them.

The director of Al-Rifa'ie came and whispered nervously to Raheem, whose eyebrows shot up in alarm. 'There is an important religious man here,' he said and launched into a list of things we mustn't do in case we offended him.

They were worried the kids might jostle him and make him angry, worried that a woman on stage with uncovered hair might provoke him. He crept out a little before the end, still laughing, leaving a message thanking us for coming, for making the kids happy: the official approval of the Sistani camp.

Later, in the hotel, we met Azzam, working with an international group on the re-flooding of the marshes. An Italian consultant and a French engineer were among the experts training Iraqi workers to break the dams which were responsible for the draining of 80 per cent of the marshes between 1991 and 1997.

Azzam left Iraq for the US years ago and continued opposing Saddam through a group called the Iraq Foundation, a human rights organization. His uncle used to get arrested every couple of weeks. His jailers would phone Azzam so he could hear his uncle being tortured, and would beg him to stop his political activity. Azzam refused. 'I did not want to let them intimidate me and if I gave in then next, well, probably about 99 per cent of people did give in and keep quiet.

'Now my uncle won't speak to me. I have lost that relationship. But I had to carry on. I did not want to have to do everything under a pseudonym like some people did. Maybe that's why he won't speak to me – because I did not protect him.' He said he hated war but couldn't see any other way of getting rid of Saddam. For him, none of it mattered now Saddam was gone.

Those of Nasariya's press that we met consisted of a friendly group of men who were also actors, directors, filmmakers, academics and writers. What began as a press conference around a long table ended with an exchange of ideas. Mr Yassir was a drama director and a founder member of the Nasariya Group for Acting, set up 12 years ago to produce drama in the city. He wanted to make links with drama groups and theater companies in Britain, was setting up a puppetry programme for the children over the summer and hoped to increase the output of the Acting Group.

Mr Ahmed was a cinematist; Mr Amir, a translator and linguist, interested in the relationship between words and democracy. His most recent article was about the need for people – the population as well as politicians – to use precise expressions, in order to build democracy, to say exactly what they meant and be clearly understood rather than using the vague and emotive language favored by the old regime. I told him words had been turned on their heads in Britain too – separated from their original meanings and spliced together into unspecific phrases which served the Government's propaganda plans.

Mr Haider was head of PR for Nasariya University, which had just had a new computer center installed, one of six in the city courtesy of the South Korean Government. The center made it possible to establish links with universities in other countries for the existing colleges of education, science and arts and the two new colleges, of medicine and engineering, which would open in the next academic year.

Yassir said his seven-year-old son Ammar had seen our show at his school. 'He talked about you the whole day and he does not only talk. He tries to imitate the clowns. Always when you give the children things to draw with, their pictures have tanks and aeroplanes and guns in, but now he is drawing pictures of clowns.'

Our last show in Nasariya was at the old aluminum factory compound where War Child's overseas workers and dozens of families lived. Just before the show, an old man outside started haranguing Luis and the kids, trying to send the children home, telling Luis to go away: 'You've got nothing to do here. You're Jewish. You're all Jewish. Go home.' It seemed that was the first assumption about every NGO and every foreigner.

The kids, though, loved the show and the parachute games that followed, despite being a bit squashed between the house and the empty swimming pool. The football pitch was too dusty for shaking a parachute on, the grumpy old man had scared the kids from the road outside and the garden was off limits because of the aforementioned landmines.

There were 39 political parties in Nasariya by late March 2004 and a significant split between the followers of Sistani and al-Sadr. Sistani apparently commanded the more support; al-Sadr commanded a militia brigade. Sistani, though, was an old man: 'We will only have him for a short while,' Raheem said. 'It all depends who takes over from him.'

Samawa

We moved on to Samawa, about 120 kilometers north of Nasariya, where at sunset swallows dived among the washing lines and satellite dishes on the flat roofs. It was also at sunset that the market came to life, dead chickens lying in trays, the insides of half sheep hanging in doorways, pungent fish and bags of sour yoghurt and cheese curd, cages of pigeons, fruit and vegetables, a tea stall here and there between clusters of stalls or shops all selling the same thing, a whole row of trays of eggs, a few selling buckets and hoses, a few selling stationery.

The taxis were the same as everywhere, white with orange panels, and the fire engines with 'Sides' printed on the sides, front and back. All the women were in black from head to foot, yet there were headscarves of every color in the market.

Peat got one of the black things that wraps around the head to hold the kaffiyeh, the men's head covering. It only led to trouble though because when he and Luis went for a narghila later, they got arrested and dragged away by four police with guns. Apparently someone reported that there were funny-looking foreigners in town, one of them wearing his kaffiyeh like a terrorist.

A man from the hotel called Akeel offered to come with me to get them out of the police station, where there was also a big bucket of cold beers seized from 'Ali Baba'. He promised to show Peat how to wear the kaffiyeh the non-terrorist way. How considerate of the terrorists to adopt a different way of dressing so as to protect other people from suspicion.

It was the second time in a day that the police had come to take us away, the first being outside the Department of Youth and Sport. They took Peat and Fisheye because they wanted to watch the film on Fisheye's camera, drove them to the police station, gave them tea, didn't notice that Fisheye was still filming and let them go again. They had to check up on all the foreigners, find out who they were and what they were doing.

Apparently the police down here once picked up three Dutch soldiers and kept them in the cells overnight. It was impossible to imagine the Baghdad police doing the same with a group of US troops.

The Dutch soldiers walked around otherwise unmolested in small groups on patrol. The Japanese soldiers I only saw in vehicles. Sabir, our translator and host in Samawa, remarked as they passed, 'They are afraid of the Iraqi people.' In Nasariya, the first guess on nationality was Italian. Here people asked if you were Japanese or Dutch. In Baghdad, for some reason, the first assumption was that you were Russian, then American. Either way, it felt much safer in Samawa than Baghdad, much quieter. There were no bombs at that time. A bit of gunfire, as in Erbil, had everyone looking out of their front doors. It was to change in a matter of weeks but nobody knew that yet.

Our street was sectioned by ditches of dirty water, the kids hopping over them, the cars slowing down to bounce through. A footbridge across the Euphrates was partly collapsed and people picked their way carefully across. The main urban center in Muthanna province, Samawa had only about half a million people, mostly Shi'a, and you were quickly out of the urban area.

On the roads to the rural youth centers we went to each afternoon were small groups of men carrying vivid green, red and black flags. They were walking to Kerbala from all over the south for the end of the mourning for the Imam Hussein. Tents of all sizes, surrounded by the same colors, offered food and rest for the pilgrims. Cars hooted in support as they passed. Mr Abu Zina tutted at the continued playing of the devotional music in Salam's car on the way to a school: 'Ashura is over,' he pointed out, apparently tired of the chanting and crashing of cymbals to mark the time for chest beating.

Again the youth centers were each used by about a hundred boys and no girls, with no facilities for anything except sport. One day about three girls, another day about nine, made little rows at the back of the theater. A family of swallows had made its nest at the front and left a pile of turd on the stage, swooping in and out of the absent windows. The day before that there had been no theater, only an unfeasibly hot tarmac games court with boys playing basketball barefoot and a crowd of non-participants leaning in the shade.

There were coaches for basketball, volleyball, handball and football, one of them the sports teacher from the boys' school, who volunteered the information that his father had died a month ago. The manager, one of three albino men I met in as many days in Samawa, looked shocked at my asking whether any girls used the centers.

The girls were in the fields either side of the road with the women, picking stuff in rows, carrying it down the dirt tracks. It was notable for its rarity when two women came into the internet center and talked to Fisheye after he did some magic tricks. Conservatism and fear mixed thickly to hide the girls and women away.

One morning we were supposed to be performing in a big sports hall on the edge of town but there were no children. The school heads had said there was no way they could take their pupils there: it was too dangerous to walk them through the streets. So instead we went to them, to a school of about 600 girls. Through the gates, as we got ready in the headteacher's office, came a constant stream of boys from their school nearby, two by two, holding hands, until the original crowd had doubled, the visitors packed into the balconies around the inside so it looked like the kids were all crammed into shelves bordering the yard.

We did manage to do the stadium show though, with a school full of girls jammed into the stands. The headteacher told them before the show to be quiet and keep still. It lasted a couple of minutes before we got them shouting and laughing, all leaning forward together when they yelled.

Much quieter, in fact our quietest show yet, was at a school for deaf and dumb children. We left out the 'boomchucka' but the advantage of a non-language-based show was that it was quite easy to adapt for people who couldn't hear us. They still laughed out loud though and did the gasp of amazement when Fisheye showed them the multicolored pictures that had magically appeared in his coloring book.

There were 71 pupils aged up to 12, after which there was nothing for them in Samawa. They studied the same primary school curriculum as all other Iraqi schools, using lip reading and sign language. The headteacher was keen to communicate with teachers of deaf children outside Iraq so as to improve their methods of working with the kids.

It is yet another of Iraq's tragedies that disabled children cannot be helped to reach their full potential. Girls tend to remain in orphanages all their lives. When boys reach their mid-teens, they become too heavy for orphanage workers to lift or too old for a children's home and there are then only two places for them to go: the street or the mental hospital.

On the street they are unprotected and destitute in a country where it's thought best to throw stones at anyone who seems 'subnormal'. In the hospital they are children, often with enormous capacity to learn, to love, to grow, locked up, stopped up, halted in the company of old men who have been there a lifetime, with no teachers and no future.

In Samawa's school for the deaf there were no other activities or arts, although the school was in a better state than a lot we'd seen, with pictures on the walls, running water and carpet. The Dutch military had embarked on a lot of school rehabilitation, but there were still no facilities for making food or for sick pupils, which means there were a lot of deaf children in the area who weren't going to the school because they wouldn't be well enough looked after.

Sabir had had four contracts from the Dutch military for school rehabilitation. He didn't have much time for the likes of Bechtel, taking contracts at inflated prices, siphoning off the money and doing the work badly, but he was more irritated still with the translators working for the Dutch army, who he said were diverting the contracts to their own relatives and friends.

'Some of these girls, I have not seen them smile since the war and today they were laughing.'

The previous day a contract worth $91,000 had been given to the translator's brother, a 19-year-old with no experience as a building contractor or engineer. The contracts brought good money and the translators knew they could get away with securing them for their own families, even when they weren't professionals. A civil engineer with 20 years of experience, Sabir felt aggrieved and wanted to challenge the decision in court.

I was dubious that there were any processes through which he could challenge it, any system of judicial review for procedural impropriety, any appeals system, any oversight. Sure enough, when I saw him later, he said the court had not been able to do anything.

All the same, Sabir said that everything was better now that Saddam was gone. He didn't care how long foreign troops stayed or what they took, he said, or who ran the country as long as the Ba'athists were gone. He had spent four months in jail in the security police headquarters in 1994 – he showed us the scar on his ankle where a cigarette had been put out. He pointed out the jail where he'd been held. 'I burned it with my own hands,' he said, miming striking a match.

The men and women in jail now without charge, trial, lawyers, without their families knowing their whereabouts, were, he insisted, all from Falluja, Ramadi or Tikrit. Nothing would convince him that there were detainees from anywhere else in Iraq, nor that merely to be from those places was not a valid reason for arrest. Everyone from those three towns was directly oppressing the people of the south, he said.

Basra

Basra started suddenly, as we approached from Samawa. On one side of the railway tracks there was nothing but desert, immense trails of oil tankers oozing along the highway, similar-sized hordes of camels trudging the other way, the Japanese troop carriers on the way out of Samawa giving way to British ones further south.

On the other side were houses, densely packed, expanding to fill all available space, washing and children and bricks erupting out of them. The central reservation, pavements and part of the road were covered with stuff for sale, old kitchenware, old clothes, old electrical goods, like a giant drive-through garage sale. After a while, stalls selling new goods started to intersperse and in a while we reached the center of the city.

Security was getting worse in Basra, people said, as unemployment rose, electricity remained erratic, and political power struggles dragged on. There had been a few attacks on British troops in recent days as frustration and the heat intensified. The soldiers used to walk the streets, much less under fire than the ruder Americans, but had stopped since the sniper incidents started.

Explosions, people said, were daily now. Kidnappings of contractors were on the increase. Security firms were making things worse by calling themselves NGOs because they thought it was safer for them. They traveled armed and created uncertainty about what it meant to be an NGO, exposing genuine NGOs to increased risk.

Reem just wanted to leave. She had lived in Cardiff (Wales) for ten years while her dad was studying for a PhD in civil engineering. What's wrong with Iraq? I asked. She pointed at the headscarf on my lap. 'That's one thing,' she said. 'I don't wear it. I won't.' In Samawa women had been threatened for not covering their hair. Not here, Reem said. 'They just whisper and point, but I am defiant. I drive a car as well.'

A computer engineer from a Shi'a family, she wanted to get a scholarship for a postgraduate degree in Britain and escape from Iraq for a while. Her dad would let her leave if it was to take up a scholarship, she thought. He wouldn't go back to Britain himself though: 'He says he likes being able to say hello to everyone in the street.'

Our first show had to be canceled. The newly opened play space set up by the Italian NGO Intersos was suffering the effects of the power wrangling. The sheikh who lived and ruled nearby thought he ought to have control over everything: he had tried to get all his friends and relations jobs in the center and to have the teachers fired.

Instead our first Basra performance was in another school for deaf and dumb children. Rehabilitated by Save the Children after a comprehensive post-war looting, the school catered for 119 children altogether. From the show in the deaf school in Samawa, we'd learned that though they couldn't hear, the kids still recognized and responded to noise and to variations in noise, so we made lots.

Luis's didgeridoo was a big favorite again and instead of communal shouting, they signed approval and disapproval in unison, very politely suggesting that I on my stilts ought to give back Luis's hat when he started to howl. A little girl called Hanaan took on translating, signing for the kids less adept at lip reading. The headteacher told us at the end that she'd never seen the kids so animated.

In the old days, a teacher called Ali said, deaf people were singled out for special persecution because they were harder to control. Using sign language, they couldn't be listened to the way everyone else could and the security police couldn't tell whether they were up to something or not. They weren't allowed to wear hearing aids because Saddam thought they might be secret communication devices and people shunned them, even taxi drivers wouldn't stop for them, for fear of being implicated. In times of war they were tortured to make sure they couldn't scream properly, to make sure they really were deaf and mute. This said, when I told him this later in Baghdad, Zaid said his brother-in-law was deaf and had worn a hearing aid since he was a small child. 'No-one has ever told him you cannot wear it. None of this happened to him. Perhaps it was only in the south.'

The next new challenge was a show for blind children and orphans in the Ministry of Social Affairs. One of the women working in the Ministry showed me a booklet of phrases and quotations which formed an exercise for teaching English, including a line about how it's possible to look without seeing, to listen without hearing. It reminded me that the reverse is also true: the deaf kids heard us through some other sense. We didn't know how the blind children would see us, how they used other senses to compensate, so we did exactly the same show we always did.

A boy of about 12 with a scarred face looked intently into the top corner of the room. His friend beside him had one eye which hardly opened at all and another which was fixed, the pupil rolled back so it was barely visible. The two sat with arms around each other's shoulders, laughing frequently and turning sometimes to hug one another. Two little girls whispered in each other's ears for the entire show, giggling.

It was different. They loved the boomchuckas at the beginning and, again, the didgeridoo. They understood and enjoyed the music box routine. The juggling was a little lost on them, but the excitement of the kids from the orphanage who could see infused the whole atmosphere. Again their teachers said they could hardly believe the effect the show had on them.

When they left, the children walked in clusters, arms around each other, the almost-blind leading the blind. Not one of them had so much as a stick to guide them. Eman said the kids at the corresponding institution in Baghdad had sticks but here there was nothing. There was a little teaching and a new project to teach them some gymnastics, but no real resources.

Outside, Rafaa watched her boy, Abdullah, laughing at Fisheye's magic tricks. In English she told me his father was dead. 'They cut off his head,' she said. 'Saddam cut off his head.' It was in 1991, after the uprising, when Abdullah was a baby. She'd brought the kids up alone since then.

One of the men outside wanted to talk about the British troops. I was curious, because in Baghdad they believed that the British troops were much better than the US ones, much more polite, fairer. 'Noss oo noss,' was his opinion: so-so. The Spanish and Japanese soldiers were good, he thought, in Samawa and elsewhere in the south. 'The Americans...' He made a brushing away gesture with his hands. 'No. No good.' He said he was glad Saddam was gone, but he wasn't sure things were better now. Human rights were not respected and the soldiers still caused many problems.

Basra had thousands of displaced people living in camps. The bombing in 1991 had destroyed countless houses. In the mid-1990s a movement had formed to overthrow Saddam. The young men had been arrested and killed, their homes burned in punishment. The latest bombing had made still more people homeless. The biggest city outside Baghdad, Basra had also seen an influx from the smaller and poorer towns and cities in the south.

Suad worked in the logistics department at Save the Children. She used to work in the community participation program and preferred that but left because she believed that one of her superiors was acting dishonestly. Before that she was in the IDP (Internally Displaced People) team at Save the Children but the program had come to an end when its funding stopped. As with IDPs throughout the country, no-one was responsible for them and no-one had funding to look after them. There were moves to evict them from a lot of the squats and compounds where they were living without services, but no real alternative housing on offer.

Like Samawa, Basra's 'youth center' was a sports club for boys with a theater for religious lectures. Two girls came in, hidden behind the abayas of mothers who worked there as cleaners. When I sat down to take off my stilts, Suad came to bring me a message. 'There is a little girl there who was really happy to see you. She told me to tell you she loves you, but she was too shy to come and say it.' In the end, though, Suha did come and chat.

Suad said life was better for women in Basra than elsewhere in the south. A bigger city, close to the border with Kuwait and to Iraq's only port, it had been more influenced by the people passing through and women were freer, could find work more easily and walk about more safely, though she still couldn't smoke a narghila in public. Nevertheless since the war she and her friends were afraid to walk outside, afraid of kidnapping, violence, robbery. Like everywhere, 'security' was the first concern, the first word on every woman's lips.

Suad was clever, funny, gorgeous, cheeky. She, her sister and another

On my stilts at the school in Samawa.

woman ran an organization called Women for Peace and Democracy. 'I don't like the word democracy in the name but my sister insisted,' Suad explained. Her sister said you got more money for projects with the word 'democracy' or 'democratization' in the title and it was true. Their funding so far had come from different sources including the CPA. They didn't like it but didn't have much choice.

Women's Centers were the CPA's latest thing. Funding was very much determined by what donors wanted to be seen supporting, not by what was needed on the ground, so all the funding was for 'democratization'. If, like the post-traumatic stress program in Baghdad, a project couldn't remodel itself to include that then its funding was cut. Likewise there was money for projects in the marshes because they were politically fashionable but much less for the other towns and villages in the province where there was more malnutrition and poverty.

'Democratization' meant teaching people, women particularly, about voting and why it was important. The local women didn't use the CPA's Women's Centers, Suad said, apparently seeing them as Western-imposed things with no relevance to their lives. Meanwhile women's rights were getting worse and conservatism was tightening its hold. Women had been receiving specific threats for being seen without abayas and head-coverings, even for wearing ones that weren't black.

Suad's group had been running computer classes, first for housewives and then for women in unskilled jobs with little education, to improve their prospects. Later they started English and literacy classes as well as providing clothes and abayas for poor women in rural areas, which helped them feel able to go out. The classes were full immediately they were advertised. 'You couldn't do that in Nasariya or Amara,' Suad said. 'The women would want to go but they wouldn't be allowed and you would find the classroom empty every week.'

They did it quite quietly, underfunded and undernoticed, but these women set the world on fire, Suad and Reem in Basra and Nafi'a in Thi Qar, fighting for their Iraq, for their women and girls.

On our last day in the south we watched TV pictures of four mercenaries from Blackwater Security, shot, burned, mutilated and dragged through the streets of Falluja. We drove back to a tense and uncertain Baghdad, where the rest of the clowns said their goodbyes and left on the last morning – though we didn't know it yet – that it would be possible to drive past Falluja on the highway to Jordan before US forces laid siege to the town.

18

FALLUJA

10-16 April 2004

Trucks, oil tankers, tanks are burning on the highway west to Falluja. A stream of boys and men goes to and from a lorry that's not burnt, stripping it bare. We turn onto the back roads through Abu Ghraib, Nuha and Ahrar singing in Arabic, past the vehicles full of people and a few possessions, heading in the other direction, past the improvised refreshment posts along the way where boys throw food through the windows into the bus for us and for the people still inside Falluja.

It's 10 April. The bus is following a car containing the nephew of a local sheikh and Ghareeb,* who has contacts in Falluja and has cleared this with them. The reason I'm on the bus is that Ghareeb and Lee, a British journalist, turned up at my door at about 11 o'clock at night telling me how desperate things were in Falluja. They'd been bringing out children with their limbs blown off and US soldiers were going around telling people to leave by dusk or be killed. But then when people fled with whatever they could carry, they were being stopped at the US military checkpoint on the edge of town and not let out, trapped, watching the sun go down.

Ghareeb and Lee said aid vehicles and the media were being turned away. They said our friend Dr Salam had been in Falluja trying to help with casualties and had come back with a bullet wound. During a declared ceasefire two ambulances went out to pick up the injured. The first was hit by a missile from a plane. Dr Salam and his colleagues were pinned inside the second by gunfire and could only watch as those in the first burned to death.

They said there was some medical aid that needed to go in and there was a better chance of its getting there with foreigners, Westerners, to get

---

* In my original blog about Falluja, I called Ghareeb 'Azzam' and otherwise disguised his identity, for his security. A few months later he was killed returning from a similar trip into Najaf during conflict there, when the Italian Enzo Baldoni was kidnapped. Ghareeb is itself a nickname, meaning 'Strange' but that is how he was known.

through the American checkpoints. The rest of the way was secured by the armed groups who control the roads we'd travel on. We'd take in the medical supplies, see what else we could do to help and then use the bus to bring out people who needed to leave.

I'll spare you the whole decision-making process, all the questions we asked ourselves and each other, and you can spare me the accusations of madness, but what it came down to was this: if I don't do it, who will? Either way, we arrive in one piece.

We pile the stuff in the corridor and the boxes are torn open straightaway, the blankets most welcomed. It's not a hospital at all but a clinic, a private doctor's surgery treating people free since the town's main hospital was taken over by US forces. Another has been improvised in a car garage. There's no anaesthetic. The blood bags are in a drinks fridge and the doctors warm them up under the hot tap in an unhygienic toilet.

Screaming women come in, praying, slapping their chests and faces. *Ummi*, my mother, one cries. I hold her until Maki, a consultant and acting director of the clinic, brings me to the bed where a child of about ten is lying with a bullet wound to the head. He's wet himself. His 18-year-old sister is being treated for a neck wound in the next bed. A US sniper hit them and their grandmother as they left their home to flee Falluja.

The lights go out, the fan stops and in the sudden quiet someone holds up the flame of a cigarette lighter so that the doctor can carry on operating. Electricity to the town has been cut off for days and when the generator overheats or runs out of fuel they just have to manage till it comes back on. David quickly donates his torch. The children are not going to live.

'Come,' says Maki and ushers me alone into a room where an old woman has just had an abdominal bullet wound stitched up. Another wound in her leg is being dressed, the bed under her foot soaked with blood, a white flag still clutched in her hand and the same story: 'I was leaving my home to go to Baghdad when I was hit by a US sniper'. Some of the town is held by US marines, other parts by the local fighters. Their homes are in the US-controlled area and they are adamant that the snipers were US marines.

Snipers are causing not just carnage but also the paralysis of the ambulance and evacuation services. The biggest hospital after the main one was seized is in US territory and cut off from the clinic by snipers. The ambulance has been repaired four times after bullet damage. Bodies are lying in the streets because no-one can go to collect them without being shot.

Some said we were mad to come to Iraq; quite a few said we were

completely insane to come to Falluja and now there are people telling me
that getting in the back of the pick-up to go past the snipers and rescue
sick and injured people is the craziest thing they've ever seen. I know,
though, that if we don't, no one will.

He's holding a white flag with a Red Crescent on; I don't know his
name. The men we pass wave us on when the driver explains where we're
going. The silence is ferocious in the no man's land between the pick-up
at the edge of the mujahedin* territory, which has just disappeared out of
sight around the last corner, and the marines' line beyond the next wall;
no birds, no music, no indication that anyone is still living until a gate
opens opposite and a woman comes out and points.

We edge along to the hole in the wall where we can see the car, spent
mortar shells around it. The feet are visible, crossed, in the gutter. I think
he's dead already. The marines are visible too, two of them on the corner
of the building. As yet I think they can't see us so we need to let them
know we're there.

'Hello,' I bellow at the top of my voice. 'Can you hear me?' They must.
They're about 30 meters from us, maybe less, and it's so still you can hear
the flies buzzing at 50 paces. I repeat myself a few times, still without
reply, so decide to explain a bit more.

'We are a medical team. We want to remove this wounded man. Is
it OK for us to come out and get him? Can you give us a signal that
it's OK?'

I'm sure they can hear me but they're still not responding. Maybe
they didn't understand it all, so I say the same again. David yells too
in his US accent. I yell again. Finally I think I hear a shout back. Not
sure, I call again.

'Hello.'
'Yeah.'
'Can we come out and get him?'
'Yeah,'

Slowly, our hands up, we go out. The black cloud that rises to greet
us carries with it a hot, sour smell. Solidified, his legs are heavy. I leave
them to Rana and David, our guide lifting under his hips. A Kalashnikov
is attached by sticky blood to his hair and hand but we don't want it with
us so I put my foot on it as I pick up his shoulders and his blood falls out
through the hole in his back. We heave him into the pick-up as best we
can and try to outrun the flies.

He must've been wearing flip-flops because he's barefoot now, no more
than 20 years old, in imitation Nike pants and a blue and black striped

* Mujahedin strictly means 'ones engaged in jihad'; this was how the local fighters referred to
themselves.

football shirt with a big 28 on the back. As the orderlies from the clinic pull the young fighter off the pick-up, yellow fluid pours from his mouth and they flip him over, face up, the way into the clinic clearing in front of them, straight up the ramp into the makeshift morgue.

We wash the blood off our hands and get in the ambulance. There are people trapped in the other hospital who need to go to Baghdad. Siren screaming, lights flashing, we huddle on the floor of the ambulance, passports and ID cards held out the windows. We pack it with people, one with his chest taped together and a drip, one on a stretcher, legs jerking violently so I have to hold them down as we wheel him out, lifting him over steps.

The hospital is better able to treat them than the clinic but hasn't got enough of anything to sort them out properly and the only way to get them to Baghdad is on our bus, which means they have to go to the clinic. We're crammed on the floor of the ambulance in case it's shot at. Nisareen, a woman doctor about my age, can't stop a few tears once we're out.

The doctor rushes out to meet us: 'Can you go to fetch a lady, she is pregnant and she is delivering the baby too soon?'

Ghareeb is driving, Ahmed in the middle directing him and me by the window, the visible foreigner, the passport. We have left mujahedin territory and are in an area held by the marines. Something scatters across my hand, simultaneous with the crashing of a bullet through the ambulance, some plastic part dislodged, flying through the window.

We stop, turn off the siren, keep the blue light flashing, wait, eyes on the US marines on the corners of the roofs. Several shots come. We duck, get as low as possible and I can see tiny red lights whipping past the window, past my head. Some, it's hard to tell, are hitting the ambulance. I start singing. What else do you do when someone's shooting at you? A tire bursts with an enormous noise and a jerk of the vehicle.

I'm outraged. We're trying to get to a woman who's giving birth without any medical attention, without electricity, in a city under siege, in a clearly marked ambulance, and you're shooting at us. How dare you?

How dare you?

Ghareeb grabs the gear stick and gets the ambulance into reverse, another tire bursting as we go over the ridge in the middle of the road, the shots still coming as we flee around the corner. I carry on singing. The wheels are scraping, burst rubber burning on the road.

The men run for a stretcher as we arrive and I shake my head. They spot the new bullet holes and run to see if we're OK. Is there any other way to get to her, I want to know. *La, maaku tarieq.* There is no other way. They say we did the right thing. They say they've fixed the ambulance four times already and they'll fix it again but the radiator's gone and the wheels are buckled and she's still at home in the dark giving birth alone. I let her down.*

Night – and day two

We can't go out again. For one thing there's no ambulance and, besides, it's dark now and that means our foreign faces can't protect the people who go out with us or the people we pick up. Or us, for that matter. Maki is the acting director of the place. He says he hated Saddam but now he hates the Americans more.

We take off the blue gowns as the sky starts exploding somewhere beyond the building opposite. Minutes later a car roars up to the clinic. I can hear him screaming before I can see that there's no skin left on his body. He's burnt from head to foot. For sure there's nothing they can do. He'll die of dehydration within a few days.

Another man is pulled from the car onto a stretcher. Cluster bombs, they say, although it's not clear whether they mean one or both men. We set off walking to Mr Yasser's house, waiting at each corner for someone to check the street before we cross. A ball of fire falls from a plane, splits into smaller balls of bright white lights. I think they're cluster bombs, because cluster bombs are in the front of my mind, but they vanish and are thus probably magnesium flares, incredibly bright but short-lived, giving a flash picture of the town from above.

Yasser asks us all to introduce ourselves. I tell him I'm training to be a lawyer. One of the other men asks whether I know about international law. They want to know about the law on war crimes, what a war crime is. I tell them I know some of the Geneva Conventions, that I'll bring some information next time I come and we can get someone to explain it in Arabic.

The planes are above us all night so that as I doze I forget I'm not on a long-distance flight, the constant bass note of a pilotless reconnaissance drone overlaid with the frantic thrash of jets and the dull beat of helicopters, and interrupted by the explosions.

In the morning I make balloon dogs, giraffes and elephants for the little one, Aboudi, who's clearly distressed by the noise of the aircraft and explosions. I blow bubbles which he follows with his eyes. Finally, finally, I score a smile. The twins, 13 years old, laugh too, one of them an ambulance driver, both said to be handy with a Kalashnikov.

---

* The editors at OpenDemocracy.net forwarded this account to the Pentagon for comment. They accused me of falsely reporting that US troops were shooting at ambulances except where ambulances were carrying weapons or fighters or have fired on them first. I can say with certainty that there were no guns or fighters in our ambulance and we did not fire on anyone.

The doctors look haggard in the morning. None has slept more than a couple of hours a night for a week. One has had only eight hours of sleep in the last seven days, missing the funerals of his brother and aunt because he was needed at the hospital.

'The dead we cannot help,' Jassim said. 'I must worry about the injured.'

We go again, David, Rana and me, this time in a pick-up. There are some sick people close to the marines' line who need evacuating. No-one dares come out of their house because the marines are on top of the buildings shooting at anything that moves. Saad fetches us a white flag and tells us not to worry, he's checked and secured the road, no mujahedin will fire at us, that peace is upon us – this 11-year-old child, his face covered with a keffiyeh except for his bright brown eyes, his AK47 almost as tall as he is.

We shout again to the soldiers, hold up the flag with a Red Crescent sprayed onto it. Two come down from the building, cover this side and Rana mutters, '*Allahu akbar*. Please nobody take a shot at them.'

We jump down and tell them we need to get some sick people from the houses and they want Rana to go and bring out the family from the house whose roof they're on. Thirteen women and children are still inside, in one room, without food and water for the last 24 hours.

'We're going to be going through soon clearing the houses,' the senior one says.

'What does that mean, clearing the houses?'

'Going into every one searching for weapons.' He's checking his watch, can't tell me what will start when, of course, but there are going to be air strikes in support. 'If you're gonna do this you gotta do it soon.'

First we go down the street we were sent to. There's a man, face down, in a white dishdasha, a small round red stain on his back. We run to him. Again the flies have got there first. David is at his shoulders, I'm by his knees and as we reach to roll him onto the stretcher David's hand goes through his chest, through the cavity left by the bullet that entered so neatly through his back and blew his heart out.

There's no weapon in his hand. His sons come out, crying, shouting. He was unarmed, they scream. He was unarmed. He just went out the gate and they shot him. None of them have dared come out since. No-one had dared come to get his body, horrified, terrified; they couldn't have known we were coming so it's inconceivable that anyone came out and retrieved a weapon but left the body.

He was unarmed, 55 years old, shot in the back.

We cover his face, carry him to the pick-up. There's nothing to cover his body with. The sick woman is helped out of the house, the little girls around her hugging cloth bags to their bodies, whispering, '*Baba*.

Baba.' Daddy. Shaking, they let
us go first, hands up, around the
corner, then we usher them to
the cab of the pick-up, shielding
their heads so they can't see
him, the cuddly fat man stiff in
the back.

The people seem to pour out
of the houses now in the hope we
can escort them safely out of the
line of fire, kids, women, men,
anxiously asking us whether they
can all go, or only the women
and children. We go to ask. The
young marine tells us that men of
fighting age can't leave. What's
fighting age, I want to know. He
contemplates. Anything under
45. No lower limit.

It appalls me that all those
men will be trapped in a city

Rana, my fellow ambulance volunteer.

which is being destroyed. Not all of them are fighters, not all are armed.
It's going to happen out of the view of the world, out of sight of the media,
because most of the media in Falluja is embedded with the marines or
turned away at the outskirts. Before we can pass the message on, two
explosions scatter the crowd in the sidestreet back into their houses.

Rana's with the marines evacuating the family from the house they're
occupying. The pick-up isn't back yet. The families are hiding behind
their walls. We wait, because there's nothing else we can do. We wait in
no man's land. The marines, at least, are watching us through binoculars;
maybe the local fighters are too.

I've got a disappearing hanky in my pocket so while I'm sitting like
a lemon, nowhere to go, gunfire and explosions all around, I make the
hanky disappear, reappear, disappear. It's always best, I think, to seem
completely unthreatening and completely unconcerned, so no-one
worries about you enough to shoot. We can't wait too long though. Rana's
been gone ages. We have to go and get her to hurry. There's a young man
with her: she's talked them into letting him leave too.

A man wants to use his police car to carry some of the people, a
couple of elderly ones who can't walk far, the smallest children. It's
missing a door. Who knows if he was really a police officer or the car was
reappropriated and just ended up there? It doesn't matter if it gets more
people out faster. They creep from their houses, huddle by the wall, follow

us out, their hands up too, and walk up the street clutching babies, bags, each other.

The pick-up gets back and we shovel as many onto it as we can as an ambulance arrives from somewhere. A young man waves from the doorway of what's left of a house, his upper body bare, a blood-soaked bandage around his arm – a fighter but it makes no difference once someone is wounded and unarmed. Getting the dead isn't essential. Like the doctor said, the dead don't need help, but if it's easy enough then we will. Since we're already OK with the soldiers and the ambulance is here, we run down to fetch them in. It's important in both Islam and public health to bury the body quickly.

The ambulance follows us down. The soldiers start shouting in English for it to stop, pointing guns. It's moving fast. We're all yelling, signaling for it to stop but it seems to take forever for the driver to hear and see us. It stops. It stops, before they open fire. We haul them onto the stretchers and run, shove them in the back. Rana squeezes in the front with the wounded man and David and I crouch in the back beside the bodies. He says he had allergies as a kid and hasn't got much sense of smell. I wish, retrospectively, for childhood allergies, and stick my head out the window.

Ambulance to Baghdad

The bus is going to leave, taking the injured people back to Baghdad, the man with the burns, one of the women who was shot in the jaw and shoulder by a sniper, several others. Rana says she's staying to help. David and I don't hesitate: we're staying too. 'If I don't do it, who will?' has become an accidental motto and I'm acutely aware after the last foray how many people, how many women and children, are still in their houses either because they've got nowhere to go or because they're scared to go out of the door.

To begin with it's agreed, then Ghareeb says we have to go. He hasn't got contacts with every one of the disparate armed groups, only with some. There are different issues to square with each one. We need to get these people back to Baghdad as quickly as we can. If we're kidnapped or killed it will cause even more problems, so it's better that we just get on the bus and leave and come back with him as soon as possible.

It hurts to climb onto the bus when the doctor has just asked us to go and evacuate some more people. I hate the fact that a qualified medic can't travel in the ambulance but I can, just because I look like the sniper's sister or one of his mates, but that's the way it is. I feel like a traitor for leaving, but I can't see that I've got a choice. It's a war now and as alien as it is to me to do what I'm told, for once I've got to.

Jassim is scared. He harangues Mohammed constantly, tries to pull him out of the driver's seat while we're moving. The woman with the gunshot wound is on the back seat, the man with the burns in front of her, being fanned with cardboard from the empty boxes, his intravenous drips swinging from the rail along the ceiling of the bus. It's hot. It must be unbearable for him.

Saad comes onto the bus to wish us well for the journey. He shakes David's hand and then mine. I hold his in both of mine and tell him 'Dir balak,' take care, as if I could say anything more stupid to a pre-teen mujahid with an AK47 in his other hand, and our eyes meet and stay fixed, his full of fire and fear.

Can't I take him away? Can't I take him somewhere he can be a child? Can't I make him a balloon giraffe and give him some crayons and tell him not to forget to brush his teeth? Can't I find the person who put the rifle in the hands of that little boy and tell him what that does to a child? Do I have to leave him here where there are heavily armed men all around him and lots of them are not on his side, however many sides there are in all of this? And of course I do. I do have to leave him, the little child soldier.

The way back is tense, the bus almost getting stuck in a dip in the sand, people escaping in anything, even piled on the trailer of a tractor, lines of cars and pick-ups and buses ferrying people to the dubious sanctuary of Baghdad, lines of men in vehicles queuing to get back into the city having got their families to safety, either to fight or to help evacuate more people. The driver, Jassim, the father, ignores Ghareeb and takes a different road so that suddenly we're not following the lead car and we're on a road that's controlled by a different armed group than the ones which know us.

A crowd of men waves guns to stop the bus. Somehow they apparently believe that there are American soldiers on the bus, as if they wouldn't be in tanks or helicopters, and there are men getting out of their cars with shouts of 'Sahafa Amreeki,' American journalists. The passengers shout out of the windows, 'Ana min Falluja,' I am from Falluja. Gunmen run onto the bus and see that it's true, there are sick and injured and old people, Iraqis, and then relax, wave us on.

We stop in Abu Ghraib and swap seats, foreigners in the front, Iraqis less visible, headscarves off so we look more Western. The American soldiers are so happy to see English speakers they don't mind too much about the Iraqis with us, search the men and the bus, leave the women unsearched because there are no women soldiers to search us. Mohammed keeps asking me if things are going to be OK.

'Al-melaach wiyana,' I tell him. The angels are with us. The cheeky angels. The feisty punk angels who are not scared of men with guns. He laughs.

And then we're in Baghdad, delivering them to the hospitals, Nuha, the Iraqi journalist, in tears as they take the burnt man off, groaning and whimpering. She puts her arms around me and asks me to be her friend. I make her feel less isolated, she says, less alone.

And the satellite news says the ceasefire is holding and George Bush says to the troops on Easter Sunday: 'I know what we're doing in Iraq is right.' Shooting unarmed men in the back outside their family home is right? Shooting grandmothers with white flags is right? Shooting at women and children who are fleeing their homes is right? Firing at ambulances is right?

Well, George, I know too now. I know what it looks like when you brutalize people so much that they've nothing left to lose. I know what it looks like when an operation is being done without anaesthetic because the hospitals are occupied or under sniper fire and the city's under siege and aid isn't getting in properly. I know what it sounds like too. I know what it looks like when tracer bullets are passing your head, even though you're in an ambulance. I know what it looks like when a man's chest is no longer inside him and what it smells like and I know what it looks like when his wife and children pour out of his house.

It's a crime and it's a disgrace to us all.

Return to Falluja

It's two days before we go back, 14 April. Sergeant Tratner of the First Armored Division is irritated. 'Git back or you'll git killed,' are his opening words.

Lee says we're press and he looks with disdain at the car. 'In this piece of shit?'

Makes us less of a target for kidnappers, Lee tells him. Suddenly he decides he recognizes Lee from the TV. Based in Germany, he watches the BBC. He sees Lee on TV all the time. 'Cool. Hey, can I have your autograph?' The cheeky angels chuckle.

Lee makes a scribble, unsure who he's meant to be but happy to have a ticket through the checkpoint which all the cars before us have been turned back from, and Sergeant Tratner carries on. 'You guys be careful in Falluja. We're killing loads of those folks.' Detecting a lack of admiration on our part, he adds: 'Well, they're killing us too. I like Falluja. I killed a bunch of them motherfuckers.'

I wish Sergeant Tratner were a caricature, a stereotype, but these are all direct quotations. We fiddle with our headscarves in the roasting heat. 'You don't have to wear those things any more,' he says. 'You're liberated now.' He laughs. I mention that more and more women are wearing hijabs nowadays because of the increasing number of attacks on them.

A convoy of aid vehicles flying Red Crescent flags approaches the checkpoint, hesitates. 'We don't like to encourage them,' Sergeant Tratner explains, his tongue loosened by the excitement of finding someone to talk to. 'Jeez it's good to meet someone that speaks English. Well, apart from "Mister" and "please" and "why".'

'Haven't you got translators?' someone asks him.

Sergeant Tratner points his rifle in the direction of the lead vehicle in the convoy. 'I got the best translator in the world,' he says.

One ambulance comes through with us, the rest turn back. There are supplies when we get to Falluja – food, water, medicine – at the clinic and the mosque which have come in on the back roads. The relief effort for the people there has been enormous, but the hospital is in the US-held part of town. They can neither get any of the relief supplies in to the hospital nor the injured people out.

We load the ambulance with disinfectant, needles, bandages, food and water and set off, equipped this time with loudspeakers, pull up to a street corner and get out. The hospital is to the right, quite a way off; the marines are to the left. Four of us in blue paper smocks walk out, hands up, calling out that we're a relief team, trying to deliver supplies to the hospital.

There's no response and we walk slowly towards the hospital. We need the ambulance with us because there's more stuff than we can carry, so we call out that we're going to bring an ambulance with us, that we'll walk and the ambulance will follow. The nose of the ambulance edges out into the street, shiny and new, brought in to replace the ones destroyed by sniper fire.

Shots rip down the street, two bangs and a zipping noise uncomfortably close. The ambulance springs back into the side road like it's on a piece of elastic and we dart into the yard of the corner house, out through the side gate so we're back beside the vehicle.

This time we walk away from the hospital towards the marines, just us and the loudspeaker, no ambulance, to try and talk to them properly. Slowly, slowly, we take steps, shouting that we're unarmed, that we're a relief team, that we're trying to get supplies to the hospital.

Another two shots dissuade us. I'm furious. From behind the wall I inform them that their actions are in breach of the Geneva Conventions. 'How would you feel if it was your sister in that hospital unable to get treated because some man with a gun wouldn't let the medical supplies through.' David takes me away as I'm about to call down a plague of warts on their trigger fingers.

Because it's the most urgent thing to do, we waste the rest of the precious daylight trying to find someone in authority that we can sort it out with. As darkness starts I'm still fuming and the hospital is still without disinfectant. We go into the house behind the clinic and the smell of death chokes me: the dried blood and the putrefying flesh evoking the memory of a few days earlier, sitting in the back of an ambulance with the rotting bodies and the flies.

The aerial bombardment starts with the night and we stand outside watching the explosions and the flames. No-one can quite recall whether it's a theoretical ceasefire or not. Someone brings the remains of a rocket, unraveled into metal and wires, a fuel canister inside it, and it sits like a space alien on display on a piece of cloth on the pavement near the clinic while everyone gives it stares and a wide berth.

Someone comes round to give us a report: the mujahedin have shot down a helicopter and killed 15 enemy soldiers. During the evening's street fighting 12 American soldiers have been killed. 600 were killed in an attack on their base but he can't tell us how, where or when. He says thousands of US soldiers' bodies have been dumped in the desert near Rutba, further east. I don't doubt that the US is under-reporting its casualties whenever it thinks it can get away with it but I suspect some over-reporting this time. Someone whispers that he's the cousin of 'Comical Ali', the old Minister of Information. It's not true but it ought to be.

The cacophony of planes and explosions goes on through the night. I wake from my doze certain that rockets are being fired from the garden outside our room. Rhythmic, deep, resonating, the barrage goes on and the fear spreads in my belly anticipating an explosion from the air to stop the rocket-launcher. I can't keep still and wait so I go outside and realize it's at least a couple of streets away.

In the morning the ceasefire negotiations begin again, centered, like everything else, in one of the local mosques. For eight days, people say, the US army has fought for control of a town of 350,000 people and now, with the fighters still armed in the streets, they're trying to negotiate the terms of a ceasefire.

A body arrives at the hospital, a wound to the leg and his throat sliced open. The men say he was lying injured in the street and the marines came and slit his throat. A pick-up races up and a man is pulled out with most of his arm missing, a stump with bits sticking out, pouring blood. He bleeds to death.

Two French journalists have been admitted to the town, under the protection of the mosque, and for their benefit the body is swaddled head to foot in bandages, carried to a van with no back doors and driven away by two boys, including Aodeh, one of the twin boys we met on the first trip. Earlier a little girl was brought out, a polka-dotted black headscarf around her face, pink T-shirt under a black sleeveless cardigan with jeans, sparkly bobbles on her gloves, holding a Kalashnikov.

She was clean, her clothes were fresh and she was very cute, 11 years old, and after the photo one of the men, her father I think, took her away as if her job was done. She was only being used as a poster child, wasn't really involved in the fighting. She's no younger than Saad, who I know is involved in the fighting, but I wish he wasn't either.

While we wait we chat with the sheikh in the mosque. He says the hospitals have recorded 1,200 casualties, between 500 and 600 people dead in the first five days of fighting and 86 children killed in the first three days. There's no knowing how many have been hurt or killed in areas held by the US. A heavily pregnant woman was killed by a missile, her unborn child saved, the sheikh says, but already orphaned.

'Falluja people like peace but after we were attacked by the US they lost all their friends here. We had a few trained officers and soldiers from the old army, but now everyone has joined the effort. Not all of the men are fighting: some left with their families, some work in the clinics or move supplies or go in the negotiating teams. We are willing to fight until the last minute, even if it takes a hundred years.'

He says the official figure is 25 per cent of the town controlled by the marines: 'This is made up of small parts, a bit in the northeast, a bit in the southeast, the part around the entrance to the town, controlled with snipers and light vehicles.' The new unity between Shi'a and Sunni pleases him: 'Falluja is Iraq and Iraq is Falluja. We received a delegation from all the governorates of Iraq to give aid and solidarity.'

The ceasefire takes effect from 9am. Those with vehicles are loading stuff from the building opposite the mosque and moving it around the town. The opening up of the way to the hospital is one of the terms of the deal, so we're not really needed any more. In addition, it's starting to feel like there are different agendas being pursued that we could all too easily get caught up in, other people's politics and power struggles, so we decide to leave.

Taken prisoner

At the corner of town is a fork, a paved road curving round in front of the last of the houses and a track leading into the desert. The latter is controlled by the marines, who fire a warning shot when our driver gets out to negotiate a way through; the former by as yet invisible mujahedin. The crossfire suddenly surrounds the car. David, head down, shifts into the driver's seat and backs us out of there but the only place to go is into the line of mujahedin. One of the fighters jumps into the passenger seat and directs us.

'We're hostages, aren't we?' Jenny says.

No, it's fine, I say, sure that they're just directing us out of harm's way. The man in the passenger seat asks which country we're all from. Donna says she's Australian. Jenny says she's British.

'*Allahu akbar! Ahlan wa sahlan.*' Translated, it's more or less, God is great.

I'm *pleased* to meet *you*. The drift is clear enough: 'I think he just said he's got the two most valuable hostages in the world,' Jenny paraphrases.

We get out of the car, which in any case feels a bit uncomfortable now there's a man with a keffiyeh round his head pointing a loaded rocket-launcher at it. They bring a jeep and as I climb in I can't help noticing that the driver has a grenade between his legs. I'm sure it's intended for the Americans, not for us, but nonetheless it's clear there's no room for dissent.

Still, it's not till we turn off the road back to the clinic and stop at a house, not until David and the other men are being searched, not really until a couple of the fighters take off their keffiyehs to tie the men's hands behind their backs, that I accept that I'm definitely a captive. For a moment, when I think they're going to blindfold us, I feel sick.

You look for ways out. You wonder whether they're going to kill you, make demands for your release, if they'll hurt you. You wait for the knives and the guns and the video camera. You tell yourself you're going to be OK. You think about your family, your mum finding out you're kidnapped. You decide you're going to be strong, because there's nothing else you can do. You fight the understanding that your life isn't fully in your hands any more, that you can't control what's happening. You turn to your best friend next to you and tell her you love her, with all your heart.

And then I'm put in a different car from her and I can only hope they take us to the same place and try in vain to notice where we're going, to recognize some landmarks, but the truth is that I'm without any sense of direction at all and have trouble remembering left from right even on a good day. In any case there's no-one on the streets but fighters, nowhere to hide.

Donna, Jenny, David, Ahrar and I are delivered to another house, cushions around the walls of a big room, a bed at one end beside a cabinet of crockery and ornaments. A tall, dignified man in a brown dishdasha sits and begins interviewing Donna, her name, where she's from, what she does there, what she's doing in Iraq, why she came to Falluja.

He decides to separate us, has the others move David, Jenny and me into the next room under the guard of a man in jeans too loose for his skinny body, trainers and a shirt, his face covered except for his eyes. It's not much to go on but I doubt he's beyond late teens, a little nervous, calmed by our calmness. After a while he decides he shouldn't let us talk to each other, signals for silence.

Jenny's not well, hot and sick. She lies down on the cushions, head on her arm. The fighter brings a pillow and gently lifts her head onto it, takes all the stuff off the cushions so he can fold the blanket over her. The other one brings a cotton sheet and unfolds the blanket, covers her with the sheet and then gently replaces the blanket around her.

It's my turn next for questioning. I feel OK. All I can tell him is the truth. He wants to know the same things: where I live, what I'm doing in Iraq, what I'm doing in Falluja, so I tell him about the circus, about the ambulance trips, about the snipers shooting at us. Then he asks what the British people think about the war. I'm not sure what the right answer is. I don't know what the national opinion is these days. I try to compute what's least likely to make him think it's worth keeping me.

If people oppose the occupation, he says, how is it that the government could carry on and do it. He's genuinely interested but also sarcastic: surely the great liberators must be truly democratic, truly governing by the will of the people? Instead of listening to the extended version of Jo's rant about the UK constitution he starts asking about Jenny. I know what her answers will be so it's easy. I dodge the issue when he moves on to David and hope he won't press me. I don't know him very well, I say, because I don't know if he wants to mention that he's American and also a journalist. His dad's Mexican, he often gives that as his nationality. I tell the man I've just met him, I just know him as Martinez.

He thanks me and we're done. David's next. Donna, Jenny and I talk quietly about the interviews and the boy guarding us doesn't object. Someone asks if we want chai. Warm giggles come from the kitchen; maybe the two young men imagining that their mates could see them now, masked, Kalashnikov-wielding, brewing tea for a load of women.

David's interview is short and when I come back from the outside toilet, still alert for an escape route, as improbable as I know it is, the others are all back in the main room again and the tea is ready. Jenny's bag comes in to be searched, a camera, a minidisc recorder. The man goes through the pictures on the camera, the missile outside the clinic and a few from Baghdad, listens to the interview with the Sheikh on the minidisc.

Donna's camera has similar pictures of the missile, some of the street kids, some from around the apartment. The tape in the video camera is from the opening of the new youth center in Al-Daura, backing up her testimony that she's the director of an organization which sets up projects for kids. The other tape contains a performance by the Boomchucka Circus, backing up mine that I'm a clown.

No-one brings in my bag or David's. I think it's best not to mention this, in case there's anything to offend them in either of them. In particular I think it's best they don't notice anyone's passport in case it encourages them to look for all our passports, David's US one – he has gone Mexican – and Jenny's containing an Israeli stamp. Actually she was working in Palestine but it's better not to spark suspicion in the first place.

Ahrar, the questioning over, is close to hysterical. She's more frightened of her family's reaction to her having been out all the previous night than of the armed men holding us. We cuddle and stroke and pacify her as best we can, saying we'll tell her family it wasn't her fault. The trouble was that, by the time we left Baghdad to come here, it was already too late for her to get home yesterday evening, and now she's afraid it's going to be a second night.

I quietly start singing, unsure whether that's allowed. The others join in where they know the words. By the end of the song her sobs have stopped and her only word is, 'Continue,' so we do, song after song until the prayer call begins and it's impolite to sing at the same time.

Ahrar gets tearful again. Donna tries to comfort her. 'I have a big faith in God,' she says.

'Yes, but you don't know Mama,' Ahrar wails.

Before the war and before we came to Falluja the first time, I remember feeling that it's impossible to know how you'll react to something like being under fire. I couldn't have imagined either how I'd react to this, this unpredictable situation, these masked and armed men, the fear, the uncertainty. Repeatedly they tell us not to be afraid, 'We are Muslims. We will not hurt you.'

My instinct tells me I'm going to be OK yet still, as well, my mind wanders to the question of whether they'll shoot us against a wall or just open fire in the room, whether they'll take us out one by one or kill us all together, whether they'll save the bullets and cut our throats, how long it hurts for when you're shot, if it's instantly over or if there's some echo of the agony of the metal ripping through your flesh after your life is gone.

I don't need those thoughts and I push them out of my way because I know the others are going through the same thoughts. What's this going to do to my mum? What's going to happen? What's it going to feel like? It wouldn't be fair to mention it aloud so there's nothing we can do but wait it out and keep our heads together.

But what I tell myself is this: I can't change the course of this at the moment and if they do point a rifle at me or hold a knife to my throat and I know it's the last moment of my life then I'm determined not to beg or flinch because I was right to come to Falluja. I was right to try to evacuate people and get supplies to the hospitals and to die trying to do that isn't ideal but it's OK. I try to shield myself with that resolution.

They bring our bags in and I make a hanky disappear. The guard, a different one now, is unimpressed. It's black magic. It's *haram* [sinful]. It's an affront to Allah. Hurriedly I show him the secret of the trick in the hope he'll let me off. Instead I make a balloon giraffe for his kids, whom he's taken away to the safety of Baghdad.

'My brother was killed and my brother's son and my sister's son. My other brother is in the prison at Abu Ghraib. I am the last one left. Can you imagine? And this morning my best friend was killed. He was wounded in the leg and lying in the street and the Americans came and cut his throat.'

That was the one who came into the hospital this morning. Oh shit. Why wouldn't they kill us?

It's boring. Hot. Frightening. That's it really. You're still just yourself, waiting. No other self comes along to replace you. No film director pops up to give you tips on being someone else. You're just yourself, waiting, trying to wait with dignity, as best you can. Awake. Hot. Frightened. Bored. Waiting. Waiting.

But the day goes by and we carry on breathing, dozing, talking. They bring food, apologize for not bringing more, promise again that they're not going to hurt us. As it gets dark, behind the windows partly blocked by sandbags, they light a paraffin lamp. The room gets hotter and hotter and it's a relief when they take us out to the car to move again, although change feels somehow threatening at the same time.

The new house is huge, with electricity. The four women are shown to a room and David has to stay in the main room with the men. This was his biggest fear all along, being separated from the rest of us. We take off the hijabs that we've kept on all day. One of the men knocks on the door and, looking at the ground, tells us they've checked everything and, *InshaaAllah*, we'll be taken back to Baghdad in the morning. They can't let us go now because we'll be kidnapped.

They feed us, bring us tea, supply us with blankets and we find pretexts and excuses to nip through the main room to check on David, bringing him half an orange, a chunk of chocolate, so he knows we're still thinking of him. He's more vulnerable than us because we've got each other to laugh and sing and talk with. Everything that's happened, although you can never be sure, says they're not going to hurt women. David's not so comfortable. His bag is in our room and I find his passport and hide it on my body.

The night is filled with the racket of what sounds like a huge dodgy plumbing system somewhere beyond the house, a rhythmic series of explosions in quick succession like an immense grinding noise: apparently it's the sound of cluster bombs. Jenny and I hold each other's hands all night. In the morning there's still a knot of doubt in my belly. They said they'd take us home after the morning prayers, more or less at first light, and it's been light for ages. Maybe they just told us we'd be released to keep us calm and quiet.

But they do let us go: they take us to one of the local imams who says he will drive us home. At the edge of Falluja is a queue of vehicles, some already turning back from the checkpoint. The passengers say the US soldiers fired as they approached. We get out of the car, hijabs off, and start the whole rigmarole again, loudspeaker, hands up, through the maze of concrete and wire, shouting that we're an international group of ambulance volunteers trying to leave Falluja, we're unarmed and please don't shoot us.

Eventually we can see the soldiers; eventually they lower the guns, tell us to put our hands down, they're not going to shoot us. 'My bad,' one says, using US slang to acknowledge that he'd been at fault, that the shots had been unnecessary. 'We're not going to fire any more warning shots.' We tell them we've got two cars to bring through and ask about the rest of the cars. They agree to open up the checkpoint to women, children and old men. The trouble is, most of the women don't drive and so can't leave unless their husbands are allowed to drive them. We persuade them to let through cars with a male driver even if he is 'of fighting age' if he's got his family with him.

The fear in Falluja is that, when most of the women and children are gone, the town is going to be destroyed completely, everyone killed. Ahrar tries to explain that the men who want to leave are the ones who don't want to fight.

'Oh, we want to keep them in there,' the marine says. 'There's fighters coming from all over Iraq into Falluja and we want to keep them all in there so we can kill them all more easily.'

But these are the ones who want to get out, those of the locals who don't want to fight. It doesn't matter to the marines though: we've got all we're going to get. We tell the crowd of anxious refugees and leave another local imam as the go-between. The road is quiet but for our small convoy until another roadblock. The imam talks to some locals, tells Ahrar there are Americans ahead. Hijabs off again, we heave ourselves out of the car for another round.

In the sickly, hot silence there are a few cracks but no responses to our shouts. Dust erupts from a house a way off and we wonder if we're walking into a battle. Shouting in English, trying to be as obviously foreign as possible is the only tactic for walking into marines' lines but it's a bit of a risk when the lines are not clear. We keep yelling for them to give us a wave if they can hear us. There's no response.

'Wait a minute,' David says. 'Are those marines or are they muja?'

Oh shit. Tell us we're not walking into a mujahedin line. We hesitate. Maybe we need to go back to the car and get the imam to come instead.

'No, I think it's OK. I think they're marines.'

'Decide! Tell us!' As if he's got any more information than the rest of us.

The men we can see start gesturing, big arm movements, pointing to their left, our right, go towards the bridge. It's a signal, which we've been asking for, but it doesn't mean they're not a group of kidnappers. Finally one yells. They're green berets, which is why they didn't quite look like

the marines we'd got used to. Jenny and I go back towards the cars to
signal for them to come. No-one fancies walking the aching gap between
us and them again, but for what seems like an endless time the cars don't
move, despite our arm-waving, my roaring through the megaphone.
Finally they shift and we scurry back into the relative cover of the bushes
around the bridge.

'Are you crazy?' asks one of the soldiers.

I am quite sane, but I have grown old these last few minutes, the
marrow in my bones crumbling from the weight of that walk into the
unknown. Mortars thunder out of their encampment. He tells me not
to worry, they're outgoing. Of course there's some comfort in this. An
outgoing mortar is preferable in many ways to an incoming one, but it
seems at the same time like a bit of an invitation, RSVP written in large
print on the end of it.

Past them, the second car leaves us. David hugs the driver like he'd
just brought him back from the dead and joins us in our car. There's still
Abu Ghraib, still Shuala, still who knows what between us and home.
Ahrar wants to stop and phone her mum from a roadside booth in the
middle of Shuala and even the imam is looking panicky as the call drags
on, his carload of foreigners just sitting waiting for someone to notice us.
Exhausted, harrowed, we selfishly drag her back to the car and escape,
trying to comfort her as we approach her home.*

It's only when we walk through the door of our apartment that we're
sure we're coming home, all of us yelling and talking at once, telling the
story, laughing over the surreal moments, hugging each other, retrieving
hidden passports.

'We're laughing about it now,' Jenny says, 'but there were moments...'

On the news they say Nahoko and the other Japanese hostages have
been released, that Yoichi Watanabe, the Japanese photographer who
hung out with us when we took the circus to Samawa, has disappeared
with a colleague. They say the ceasefire is holding in Falluja. Lee and
Ghareeb arrive back a few hours after us, having been held separately.
Harb comes round to tell me off, but I'm unrepentant. I still think it was
the right thing to do.

They took us because we were foreigners acting strangely in the middle
of their war. They found out what we were doing and let us go. On the way
out we were able to open up the checkpoint which meant people were able
to get out of Falluja to safety. Even if that was all we did it would have
been worth it. But still in a quiet moment later on I whisper a thank you
to the cheeky angels who look after clowns and ambulance volunteers.

---

* Ahrar was right, she was beaten by her brothers for being out all night, despite having been held
against her will.

19

FALLUJA'S REFUGEES

April-May 2004

'This is my honeymoon,' Heba said, in the crowded corridor of Bomb Shelter Number 24 in the Al-Ameriya district of Baghdad. Married just under a month, she fled Falluja with her extended family. 'There were bombs all the time. We couldn't sleep. Even if you fell asleep, nightmares woke you up. We just gathered the whole family in one room and waited.

'It is better here than in Falluja. We hear bombs but they are far away and not so many. But there is no water in here: we have to go outside for water for drinking, cooking and washing ourselves and our clothes and we buy ice. There is no fridge, no fans, no air-conditioning, no generator and only one stove for us all. We have to go to the garden for a toilet and that's a problem at night. Everyone has diarrhea from the ice that we bought.

'Now I am a bride but I couldn't bring any of my clothes.' As if there would be any privacy anyway, 88 members of 18 families piled on mattresses in the long narrow passage from the door to the kitchen at the end, from where a stream of tea and sweet sesame biscuits is flowing, part of the commemoration of Heba's uncle.

He died seven days ago, the day after they arrived in Baghdad. Heba's dad Rabiia said his brother died of sadness. Because all the family's identity documents were in Falluja, they were unable to get the body from the hospital. Rabiia met some friends, doctors who worked there, and they were able to help him get the body back after a day.

He'd sent two of his sons back to Falluja with their families the day before and they'd phoned him at seven in the evening to tell him not to come back. Things were worse. They were trying to get back out but all the roads were closed. 'Now everyone in Falluja is in prison.'

'We left because of the bombs,' Rabiia explained. 'The kids were frightened, crying all night. We left on 9 April. Lots of our relatives had cars but there were problems getting fuel. We got all 18 families together and then waited at the checkpoint. The Americans made us wait hours in the sun to exhaust us. The children were crying with hunger. Then the

Americans changed the route we had to take and made us travel by a long side road.

'We all arrived at different times – some slept in the cars at the checkpoint and arrived in Baghdad the next morning. They would only let through one young man as the driver with each car and only if there was no old man. Some of the families here couldn't get their young men through so they had to come by the river.* There was no fuel, no water, no generators, no hospitals there, so families couldn't live.'

His youngest son Mustafa was 11 and woke up crying every night, saying there was going to be a bomb. Miluuk said all the kids were having nightmares. Her brother-in-law's child had started sleepwalking. Miluuk's daughter had developed a blood pressure problem and a stomach microbe that was caused by the bad water.

A nurse called Hadil from Falluja visited them and gave them a list of medicines they needed, a couple of injections for one of the women who was pregnant, some medication for stomach ulcers. He ran a pharmacy but had already donated all his medicines. Rabiia had built a toilet with his own money but there wasn't much left. Miluuk's sister Sabriya taught disabled people in Shuala. She never married because of all the wars: 'Wars eat your youth. When I was in college we made a census, boys and girls. There were about half girls and half boys but now there are maybe ten times as many women.

'I can't explain to you. I feel hopeless. I don't know what the future will bring. I thought life would change, things would settle down, this war would be the last for Iraq. They said they came to give peace and human rights but now we're figuring out that that's not true. They don't understand Iraq so they make problems that lead to conflict. They said they would rebuild but they're destroying. Clean water and electricity would be enough.'

Ikhlas, a Kurdish woman with a tiny daughter, Jwana, explained in a cracking voice that her sister Sena's husband died two years ago and now her husband was responsible for all of them, without work, crammed into a room in a house which a local man opened up to families fleeing Falluja, near to the bomb shelter where the rest of the family were staying. There was no kitchen there for eight kids, six women and a man. Sena too started to cry. Four of her children were with her; the fifth had stayed in Falluja with an uncle.

Sena's daughter Sheyma sat still white with shock, unspeaking, unsmiling, 14 years old and utterly despairing. She'd left school. There didn't seem any point in it, any future. Beyda, at 18 the youngest sister,

---

* During the November 2004 attack on Falluja US soldiers were reportedly killing people who tried to swim out across the river as well.

fled Falluja with them; another stayed in Falluja where her husband, only 33 years old, had died a couple of days earlier from a heart problem. He'd had to be taken by boat across the Euphrates to the hospital because the roads were closed. He'd spent a day there and then died.

The little ones, when I gave them drawing things, would only draw aeroplanes dropping missiles on houses, some kind of structure with an Iraqi flag firing back at the aeroplanes. The violence starts to pervade everything: the kids on our street were playing Hostages as we left in the morning, Ahmed holding one hand over Karlu's eyes and making sawing motions at his throat with the other hand, acting out the pictures from TV.

Because they fled with so little, they needed almost everything now. Heba and Israa sneaked me away to tell me they needed underwear and sanitary towels. Living from hand to mouth, their jobs left behind in Falluja, there wasn't even enough for basics. Rabiia said he was running out of money to feed the extended family.

He was in the Iraqi Civil Defence Corps (ICDC), which used Shelter Number 24 as a station, so he'd known the building would be unlocked and that he could take the family there. He was told to go to the local assembly to register in order to get help but refused, convinced that there was a plot between the local assembly and someone from the Red Crescent to get aid and keep it for themselves.

Of another agency, he said they made people stand in a line for supplies every four days. It's embarrassing, he said, and he wouldn't do it. I kept telling him it was the only way the family could get any meaningful supply of aid, that there were no NGOs left, but still he repeated: 'I cannot.'

Ali, Heba's new husband, had been in the army for two-and-a-half years, until the war. He'd had no desire to fight anyway and when two bombs fell nearby and didn't explode, he'd got in the pick-up and left, taken off his uniform and come to Heba's family's house.

Israa was 23, a philosophy student in Baghdad University, planning to be a teacher when she finished. She normally stayed with family members in Baghdad during the week and the universities had reopened after widespread fighting, so she could have gone to study, but most of the Falluja students had boycotted lectures in protest. She had decided to join the boycott, partly as a protest but largely out of exhaustion, depression, homesickness, warsickness, hopelessness.

A few days later there were 24 branches of Rabiia's extended family staying in Baghdad, three of them headed by widows, totalling 121 people. One son, Ahmed Firas Ibrahim, was still trapped inside the town after he went back. Rabiia had advised all the other families not to go back yet. The Al-Jolan district was attacked, he said: the locals were not fighting that day, but the Americans came and started raiding houses. The women were screaming and the mujahedin came out to try and defend them.

'We had to leave our houses unguarded,' Rabiia said. 'We have heard that the Americans are going into empty houses but not taking anything. We have heard that there are some people starting to steal stuff from the houses but the imams are forbidding it and punishing people who do it.'

Rabiia was no Saddam loyalist: 'I used to be in prison for many years. They put me in a room where I could not see the sun. It started in 1971 and I stayed in Syria for four years in exile because my party, the Arab Nationalist Party, was banned. Then Saddam excused us and we came back to Iraq but I was arrested in the mosque and jailed for 15 years for being in the party. They put electricity in my ears. I told them I no longer had contact with the party.

'There are Ba'athists in Falluja and Ba'athists everywhere in Iraq, but the people fighting in Falluja are just defending their homes and families. I was hoping for something positive from this occupation, but I used to have work, at least, and now there is none. We could throw them out with violence but the violence wouldn't stop there, once it started.'

The phone had been their main source of news from Falluja, getting through when they could to family and friends still inside, but the landline to the shelter had been cut off. When the terms of the ceasefire permitted a certain number of families per day to return, people hesitated, unsure the ceasefire would hold, reluctant to drive back into the aerial bombardment.

There were thousands of similar stories. Faris Mohammed, secretary general of the Iraqi Red Crescent, believed that about 65 per cent of Falluja's 300,000 population had left during the siege. Of these 200,000, most were staying with extended family in Baghdad or elsewhere or had been given shelter by strangers with space to spare. About 200 families were homeless.

The Red Crescent camp

Two men, two women and eight kids sat in one of the white tents of the new Red Crescent camp on two dusty football fields. Of the 40 families who had registered, these two were the only residents so far because there was no sanitation. UNICEF had promised to provide it, according to camp manager Qasim Lefteh, but had so far failed to show up. Meanwhile they were using the toilets in the neighboring school.

Their house had been in the heavily bombed Shuhada district. The 58-strong extended family left after aerial bombing killed several of their neighbors. 'Two of my relatives died and I buried them with my own hands,' Adil explained. 'There is no way to the hospital so, even if they are not killed, injured people are treated at home and there are no medicines so they die.

'Even if the ambulances tried to come, the Americans tried to shoot them. I saw the Americans shoot at a man and he stayed there from morning till night and no-one could help him. The Americans shot at the ambulance. I could see them. They were on the tops of the buildings.

'Many times it happened. Whenever we saw ambulances the Americans shot at them. They even took over a minaret. They shot a family of women and children going to the market and killed them. A family of 25 people were killed when the Americans bombed their house. We saw a fighter plane firing rockets at their house.'

The kids were listless. Sara, who was 13, kept giving me shy smiles and when the grown-ups had gone, she came and sat with me. She asked: 'Why did the Americans destroy our homes? This is not their country. Why did they invade our town? They made us homeless, to wander from house to house asking for help. Bombing went on all day and night and people sent cars from Baghdad to get the people who needed to leave.' Her brother Hadil was only four but troops raided and searched their home because he was playing with a toy gun in the street. Sara was full of fury.

It took a while to coax a smile out of any of the little ones. When the others went off to look at some of the aid that had been given, I started blowing bubbles and making balloon animals. Hadil, Hamoudie and Mustafa sat for a couple of minutes, edging closer. Hamoudie popped one first, his face transforming as the soap splattered on his face. The adults' faces relaxed into smiles too when they came back and saw the kids dancing in the middle of clouds of shiny bubbles.

'If they open the roads we will go back,' said Eman, Sara's mum. 'Life here is miserable. The Red Crescent are nice to us but there is no work, even for the men.'

The Red Crescent had decided to set up a camp in Namiya, about seven kilometers south of Falluja, as worker Faris Mohammed explained. 'But when we arrived to start setting up, the area was already a battle zone. We withdrew another 10 kilometers but then the battle spread to there too.

Sara: 'Why did the Americans destroy our homes?'

When we returned we found some of the tents already burnt.'

'We tried to choose sites that were near the road but the problem is that sometimes in these situations the insurgents shoot at troops as they pass and the troops shoot back at the insurgents, so we decided to set the camp up in Baghdad instead, away from the borders of Falluja.'

But he was adamant that US claims about Red Crescent ambulances being used to move weapons and insurgents were false. 'None of our ambulances has gone missing and we have not been using them to move weapons. During the conflict we were the only Iraqi organization with permission to go in and out of Falluja. There were no problems from either side until Wednesday, when we had supplies coming in from Dubai. We sent them straight to Falluja but the Americans sent them back saying each vehicle had to have specific permission 24 hours in advance.'

Within a few days there were 67 families at the camp, with the toilets finally in progress. Red Crescent spokesperson Qusay Ali Yasseen said many were suffering from diarrhea, either from unclean water they had drunk in Falluja and on the journey or from unhygienic conditions since they arrived in Baghdad. Their immune systems were suppressed by trauma and shock. Chest infections were also rife among the kids because of the heat. Some had walked for a day or more to reach safety.

In the middle of each day, local people arrived and unloaded trays, boxes and pans of food. They'd taken on the responsibility of feeding the increasing numbers of homeless, Qusay said, everyone bringing what they could. Through the day, other locals arrived in cars to offer help. A three-truck convoy flying UNICEF banners unloaded boxes of parts for a water tank, a 20-meter tent for a children's area and several crates of crayons and paper and other kids' stuff to put in the tent once it was up.

For the time being, though, we played parachute games, blew clouds of bubbles and did a good bout of therapeutic 'Boomchucka' shouting on the dusty gap between tents, the kids bursting with nervous energy, the trauma still fresh: you could see it whenever planes and helicopters screamed overhead.

A friend of a friend, who worked for CNN, asked me to come out with them to interview people at the refugee camp. Pleased that they were going to cover it, I went with them, all of them flak-jacketed and carrying helmets. Going through Shuala, we passed a burnt-out truck at the roadside. It wasn't smoking any more, clearly a remnant of the fighting all over Baghdad a week or so earlier, not a sign of current unrest. I didn't even notice it at first. But CNN's security man did and ordered the driver back to the Red Crescent HQ immediately. So there you have it: the CNN News agenda, determined not by what actually happened, but by fear, by what's easy, what's safe, by a security man who's spooked by less than a shadow.

Back to Falluja

On the outskirts of Baghdad on 2 May, a US army fuel tanker was burning furiously as Rana and I headed back to Falluja. At the checkpoint on the main highway beside Falluja's Hay al-Askeri [Military Quarter], US soldiers were turning away an exhausted-looking family crammed into a Kia, a small Chinese-made minibus. Their orders, in the last couple of minutes, were not to let the press in either. Gunfire sounded. They said there were still snipers over there, indicating the buildings of Hay al-Askeri, but couldn't say whether they were their snipers or Falluja's.

Iraqi soldiers wearing Iraqi Civil Defence Corps (ICDC) armbands, camouflage uniforms and assorted shoes stood at the checkpoint. Coalition failure to equip the Iraqi Police and army properly throughout the occupation had made it hard to tell a genuine checkpoint from an *Ali Baba* one.

The checkpoint was, apparently arbitrarily, only letting through 200 families in a day, of around 8,000 thought to have left, so the thin dusty back roads that we'd used during the fighting were the main route for returners. Saif, the driver of a pick-up, had come through earlier in the day to check that it was safe and that the houses were still standing. There was no fighting on Friday or Saturday and no checkpoints this way, he said.

In the pick-up 17 family members were traveling back together, 26 days after they had left, fleeing the air strikes, on the fourth day of fighting. They'd been staying, crowded, with relatives in Abu Ghraib. They turned off the road onto a riverside track, two men and a woman in the front, another man in the back holding up a white cloth, 13-year-old Hussein leaning on the bare pole behind the cab. One of the boys held his arms in the air in celebration as we drove into Falluja.

Everyone raised a hand in greeting to the ICDC guards who waved us straight through a checkpoint. Everyone raised a hand also to the mujahedin fighters in ones, twos and little clusters around the town, their faces still cloth-covered, Kalashnikovs still at hand, walking in and out of houses; one held up the Iraqi flag, another guarded a corner in a black balaclava.

'They are waiting,' Saif said. 'They will shoot the Americans if they come back. We will not accept their patrols. We blame only the Americans for what happened. The fighting in Falluja was because they were shooting civilians. Let them have our oil, we don't care, but let us live in peace. This is only people from Falluja fighting, not foreigners, because of the clans. If the Americans kill a father or a brother then the clans want revenge, but we don't let strangers in.'

A car flashed its lights, slowed down, passed bags of food to the people in the pick-up, offered another to us. Women, men, small children stood by a shop, its shutters open, food on sale in scales and bags. As the pick-up slowed down, the kids jumped out, ran in through the gate as if to

The family of 17 in their pick-up.

check, then dashed back out to fetch me. Hussein and Betul wanted me to see their garden, a small green space with slender trees growing up poles. They pointed out where flowers had been in the spring and asked for their photo to be taken: two brothers and two sisters.

There were hugs, there were greetings, there were children watching the town refill from gateways that looked out onto the roads where we had run and ridden with stretchers and bodies and terrified families. Boys waved at each other across roofs that had been, for the last month, the preserve of snipers. The patchwork of territories and no man's lands was home again, for now, for those whose homes were still there.

Hussein's best friend and next-door neighbor had been back a couple of hours, a tall thin boy with dark smudges of malnutrition under his eyes. They shook hands, Hussein bouncing with excitement, Ali looking nervous and exhausted. Their dad showed us the hole in the ground that they'd had to use as a well after the electricity had been cut as a collective punishment.

Abdulbakr's house was just around the corner, a pile of refilled plastic water bottles in the corner of a room whose floor was covered with pebbles. A trench ran through the hallway because there was no drain, a couple of blankets spread out beside it. The back of the house was open, steps leading up to the roof. It wasn't damaged by the bombing, they said: 'We were already poor, without them attacking us.'

The last drop-off was a few streets away, the children running across the road to reunite with the other part of the family who had got back earlier in the day, having stayed with a different set of relatives. The baby was cuddled, children checked that things were still where they had left them, and Safa'a wiped her eyes on her abaya amid her laughter, embracing her own children and everyone else's. You have to come back, she insisted to us, when we've straightened things out.

Before we left they gave us a list of phone numbers for the rest of the extended family still in Baghdad, so we could call them and tell them it was safe to go home. The fuel tanker was still burning as we drove back at sunset and still next morning, as aid vehicles and families flowed towards the checkpoint.

Again the seemingly arbitrary limit of 200 families a day was in place, a family comprising up to 25 individuals. All but the driver, women with infants and invalids were required to walk through the checkpoint, to be frisked with a wand while the vehicle was checked with mirrors on the underside. Lots of the people had left a month ago, just as the fighting started, and had moved between relatives ever since.

Almost as many were leaving as coming in, driving out to fetch family members still outside. Nazar was going to fetch five surviving relatives from hospital. His mother Zahra and his one-year-old nephew Sejad had been killed by a missile that landed among them, fired from a US plane as they tried to flee their home.

Salam had already brought back his own family in a small minibus and had started ferrying others back in. He'd brought two families from Baghdad that morning, was returning for more, and hadn't heard that only 200 would be allowed through in the day. The round-trip would take him another couple of hours so he'd have to go in the back way.

Salam had stayed in farms around the town during the fighting; his own house was fine but there were many, he said, whose houses had been destroyed in Hay Julan, Hay Shuhada and Hay Askeri. Maki at the clinic said there were still people missing, who hadn't yet turned up either living or dead, and the casualty figures from the different clinics, hospitals and mosques had yet to be collated: several hundred, at least, would never come home.

The atrocities repeated

Yet it was all to happen again, in November 2004, with fighting going on throughout and since, with white phosphorus used in residential areas, civilians killed and hospitals closed again. Appallingly, British troops moved north to free up US ones to savage Falluja again. Thousands of survivors subsisted in camps and shelters indefinitely. Shi'a and Kurdish militia forces were unleashed on Sunni areas, deliberately provoking sectarianism, seeking to undermine the unity spawned when US forces also attacked Shia Najaf and Thawra.

There were reports that Sharia law had been imposed in Falluja, with hairdressers and alcohol sellers, among others, under attack. Far from vindicating the US assault, the siege had opened the way for armed enforcement. There were many sides, not two – many individuals formed into groups to fight, some of them fighting for things I would not have agreed with, like Sharia law, and using methods I wouldn't agree with, such as allowing children to fight. But the fact remained that, from the start of the occupation, the Fallujans had been brutalized by troops and mercenaries and these major and ongoing attacks have been appalling massacres for which, at the time of writing, no commander has yet been brought to justice.

There is much more to say about mercenaries but little space. Private companies recruit mainly former military personnel, especially British and South African, to perform essentially military jobs under contract. Their deaths and injuries are not recorded as military casualties, which helps the domestic propaganda. They are not subject to military law. They travel armed and kill people, including civilians, with impunity. In the mass media and in politicians' speeches they are called 'civilian contractors' but they are in truth hired assassins, soldiers to whom no law at all applies.

Not only Falluja but Ramadi, Hit, Haditha, Al-Qaim, Tal Afar, Rawa, Parwana have been surrounded and bombed from the air, with electricity, water, food and medical supplies cut off as collective punishment, with hospitals closed and doctors arrested and beaten.

Each time, ordinary civilians, unarmed, have been killed, maimed, displaced, have had their homes destroyed. Each time the embedded media has fed out, at best, scraps of the truth – the BBC did not report the use of napalm in Falluja in November 2004 because their correspondent 'did not see it', though US military spokespeople had announced that it was used. Meanwhile Doctors for Iraq and International Peace Angels, Iraqi-led organizations, struggle to get emergency supplies in and civilians and information out.

All this in the name of 'pacification', of making the towns peaceful for the new democracy. But citizens in some of those towns reported being prevented from leaving their houses to vote in the constitutional referendum, prevented by armed force. All this death, all this rubble, all this outrage, to be still denied a voice.

20

THAWRA

April–May 2004

Israa's mother, her sisters, sisters-in-law and cousins heard an explosion at about eleven in the morning and another at about three in the afternoon. They heard a couple every day, just in their small area of Thawra, or Sadr City. But on this day the second one, the afternoon one, went through Israa's bedroom ceiling.

'I was in my house,' Israa's husband said. It was around three on Saturday 24 April. His friend had come to visit, so he was sitting with him in the visitors' room, with Nuredin and Huda, the older two children, playing in the same room while Israa lay down with the youngest child, Abdullah.

'I went to ask her if she would make tea for us but she said she was too tired, so I went back to my friend. After a while I heard a horrible explosion. My friend went out to see what had happened. I thought our house was OK because nothing happened to the room I was in. My friend said don't come out, stay in the house. I pushed past him. I tried to go out but there were people coming up the stairs towards me saying the explosion is in your apartment.

'I opened the door to the bedroom and saw light coming in through the ceiling but it was full of smoke and dust. I couldn't see anything. I was trying to feel my way, to touch something, calling Israa, Israa. I found her body with her belly open and her bowels outside her body. I went out of the room and told my friend she was not there.

'Two of my friends went in and took the little one from her arms. She was still cuddling him. I couldn't believe something bad had happened to the person I loved. I said if my son was fine then my wife was too. I kept telling myself I didn't see her body. I gave Abdullah to my friend and then went to check on the other two kids, still in the room I was in before. They were very frightened.

'When I came out I heard one of my friends telling another that Israa was dead. I can't remember anything else until I woke up with the kids beside me and people crying all around. I can still hear the explosion in

Huda and Nuredin, whose mother died in the explosion.

my ears. I didn't see the mortar but I'm sure it was the Americans. They came to the house later and took away the shell pieces. They couldn't say it wasn't them that fired it.

'They told the owner of the house they will pay compensation if they prove it's an American shell. But what could they have been aiming at? In my neighborhood there is a hospital, a school, houses, an electricity plant. Do they want to attack those? I believe it was the Americans who fired it, but even if it wasn't them, it's because of them. Even if someone else fired it, it's still because of the occupation.'

Nuredin, at six the oldest of the three kids, lay in his dad's lap chewing a plastic ruler. Abdullah just cried and cried. 'No-one can comfort him,' his grandma said. 'He needs his mother.' The children were staying with Israa's family; their dad sometimes with her family, sometimes with his. Israa was 30, working in a nearby tax office.

'What am I going to tell my children when they grow up and ask what happened to their mother? That she died defending her country? She died asleep in her bed.'

From the roof of the house, you could see the monument to the Unknown Soldier, two blue halves of an egg shape, which had been taken over as a US base. The owner of the house said all the neighbors who saw it happen told him the mortar had come from that direction.

The other explosion that Israa's sisters heard was around the corner, a mortar hitting the sidewalk outside the front of another residential house, killing a grandfather and a little girl, an hour or so after the explosion in the Chicken Market which killed 12, maybe 14 people and injured at least 35 more.

Each story, each individual family: the total numbers are important in themselves. Their names, their ages, their histories ought to be known all over the world, even if they are not very different from thousands of other stories from Iraq.

But there is also this: Thawra is described by the Western media as a 'slum city', home to between two-and-a-half and four million Shi'a people, mainly poor, densely crowded and bullied ferociously by Saddam. A dozen men gathered in the room to tell us about the death of the grandfather and the little girl and one, Mohammed, told me how they had welcomed the Americans when they first arrived. 'I gave them cigarettes. We thought anything would be better. But even Saddam at his worst was better than the Americans.'

Another son pulled shrapnel from his pocket. It had filled the houses, shattered all the glass, killed three people and injured ten. Jassim, the grandfather, was a 58-year-old builder who'd been unwell and was walking in the street because it was supposed to be good for his health. Six-year-old Zainab was heading for the shop to buy eggs with her three-year-old sister Noor and their grandma, Thanwa, both of whom were injured when Zainab was killed.

'All we know is it was a US mortar,' Faisal said. 'It had the markings on the shell pieces. We don't know which direction it came from. It was calm and quiet that day. They bombed to try to provoke us so then they can kill us. But there are no foreign fighters here. We don't accept strangers here. They raid houses saying they're looking for foreign fighters.

'All this trouble is because they closed a newspaper,* because it exposed the truth about Bremer. Why didn't they close the newspapers that exposed the scandal about Bill Clinton and Monica? We didn't do anything to them. They drive through here on patrols all the time and there haven't been any attacks from us because we are waiting for orders from Najaf.'

A vehement debate broke out over Sistani and Al-Sadr, over whose orders were to be followed. 'Why do you differentiate between Sistani and Al-Sadr?' one demanded. 'They are the same,' another insisted. They differed a bit over whether there were differences; they also differed over whether the Americans were unequivocally worse than Saddam. The latter, in his time, closed more newspapers, for example.

Still they were unanimous in wanting the Americans to leave now. 'Immediately,' Hussein said. 'They didn't do anything for us. They only invaded. They only brought terrorism.' They talked about the impossibility

* Moqtada al_Sadr's newspaper, *Al-Hawza*, which was suspended by the US authorities.

of sleeping with helicopters constantly overhead, about the nightly house raids and arrests of young men, about the frequent explosions, mortars falling close to the hospital.

Kerim wanted us to see his mother in the hospital. Rana, David and I didn't have the proper permission to go in but the (Iraqi) guards who had seen all the bodies come in didn't much care for the sensitivities of the Ministry of Health and its procedures. They just wanted the world to know what was happening. An old man was sweeping the floor with a palm branch as the guard told us about another mortar that had hit the neighborhood next to the hospital at 5am two days before.

Thanwa pointed through her abaya at the places where shrapnel had pierced her body. Kerim's cousin was lying nearby. In front of the house when the mortar hit, he had serious internal injuries, part of his bowel severed. 'Most of the women in here were hurt in the chicken market explosion,' she said. The market actually sold scrap metal rather than birds.

'It was only a mortar,' Saad the security guard explained, but they heard the explosion from the hospital. People bought refilled gas canisters from flatbed vehicles or horse-drawn carts which trudged around the city, the drivers hooting or banging a stick on a canister to advertise their arrival. The mortar hit one of those. 'They found the driver's head on the roof of the market.'

People were adamant that they hadn't heard any shooting before the explosion, any provocation. Mayada Radhi was washing clothes at home, opposite the market, when she heard the explosion. Shell fragments blasted through the door. She went outside to look for her two children, didn't find them and came back indoors, then saw the blood on her own body, felt the pain and passed out. Hamid, a boy in a football shirt and baseball cap, her brother-in-law, was woken up by the explosion, and came out of the house to see pieces of bodies lying in the street.

The hole in the road, the pitted walls of the buildings, the strainer-like front of the truck standing in the middle of the marketplace, the dried blood spatters: all these told a story which rated a brief mention on the main networks but little more. The other two bombings which killed civilians in that small area on that single day were not news at all.

Al-Sadr's office in Thawra was bombed several times by the US and at dawn the boys and men came out and began rebuilding it, the children mixing cement while the adults laid bricks. Every time the office was damaged by bombing, the locals rebuilt it. Shi'a people in Thawra collected aid for Sunni Falluja, later for Shi'a Najaf. Men stood defiantly on the roof declaring their new unity, all Iraqis against the invaders. Not the liberators – the invaders.

That's what became – in a little over a year – of the place that welcomed the Americans.

21

WHERE HAVE ALL THE WOMEN GONE?

April-May 2004

Alaa lied to her family about where she was going when she came to meet us. They were scared for her and tried to persuade her to stay at home. 'But if I just stay at home I am already dead. Women who have no jobs don't go out, they don't do anything, there's no entertainment. They just cook and clean and wash clothes.'

'I see my friends across the fence or in the street but not to sit down and drink tea and talk for hours, maybe once or twice a year.' There was no money for leisure and nowhere safe to go. Those without jobs disappeared into the home.

For lack of anything but housework to do, lots of women were losing their minds. My friend Asmaa had been looking for work but couldn't find any. She taught computing in a public college until her first child was born and then in private lessons. It was boring and frustrating for someone used to being out working, someone with good qualifications and work experience to be at home all day.

'We do all the work of the house and then we chat on the internet and we download music and we dance and watch TV.' She knew they were among the luckier ones, being able to afford the internet in their house. At one of the first talks I gave after returning from Iraq in April 2003, someone remarked that, in all the images from this war, women were either invisible or victims.

Women hadn't completely disappeared: you still saw them in the markets, on the buses, working in the banks, begging in the traffic queues. The mainstream media didn't notice them and most of the few independent journalists in Iraq were male,* so they often didn't have much contact with Iraqi women. You still saw them inside the universities. In Karrada you still saw a few wealthy ones dressed up and shopping.

But, as Asmaa said, there was nowhere to go. The coffee shops were the

---

* Notable exceptions included the filmmakers Julia Guest and Tara Sutton and the writer Wendell Steavenson

preserve of men. The streets were dangerous, far too dangerous to walk just for leisure. The shops were just depressing if you hadn't got any money to spend. There were no cinemas. There were few places where women could meet and just share gossip and company. A woman could quite literally be bored out of her mind. Confinement was exacerbated by the greater impact on women of shortages of electricity, food, water, health care and so on with their responsibilities for the home and family.

In the Sufi mosque at Friday prayers the women greeted each other with hugs and hundreds of kisses, whispering eagerly at the back while the kids frisked about, until a woman in a huge white outfit, the Prayer Police, came past to tell them to face the front, be quiet, keep their children under control. When she'd gone the chatter would start again.

Lines of women prayed, standing, bowing, kneeling, a young girl praying next to her mum, a smaller one going through some of the motions but mostly trying to balance on her head in some semblance of the bow from a kneeling position. A tiny, curly-headed girl in a white frilly dress danced about, tumbled over one of the grown-ups.

Everyone moved to the front to stand close together for the final prayer and then the real business began of exchanging the week's news. Men gathered outside waiting for wives and sisters and in-laws who were queuing for the return of their shoes, reluctant to cut short the only social occasion of the week.

'I had a letter from some women students in one of the colleges,' Layla Mohammed said. 'They are being threatened with suspension if they do not wear a veil. There are also some women students in the Fine Art College who have had threats and been stopped from making music and singing and putting on theater shows. They want to stop them making any art unless it is religious.'

There was a billboard near one of the colleges advertising the opinion that veils made you beautiful and respectable. It was not, of course, 'the veil' per se that was the problem but enforcement, the denial of women's right to choose. But by late April 2004, women were being physically prevented by armed men from entering some colleges unveiled and it was increasingly rare to see a woman on the street without an abaya, let alone with her head uncovered.

Layla, one of the directors of the Organization for Women's Freedom in Iraq (OWFI), said violence against women had increased dramatically since the occupation began, both domestically and publicly. Rising levels of abuse in the home were bound up with the social and economic chaos unleashed by the invasion and the poverty caused by sanctions and war.

Public violence was directed at men as well – murder, robbery, car-jacking, kidnap for ransom and so on – but certainly impacted more on women who were not only targets for sexual violence but also politico-religious attacks on, for example, those whose hair was visible or who wore trousers. In Mosul, a doctor, a pharmacist, a vet, three public servants and two university lecturers were killed within a few months, apparently because they were professional women, though it is not proven that these attacks were religiously motivated. Impunity for perpetrators, even suspected police complicity in some cases, has contributed to the carnage.

OWFI set up a shelter for women fleeing domestic violence or the threat of 'honor killing' and both Layla and Yanar Mohammed were trying to raise funds to keep it running, to keep an armed guard outside all the time. Domestic violence wasn't talked about in public and Layla had been discussing it with women in some of the squatter camps, trying to raise consciousness that it happened and was wrong and that women did not have to accept being beaten.

I learnt some of my first Arabic, with Sura and Imad's help, from *Equality*, OWFI's newspaper, so even while I could barely ask for directions I could say: 'We demand a secular constitution guaranteeing equality between women and men; end honor killings and no to forced veiling'. Those, as well as determined enforcement of the gender equality laws and incontrovertible criminalization of violence against women, were OWFI's main demands.

Some women criticized OWFI for an excessive focus on domestic violence and the veil, to the exclusion of issues of representation, for example, while other women expressed frustration that certain groups concentrated all their energies on lobbying for 40 per cent representation of women in any new government.

OWFI was allied to the Workers' Communist Party, which did not believe there could be valid government under occupation, and this perhaps explains the different priorities. Most groups were allied with one political party or another for historical and financial reasons. OWFI also focused more on threats from political Islamists than those from non-aligned criminals, which enraged some because it seemed to agree with the occupying forces' version of events. In reality, of course, the situation is enormously complicated and violence came from many sides, with ordinary and extraordinary women crushed in between.

I, meanwhile, felt like a traitor every time I put a headscarf over my hair. I felt like a traitor because women were risking their lives to go out without one and publicly to oppose forced veiling but sometimes I wore one just to minimize hassle, to be shouted at less, to be less visibly foreign, less visible at all. By April-May 2004, though, I was wearing a headscarf for simple safety – foreigners were at risk of kidnapping and all women were at ever more risk of attack if they were uncovered.

Layla, Yanar, OWFI itself and other leaders had been threatened, as had labor organizations, individual women and women's groups. The threats were reported to, and ignored by, the Coalition Provisional Authority (CPA). Extremist cleric Moqtada Al-Sadr's *Al-Hawza* newspaper, which opposed OWFI's calls, was suspended only when threats were extended to the occupying forces, a ban which lent credibility to what had been a relatively marginal publication with a circulation of around 10,000.

The practice of declining to protect women's rights was not new. The CPA appointed thousands of judges, including only 15 women. When male lawyers protested, at the swearing-in ceremony of one of the women, against the promotion of women to the judiciary, the CPA suspended her appointment, acquiescing in the denial of women's rights to participate in high-level public life.

Zakia Hakki was Iraq's first woman judge, appointed in 1959, the year the Personal Status Law was passed, making women and men substantially equal under law. The constitution declared formal equality in 1970. Iraqi women were among the most advanced in the region in terms of education and rights: working mothers received five years of maternity leave.

By 1980, women could vote and run for election. Some 20 per cent of Saddam Hussein's government were women compared with 14 per cent in the US and 3.5 per cent average in Arab countries. On the other hand, the death sentence for prostitution was used to punish women dissidents and the female relatives of male dissidents. In 1991, UN sanctions and consequent poverty were followed by an increase in politico-religious influence, prompting Saddam to close down the night-clubs and to decriminalize 'honor killings'.

As for the 'new' Iraq, in January 2003, the then-Governing Council passed Order 137 which reversed the Personal Status Law and submitted family, matrimonial and related financial matters to religious, rather than legal, jurisdiction. In the face of protest the Order, passed by only 11 of the 25 Council members, was dropped but it perhaps illustrates the remark made by a representative of the interim Interior Ministry to the *New York Times* in September that year: 'We don't do women.'[1]

Dina's house

Back in November 2003, Michael Birmingham had been helping several tenants to fight eviction and I went along with him. Dina made us thick coffee flavored with cardamom in the usual tiny, dainty cups, served on a table improvised from the tray and a plastic spool in a room containing two wooden chairs, a bed made of cardboard on the floor and a calendar on the bright yellow wall with a picture of a pink-skinned blonde baby. Dina's daughter Aya and two cousins carried out the remaining furniture – a bookcase, a small TV, a square cupboard. It was going to Dina's sister's house because they hadn't got anywhere to go yet.

They were the last of 11 families being evicted by the landlord Abdul

Aziz, a member of one of the richest families in Iraq. He lived in Texas and had come back to Iraq a few days earlier to finish the process his agents had been carrying on. Dina went through the courts, the Ministry of Labor and Social Affairs and the Coalition Provisional Authority. The first told her only Paul Bremer – US Administrator of Iraq following the invasion – could help her. Bremer, however, said her case was 'irrelevant' – it didn't fall within the special circumstances in which protection from eviction could be given.

This was social housing in Betouin, one of the poorer parts of Baghdad, rented by the Government from the owner and free or very cheap to tenants. During the years of economic sanctions the rent paid had been nominal. Now, however, Abdul Aziz's agents expected him to knock down the buildings and either speculate or build something else on the land.

The agents had been round to harass and intimidate the women living there. Sometimes they brought the Iraqi police, once even some US troops. Michael had been threatened and then arrested. With cameras from Canadian television watching, Aziz promised Dina would be given an apartment and a job. When she went, as agreed, to see him the next day, his promises, like the cameras, were gone.

Dina was divorced. Her family disapproved. Her brother sorted himself out a new apartment through the ministry but did nothing to help the rest of his family. She didn't want to live with her mother because she didn't want Aya to grow up internalizing the same oppressive attitudes towards women that had been foisted on her throughout her life, both by society and her own family. She agreed, finally, to be rehoused with her mother if it was the only way to get somewhere to live.

Dina was Palestinian. Aya was born in Iraq. Now it was difficult for them to get apartments even if they had the money to pay a market rent because of discrimination against them. One contact told us he'd ask about an apartment in a nearby block but looked doubtful when he heard they were Palestinians. He could try, he said, but the landlord might not agree.

Sami, the landlord's agent, had come round while we were away. We explained about the apartment and tried to dream up more possibilities. Dina called us into the kitchen away from Sami and asked us to come to dinner in New Baghdad. She'd put her hair up, done her make-up, was dressed in a bright shirt and cotton lycra leggings. We'd already turned down staying for lunch, earlier in the day, and she was really keen. Sami was going to take us all. Sami, the agent of the landlord who was evicting her in the morning, was going to take us all for dinner.

We all got into Sami's car. In a street of small cafés he left the engine running and fetched a carrier bag. The next stop yielded bottles of fizzy drinks and the third was outside his apartment. This was a long wait and he came back carrying a tall glass which he handed to Dina. She held it a while and then put it in the glove box, where it rattled. What would a woman want with fancy glassware when she was about to be evicted from her home in the morning by your employer?

Back at Dina's, Sami disappeared. His car was still outside but we saw no more of him. Dina urged us to eat, in the eye-straining paraffin glow because there was no electricity. Where was Sami? we asked – the food was getting cold. He was sleeping, she said. Sami, the landlord's agent, was sleeping in Dina's house.

What could we say? We'll find you an apartment. We'll pay for it or help you pay for it if necessary. Hang on, we'll sort something out.

We made to leave. It was late: too late, Dina said. The street would be closed. There was no curfew now, because it was Ramadan. There weren't any taxis, she said, but it was only a 10-minute walk. Guns fired again and she wagged a finger triumphantly, waiting for another rattle which didn't happen. Michael walked me back and then returned to stay at Dina's.

It didn't help though – none of it helped. In the morning Dina and Aya moved out of the house Dina had lived in for 34 years. They went, for the time being, to the damp, ratty apartment which their old neighbor, Abu Nidhal, had just moved into.

Despite their education and professional positions, despite their theoretical legal rights to divorce, to choose whom they married, women still faced issues of violence and control. Rape remained the woman's disgrace, for which she might be killed by her husband, father or brothers, even by female relatives. It took a *fatwa* from the Committee of Islamic Scholars to establish that women held and raped in US detention were victims, deserving of care and sympathy, rather than blots on their families' honor, an apparently unprecedented acknowledgment in Islamic countries.[2]

But, as Naomi Klein wrote, the occupying forces have been 'using feminism and women's issues to advance the occupation in a really dangerous way, because they are sullying the reputation of women's issues, which could be seized upon by anti-women forces in Iraq. It is easy then to say: "if you are advocating women's rights, you're for the occupation."'[3]

The US State Department trumpeted a 10-million-dollar Iraqi Women's Democracy Initiative to train a small number of women before the Iraqi elections. The money went to US agencies, as Haifa Zangana put it: 'organizations embedded with the US administration, such as the Independent Women's Forum (IWF) founded by Dick Cheney's wife Lynn'.[4] Meanwhile, Haifa pointed out, unemployment at 70 per cent was exacerbating poverty, prostitution, backstreet abortion and honor killing.

More expensive fiddling while Iraq's women burned.

1 *New York Times*, 16 September 2003.
2 Tahrir Swift, personal communication, 2004.
3 Naomi Klein and Haifa Zangana, *Killing democracy in Iraq*, Red Pepper, January 2005.
4 Haifa Zangana, *Quiet or I'll Call Democracy*, Guardian, 22nd December 2004.

22

UNIVERSITIES

May 2004

The highway towards Baghdad University's College of Languages was partly on a flyover which afforded a perfect view of the layers of smog that enveloped the city. For much of the way the road was quiet, which wasn't common. 'I hope there's not another *fatwa*,' Anna said, referring to the order not long ago from Moqtada Al-Sadr that students should not go to university. Anna taught English conversation to final-year students at the university and they wanted to talk to someone with a British accent.

The young women were all immaculately dressed, not a hair astray between them, let alone an eyebrow, black lines around their eyes, lips painted. This was the only place they got to meet up with their friends, the most likely place to meet a future husband, so apparently it was worth the effort. Headscarves, for some, must have saved hours of hair styling.

Anna had to tell them about their final test, the next week. There'd been one a couple of weeks earlier, accompanied by an array of unusual but feasible excuses for not turning up: 'There was a bomb at the end of my street'; 'The highway was blocked by the Americans'; and 'It was my wedding'.

Shayma said her husband heard of her by reputation and came to ask the family for her hand in marriage. The family agreed and the couple met just once before getting engaged. The engagement lasted eight months and they were married a couple of weeks ago, just before her university finals.

All the young women said they wanted to get married. 'Of course.' It wasn't even seen as optional. It was like asking whether they wanted to graduate. 'Your family will choose your husband,' Beyda explained. 'It could be someone you chose, who went to your family to ask them. You have the chance to say no to the man they suggest, but you don't want to risk that no-one else will want you.'

The university was not obviously filled with radicalism and student politics but still you could see the boundaries of society being pushed on and around the campus. There were young women in knee-length skirts and figure-hugging clothes that you rarely saw elsewhere, perhaps a reflection of the relative safety of this particular campus where young men and women were able to meet and talk openly in a way that was unusual outside.

Equally, though, there were women in full abayas, hijabs and black gloves, with their normal clothes underneath. There was no electricity in all the time I was in the university, which meant no fans and certainly no air-conditioning. Exams must have been unbearable.

Taif, a student on the MA course, wouldn't be 23 until July, but she wouldn't be able to invite both male and female friends to her house for a party. This, the end of the academic year, was as close to her birthday as she could celebrate with the whole group. Even in the university Taif stood out, with curly reddish-brown hair, a bright yellow patterned skirt, short sleeves and loud, rapid speech in accented but excellent English.

Among my projects was setting up solidarity links between schools, universities and other institutions in Iraq and outside, so that people in other countries could help those in Iraq rehabilitate their own libraries, labs, curricula and so on. It was a problem for a huge number of students that they couldn't get the books, journals and subscription web resources they needed. Farah was writing a thesis on the political discourse of the Iraq debates between Tony Blair and Ian Duncan Smith because she was fascinated by their use of words to play around with the facts and people's beliefs. She didn't even have access to the Hansard transcripts of the debates. On a lighter note Farah also said her favorite band was Blue because, in their videos, they were naked and her parents let her watch them because they were only pop videos.

Some 84 per cent of Iraq's higher-education institutions were burned, looted or destroyed, according to the UN, but even Nahrain University, which had escaped, was short of everything. The Dean, Professor Fawzi, said the college had the finest librarians it could have – very dedicated, well trained and fluent in English. The science and engineering books used in Iraqi universities were mainly in English.

They had books, although not usually the most up-to-date editions, but they had no journals more recent than 1991. There was only one computer for the whole science library for cataloguing, internet and other work. Baghdad University students also used the college's library, so the shortage of resources was acute.

Another young woman called Farah said laboratory equipment was the biggest problem on her course, electronic and communications engineering. 'It is a practical course but there isn't enough equipment to do practicals, so it is mainly theory.' Her friend Tegrit agreed. She studied civil engineering and wanted to work in construction.

The graffiti on the walls was officially sanctioned 'tagging' by graduating groups, Science Class of 2003, King of Electronics, as well as the ubiquitous 'mind the bomb' posters warning against stepping on landmines and unexploded cluster bomblets. Everyone said there was no political activity on campus. There were no students' unions now that the old Ba'athist ones had gone. The political parties were not recruiting there and none of them were aware of any student organizations. Both Farah and Tegrit said all that mattered was to be safe.

Dr Fawzi, though, summed up safety in Iraq: 'The soldiers shot one of our lecturers, Dr Imad, by accident. We had a demonstration on the campus. You know today there is a demonstration against terrorism. I am not sure whether it is against US terrorism or some other kind. In the student halls of residence here on the campus they have had no electricity for the last 10 days.'

In fact, over 250 teachers, lecturers and professors were assassinated between the start of the occupation and the end of 2005. Hundreds had disappeared and thousands had fled the country. There was no pattern: male and female, all sects and religions, all academic subjects had been targeted. According to Robert Fisk: 'University staff suspect that there is a campaign to strip Iraq of its academics, to complete the destruction of Iraq's cultural identity which began when the American army entered Baghdad.'[1]

Aside from the obvious consequences for individuals, families and the education system, Dahr Jamail writes that: 'The secular middle class – which has refused to be co-opted by the US occupation – is being decimated, with far-reaching consequences for the future of Iraq.'[2]

1 Robert Fisk, *Independent*, 14 July 2004
2 Dahr Jamail, *Urgent Appeal To Save Iraq's Academics*, http://dahrjamailiraq.com

23

DE-BA'ATHIFICATION

2004-2006

'The US fought the people of Falluja because it said they were Saddamis. Now they are letting the real Saddamis have their old jobs back. For a year we have been told there are no jobs, but suddenly there are 6,000 jobs for Ba'athis.' Saleh was one of a few thousand men – all men – at a demonstration that marched from Kahromana Square to Firdos Square, the day before I left Iraq, protesting against the re-employment of all but the highest-ranking former Ba'athists.

'The Governing Council decided this without consulting the people. Now the Ba'athis will be representing us. They started killing people before. They never did good things before. It is impossible. There are not enough jobs. They have to give the chance to new people.' Taalib was a politician in the Daawa Party, forced out of work by the Ba'athists.

Mehdi was once employed by the Ministry of Information but was fired along with 50 other workers because he did not join the Ba'ath Party. 'Now they are bringing the Ba'athis back we will face the same problem.' The same was true for teachers. Hassan graduated in 1991 and applied for a job as a teacher but was refused because he was not a Ba'ath Party member.

'The employees who humiliated us are now Ministry of Education employees. After the war they said all the politicians and teachers and others would get our old jobs back but none of us did,' Hassan said.

The decision was only a public announcement and a larger-scale advancement of a policy which had been pursued ever since the US took over in Iraq. Adil went to apply for a job in the Ministry of Foreign Affairs when it reopened after the war and found the same Ba'athi still there on reception, refusing to let him in, telling him no, there were no jobs there for him.

Neo-Ba'athism, the process of slipping the old party back into power, was predictable. When the US and UK talked about De-Ba'athification they hinted at a massive operation but appeared to plan for much less. The regime's figureheads were to be changed, its loyalties, but not its power base. The people were expecting more, especially those who had lost someone to the Ba'athists.

Adil's daughter was pushed down the stairs when the Ba'athis raided his house to look for his brother and the head injury is still causing her problems. He was carrying a set of papers, black-and-white pictures of men murdered. One cousin died during torture. One was in a high position and was killed by them. His brothers too: in all, 13 of his relatives were killed for being Daawa Party members. He was not a member but was nonetheless sacked from his job as an engineer in the Electricity Ministry because of his brothers' affiliations.

Likewise Hadi found himself pointed at in the street as a child: 'There's the boy whose brother was in the Daawa Party.' His engineer brother was arrested in 1981 and his body was brought to the family ten months later. For 20 years Hadi was pointed at. 'Now they are trying to bring it back,' he said. Worse, Fadhil's wife was arrested and spent seven years in jail while he was in exile in Iran, where he spent 25 years altogether. He said he came from Iran and got her out of jail with bribes.

'Why put the criminals back into power?' Jassim demanded. 'You have to give rights first to the victims and their families.'

The difficulty was, as with all such regimes, that the majority of the qualified, experienced people, the people who knew the workings of the ministries, were members of the Ba'ath Party. As the men explained, you could lose your job for refusing to join the Party, whether you were a teacher, an engineer or a journalist. Even students, even children, especially those in orphanages, faced coercion to join the Party.

Yasser was adamant that all of them, every person who joined the Party, were criminals, no matter if they only joined to get or keep a job. Not one of them, for him, ought to be given a job now. Who would teach the children? I asked. People from the Daawa Party and other parties, he said. It didn't matter: better to have an unqualified person teaching the children than a qualified criminal, better anyone than a Ba'athi.

There's something in that, of course. The choice in the end is a difficult one. In some former communist countries everyone who had been a member of the party was sacked. The new teachers were young graduates, inexperienced but quick to learn and, although the transition was painful, it created a clean break from the past. The young graduates do not pick up the bad practices and corruption that have become second nature to the old ones; the old policies are not maintained by default or by habit.

But imagine. You're well educated. You've studied for years and got a qualification. You've got a family to support: parents, perhaps an unemployed wife or husband, children, maybe some nieces or nephews or siblings who depend on you financially. You're obviously aware that the Government is a dictatorship, but you've got no particular political allegiances.

Your choice is this: to join the Ba'ath Party and get or keep a job or to refuse and to lose it, to have no job at all or drive a taxi. That, at least, is the beginning. That's the only immediate decision. Perhaps later you're called upon to report on colleagues, students, customers but in any case you're already expected to keep an eye on your neighbors. Is it so different? You're not a party leader, not joining the security police or anything like that. How would you have fed your family otherwise?

It's easy to judge. And, of course, judgement is needed. But can you, in all honesty, say you would have resisted, paid that much for the principle, risked everything just to be a non-member? How many of us have done something unethical and justified it with the words: 'I'm just doing my job'?

But if they are not sacked, where is the justice for the ones whose jobs were taken away all those years ago, who did resist? I make no claim to have an answer. The promise of De-Ba'athification was held out, the promise of exorcism. Fulfilment of the promise would have caused hardship to some, might though have brought healing and restoration, maybe retribution, for others.

Of course, the former Ba'athis who'd been re-employed were not there to tell me their stories. The men there were all like Abdelhassan, sacked from the Ministry of Housing for not joining the party, fighting for ten years to get his job back and now watching it going back to the former Ba'athi. The men there were saying nothing had changed.

Soon people would start finding it hard to get a job unless they had a letter of recommendation from one of the new parties. There was a choice of parties rather than just one, but still if you refused to align yourself with any of them you stayed unemployed.

Nothing Had Changed. Things had come full circle. The New Iraq was the Old Iraq with added rampant crime, soldiers and mercenaries on the streets, devastated infrastructure but still the same fear, corruption, party-nepotism, torture, imprisonment without charge, poverty. Only the economic control had shifted. Only the economic control.

24

EPILOG

May 2006

This book has not been an analysis of policy or politics but has, I hope, illuminated their effects, the real and practical meanings of those things. It has been about an enormous number of people with myriad stories to tell, stories which help define the words 'dictatorship', 'UN embargo', 'war', 'invasion', 'occupation', 'liberation' and 'weapons of mass destruction'.

Language has been commandeered as a weapon. The Pentagon's 'Office of Special Plans' produced 'talking points', lists of phrases which would appear in presidential speeches.* The same sets of words would be repeated over and over in press briefings until they were sold to the journalists, who passed them on to the public by repetition in print and broadcast media. Ordinary people then began using them in their everyday conversation because they had insinuated themselves into public consciousness and from there they became ubiquitous. Words meant – as Lewis Carroll and Humpty Dumpty might have put it – what the Pentagon said they meant.

Mr Amir, the journalist and linguist we met in Nasariya, wrote and talked about the need for precise language in order to build democracy, in contrast to the vague, emotive slogans of the old government. Things are always more complex than good against evil and the vital challenge is to question those phrases from the media, the military and the politicians and to examine the substance behind them.

I think of the lies that have been told, the deliberate, outright falsehoods, the half-truths, the misleading soundbites, the omissions of truth and the self-delusion. I think of the crimes committed with impunity. I think of the countless opportunities that were missed to question, to stop all this: the media complicity which kept too many people too ignorant for too long.

* Karen Kwiatkowski, a former USAF Colonel, spent four years working for the Pentagon and became a 'whistleblower', writing among other things about the OSP and its tactics.

But questions can be passed up, challenges can be passed up, along the same pathways that 'talking points' are handed down. Language need not be surrendered; it can be fought for.

*   *   *

Zaid and Asmaa were always my beacons of hope, so optimistic about the liberation of Iraq that they could put a positive interpretation on anything. Within two years of the war, Zaid told me: 'I'm not pro-occupation any more but what other options have I got? The Government and especially the Interior Ministry are taking us and torturing us then our families find our bodies in a trash field, the situation is terrible. Baghdad is a city of ghosts after five o'clock, you don't know who is your enemy. Security completely fell down. There are no local services at all, electricity, water, fuel and sewage services; you have to wait in a fuel line for nine hours and you may get nothing.'

And Fuad Radi had been beaten to death for making children laugh.

Two years. Was that all it took to do away with hope?

And I remember Akael's father, during the war, who, even as his son lay critically ill, expressed his thanks to the people of the world, and especially those in Britain and the US, for marching in our millions against the invasion. Those marches were big enough to be visible across continents, to ease the sense of isolation.

But they were not enough. Where is the outrage on the streets every time Falluja or some other town is surrounded and its people, ambulances and hospitals targeted? Where is the outrage – even the sabotage – at the doors of the arms traders and manufacturers, the mercenaries, the companies that seek profit out of war, the investors that fund them all?

At hospital bedsides, on the streets, in their homes, people asked often that I take their stories with me and tell them all over the world. They asked because they were isolated. A few Iraqis were able to represent themselves via blogs, and a few more could afford to contact family or friends abroad via internet and telephone centers, but overall the sense of invisibility was pervasive.

Now I am one of those distant friends and I am telling those stories I've been given. Please pass them on until everyone knows the real meaning of war.

FURTHER READING AND RESOURCES

Paper

Christian Parenti, *The Freedom: Shadows and Hallucinations in Occupied Iraq*, New Press 2004. ISBN 1-59558-037-9.

Riverbend, *Baghdad Burning: Girl Blog from Iraq*, New York: Feminist Press and London: Marion Boyars. ISBN 0-7145-31189. The book is a paper archive of the exceptionally good weblog written by an Iraqi woman in Baghdad at www.riverbendblog.blogspot.com

New Internationalist magazine tackles one globally important issue each month, such as terrorism, corporate power, trade justice and nuclear power. Available worldwide by subscription. Visit www.newint.org

Film

Iraqi filmmakers are bringing out documentaries and dramas representing their own situation but there's no central point I can direct you to for those.

A Letter to the Prime Minister, directed by Julia Guest, Year Zero Films. www.alettertotheprimeminister.co.uk

Iraq in Fragments, directed by James Longley www.iraqinfragments.com

Occupation: Dreamland, directed by Garrett Scott and Ian Olds, distributed by Rumur Releasing.

Online

There are now a lot of blogs by Iraqis – for an overview and links, see http://iraqblogcount.blogspot.com Everything from individuals and families writing about their lives to a group blog bringing together expat Iraqi academics – http://iraqiscientists.blogspot.com

Iraqi Economy – www.iraqieconomy.org – information about all sectors, including news articles and other information, as there are no official sources of this information.

Corpwatch – US-based website of information about corporations' unethical activities generally, including war profiteers. www.corpwatch.org

Corporate Pirates site for information about the corporate plunder of Iraq. http://corporatepirates.gzzzt.net

International Co-operative Alliance – www.ica.coop

Dahr Jamail's reporting on http://dahrjamailiraq.com

Open Democracy – an independent online political magazine: www.opendemocracy.net

Raed's survey of civilian deaths and injuries during the invasion www.civilians.info/iraq/

There are a great many activist websites based all over the world. Most networks are locally based, so for information about what's going on in your area, try googling.

About the New Internationalist

The **New Internationalist** is an independent not-for-profit publishing co-operative. Our mission is to report on issues of world poverty and inequality; to focus attention on the unjust relationship between the powerful and the powerless worldwide; to debate and campaign for the radical changes necessary if the needs of all are to be met.

We publish easy-to-read, informative current affairs titles and popular reference, like the *No-Nonsense Guides* series and the *World Guide*, complemented by world food, photography and alternative gift books, as well as calendars and diaries, maps and posters – all with a global justice world view.

 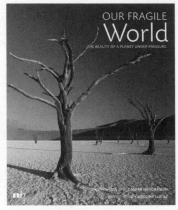 

We also publish the monthly **New Internationalist** magazine. Each month tackles a different subject such as Climate Change, Trade Justice, Venezuela or Iraq, exploring each issue in a concise way which is easy to understand. The main articles are packed full of photos, charts and graphs and each magazine also contains music, film and book reviews, country profiles, interviews and news.

 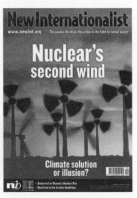 

To find out more about the **New Internationalist**, subscribe to the magazine or buy any of our books take a look at **www.newint.org**